Brazilian Foreign Policy after the Cold War

UNIVERSITY PRESS OF FLORIDA

Florida A&M University, Tallahassee
Florida Atlantic University, Boca Raton
Florida Gulf Coast University, Ft. Myers
Florida International University, Miami
Florida State University, Tallahassee
New College of Florida, Sarasota
University of Central Florida, Orlando
University of Florida, Gainesville
University of North Florida, Jacksonville
University of South Florida, Tampa
University of West Florida, Pensacola

Brazilian Foreign Policy after the Cold War

✳ ✳ ✳

Sean W. Burges

University Press of Florida

Gainesville Tallahassee Tampa Boca Raton
Pensacola Orlando Miami Jacksonville Ft. Myers Sarasota

Copyright 2009 by Sean W. Burges
Printed in the United States of America on acid-free paper
All rights reserved
First cloth printing, 2009
First paperback printing, 2011

Library of Congress Cataloging-in-Publication Data
Burges, Sean W.
Brazilian foreign policy after the Cold War/Sean W. Burges.
p. cm.
Includes bibliographical references and index.
ISBN 978-0-8130-3333-4 (alk. paper)
ISBN 978-0-8130-3729-5 (pbk,)
1. Brazil—Foreign relations—1985– I. Title.
F2538.3.B86 2006
327.81009'0499–dc22   2008040218

The University Press of Florida is the scholarly publishing agency for the State University
System of Florida, comprising Florida A&M University, Florida Atlantic University, Florida
Gulf Coast University, Florida International University, Florida State University, New
College of Florida, University of Central Florida, University of Florida, University of North
Florida, University of South Florida, and University of West Florida.

University Press of Florida
15 Northwest 15th Street
Gainesville, FL 32611–2079
http://www.upf.com

Contents

Tables

Acknowledgments

This book could not have been completed without the help and encouragement of a large number of people. Inevitably I will forget to mention many who deserve thanks.

Development of the ideas in this book benefited greatly from discussions with a number of people. Nicola Phillips and Jean Daudelin were tireless sources of advice and invaluable constructive criticism and were always ready to provide the necessary nudge to keep the project moving forward. My colleagues at the University of Warwick, the University of Wales, Aberystwyth, and Carleton University's Norman Paterson School of International Affairs provided essential critical commentary on a number of discussion papers that I used to shape this book. A Brazilian perspective on various aspects of my ideas was provided by, Maria Celina D'Araujo, Renato Flores, Joanisval Brito Gonçalves, Terrie Groth, Ricardo Markwald, Bernardo Mueller, Amâncio Jorge de Oliveira, Janina Onuki, Matias Spektor, Alcides Costa Vaz, Eduardo Viola, and a large number of Brazilian diplomats and government officials who supplemented interviews with more speculative discussions about the nature of Brazil and the country's foreign policy. While I am quite certain that the connection of "hegemony" to Brazilian foreign policy will raise hackles in Itamaraty (Brazil's Foreign Ministry), I hope that my findings will prove productively provocative.

The stimulating discussions about South American politics and the realities of planning and completing fieldwork that I had with fellow members of the Society for Latin American Studies—especially Mahrukh Doctor, Claudia Fabbri, Gian Luca Gardini, Peter Lambert, and Fiona Macauley—breathed life into what for the longest time seemed a book-ridden research project. Invaluable feedback and encouragement on the theoretical thinking driving this text came from Andrew Hurrell and Shaun Breslin who read complete versions of the first draft of this book. Later versions of the theoretical structures that I use here benefited from the critical commentary of Jenny Edkins, Randall

Germain, Cornelia Huelsz, Justin Robertson, and David Smith. The discussions and seminars to which Leslie Bethell welcomed me at the University of Oxford Centre for Brazilian Studies proved an invaluable learning experience and testing ground for my half-formed ideas.

Financial support for the various stages of this project came from several organizations. Larry Birns at the Council on Hemispheric Affairs helped with research trips and has long proven unflagging in his support of my research, particularly when he disagrees with my findings. The Canadian Women's Club in the United Kingdom provided the funding to get the project off the ground. Additional support for field research came from the Gilchrist Trust, the Sir Richard Stapley Trust, and the Society for Latin American Studies. The Canadian Social Science and Humanities Research Council provided substantial funding to complete the book project. Blackwell Publishing graciously consented to the reproduction of large parts of an article (Burges 2006) that I previously published in *The Bulletin of Latin American Research*. Time spent with the Government of Canada's Department of Foreign Affairs and International Trade as the 2006–2007 Cadieux-Leger Fellow gave me a great deal of insight into the nuances of the actual practice of foreign policy. Needless to say, there is no connection between the words and ideas in this book and the policies of the Government of Canada. Colleagues at the Universidade Nacional de Brasília and the Fundação Getúlio Vargas in Rio de Janeiro offered a sense of home and source of support during multiple research trips to Brazil.

Completion of this book is largely due to the support of family and friends. Their unflagging belief in the project as well as the practical support they provided greatly eased the mundane worries of research and writing. A growing group of athletes in Coventry, Oxford, and Ottawa provided a chance to relieve stress by submitting to vigorous workouts; the chuckles of amusement from my fellow coaches helped keep everything in perspective.

It is simple, really: run fast, jump far. This, by the way, is something that Brazilians know well.

Abbreviations

ALADI	Associação Latino-Americana de Integração (Latin American Integration Association)
ALALC	Associação Latino-Americana de Livre-Comércio (Latin American Free Trade Association)
BNDES	Banco Nacional de Desenvolvimento Econômico e Social (National Social and Economic Development Bank)
BRIC	Brazil, Russia, India, and China (emerging-market countries)
CAMEX	Câmara de Comércio Exterior (Foreign Trade Council)
CAN	Comunidad Andina (Andean Community)
CASA	Comunidade Sul-americana de Nações (Community of South American Nations)
CEPAL	Comisión Económica para América Latina (Economic Commission for Latin America)
CET	Common external tariff
CCM	Comisión de Comercio del Mercosul (Mercosul Trade Commission)
CCR	Convênio de Pagamentos e Créditos Recíprocos (Reciprocal Credit and Payment Convention)
CMC	Consejo Mercado Comum (Common Market Council)
CONAIE	Confederación de Nacionalidades Indígenas del Ecuador (Confederation of Indigenous Nationalities of Ecuador)
EAI	Enterprise for the Americas Initiative
EU	European Union
EXIM	BNDES Export-Import Financing Program
FARC	Fuerzas Armadas Revolucionarias de Colombia (Colombian Revolutionary Armed Forces)
FDI	Foreign Direct Investment
FIESP	Federação das Indústrias do Estado de São Paulo (São Paulo Federation of Industry)

FTAA — Free Trade Area of the Americas
FUNCEX — Fundação Centro de Estudos do Comércio Exterior (Foundation Center for the Study of Foreign Trade)
GATT — General Agreement on Tariffs and Trade
GEIPOT — Grupo Executivo de Integração da Política de Transportes (Executive Group for Transport Policy Integration
GMC — Grupo Mercado Comum (Common Market Group)
IADB — Inter-American Development Bank
IBSA — India–Brazil–South Africa Dialogue Forum
ICONE — Instituto de Estudos do Comércio e Negociações Internacionais (Institute for International Trade Negotiations)
IIRSA — Iniciativa para a Integração da Infra-estrutura Regional Sul Americana (Initiative for the Integration of Regional Infrastructure in South America)
IMF — International Monetary Fund
LIBOR — London Interbank Offered Rate
M&A — Mergers and acquisitions
MDIC — Ministério do Desenvolvimento, Indústria e Comércio Exterior (Ministry of Development, Industry, and Foreign Trade)
Mercosul — Mercado Comum do Sul (Common Market of the South—Mercosur is the Spanish acronym)
MRE — Ministério de Relações Exteriores (Ministry of Foreign Relations, Itamaraty)
MNC — Multinational corporation
MOMEP — Missão de Observadores Militares Equador/Peru (Military Observer Mission Ecuador/Peru)
NAFTA — North American Free Trade Agreement
NGO — Nongovernmental organization
OAS — Organization of American States
ONPE — Oficina Nacional de Procesos Electorales (National Office of Electoral Procedures, Peru)
OPA — Operação Pan Americana (Pan American Operation)
PDN — Política de Defesa Nacional (National Defense Policy)
PDVSA — Petróleos de Venezuela, SA
PICE — Programa de Integração e Cooperação Econômica (Program of Economic Integration and Cooperation)
PSDB — Partido da Social Democracia Brasileira (Social Democratic Party of Brazil)

PSCI	Programa de Substituição Competitiva de Importações (Competitive Import Substitution Program)
PT	Partido dos Trabalhadores (Workers' Party)
SAFTA	South American Free Trade Area
SECEX	Secretaria de Comércio Exterior (Foreign Trade Secretariat of the MDIC)
Sivam	Sistema de Vigilância da Amazônia (Amazon Vigilance System)
UNCTAD	United Nations Conference on Trade and Development
UNSC	United Nations Security Council
WTO	World Trade Organization

Introduction

Brazil started the twenty-first century by raising its global foreign-policy profile, catching attention as one of the four BRIC emerging-market countries—Brazil, Russia, India, and China—preoccupying foreign ministries in the G-8 nations. As part of this group of emerging powers Brazil has played an increasingly vocal and central role in the evolution of major international institutions such as the World Trade Organization (WTO) and adopted an important position as provider of economic, political, and physical security in the Americas.

This characterization of Brazil as a nuanced and sophisticated actor on the international stage strikes many outside of South America as unlikely not only because of the scant attention the country has received from international-affairs analysts and scholars, but also because of the manner in which Brazil pursues its international agenda. The country has a long history of acting to protect its own interests in the Americas by quietly influencing and pressuring its neighbors, a process that accelerated toward the end of the twentieth century. That such actions have often gone largely unnoticed is not just a by-product of broad international indifference to Brazil's foreign policy, but also a result of the methods that the Brazilian Foreign Ministry, Itamaraty, uses to pursue the country's international agenda. Overt action or intervention has not been the norm. Rather, the strategy has been one of secreting the country's integrated and sustained ambitions for hemispheric and global leadership behind a cloak of indirect and ostensibly technocratic apolitical programs, well wrapped in an added mantle of multilateralism and often run through other government ministries and agencies. This book will unravel the tangled threads of Brazil's continentally oriented actions and ambitions between 1992 and 2002 to explain why sometimes seemingly unrelated initiatives have been pursued in the South American context and, more significantly for the wider study of Brazilian foreign policy, provide a clear picture of how Itamaraty goes about advancing Brazil's international agenda.

Although not often officially framed in such explicit terms, the perennial goal of Brazilian foreign policy remains the preservation of national autonomy and the prevention of external interference in internal domestic affairs (Lampreia and Cruz 2005; Bernal-Meza 2002; Lampreia 1998a, 8). The central research question driving this book therefore asks what foreign-policy strategy Itamaraty implemented between 1992 and 2002 to continue preserving and protecting national autonomy amid the changing pressures created by the end of the Cold War and the acceleration of globalization. An added complication is that Brazil faced a succession of economic crises throughout the time period covered by this book, severely limiting policymakers' freedom to engage in activities requiring much more than symbolic resource expenditure. In short, the answer is that after 1992 Brazilian foreign policy was based on a strategy of achieving and exercising a quiet style of leadership in South America, seeking to develop and lead regional groupings as a defensive response to the new realities that rapidly followed the fall of the Berlin Wall in 1989. These regional groupings were pursued in a decidedly self-interested manner, one that was relatively benign and that explicitly left space for the advancement of the interests of other South American states provided those interests did not contravene Brazil's core interests.

The story told is thus one of how Brazil rose from being a significant actor in the Americas to one of two dominant players in all hemispheric discussions despite lacking the economic and military muscle of the United States. An understanding of the techniques and strategies deployed by Itamaraty to position Brazil as the leader of South America, albeit a sometimes shaky leader, is essential for a comprehension of Brazilian action in the extrahemispheric global context. Efforts to secure and consolidate leadership in South America were the proving ground and finishing school for tactics and strategies that would be deployed tentatively at first on the global stage after 2000, and with increasing confidence and vigor after the 2002 presidential succession.

The temporal period I have chosen for the study of Brazilian foreign policy begins in 1992 and extends to 2002 because it encompasses a time of important changes and innovation: the decade in which Fernando Henrique Cardoso had enormous influence on or direct control over Itamaraty, first as foreign minister (1992–1993), then as the finance minister attempting to rescue the embattled national economy (1993–1994), and then as president of the republic (1995–2002). As a sociology professor Cardoso authored some of the seminal contributions to the study of Latin American politics and development, most notably through his elaboration of dependency theory (Cardoso and Faletto 1979) and work on authoritarianism and democracy (Cardoso 1973; 1975; 1979; 1985; 1989). The ideas at the core of his academic research continued to inform not only his own view of both Brazil and the wider international system (Cardoso 2006, chapter ten), but also those of his chief advisors and international-policy assistants. As one Brazilian diplomat noted, many of Cardoso's key advisors in the Planalto presidential palace were diplomats well versed in the nuances of the president's version of dependency theory, and they actively used the theory as an analytical lens through which to understand the international dimensions of the challenges facing the country.

In a policymaking context this intellectual trajectory was immediately felt when Cardoso began his tenure as foreign minister by initiating a series of detailed seminars to reappraise and reformulate Brazil's foreign policy in the new world order (Brazil 1993). Two items of central importance emerged from this initiative. First, the notion of South America as a distinct geoeconomic and geopolitical space moved from an interesting point for internal Itamaraty discussion to a concept that would form the core of Brazil's foreign policy. Second, an updated dependency worldview, as described by Cardosa in *Dependency and Development in Latin America,* caused Cardoso to seriously engage in a reformulation of foreign policy as an integral part of the wider policy changes necessary to address Brazil's enormous developmental challenges.

This carried through to Cardoso's presidency (Cardoso and Font 2001), during which he effectively combined the roles of president and foreign minister in an archetypical example of what has become known as presidential diplomacy (Danese 1999). While the idea of foreign policy being used by the president as a developmental tool is not new (Hirst and Lima 2006), the innovation that Cardoso's dependency worldview introduced was an explicit attempt to reframe and reorient global, hemispheric, continental, and regional political-economy structures to advance the Brazilian development process.

While there is active debate over who first came up with the idea of South America as an organizing principle—credit in interviews I conducted was variously given to Samuel Pinheiro Guimarães, Celso Amorim, Celso Lafer, Rubens Barbosa, and Cardoso—the continental focus was ultimately given practical substance, implemented, and entrenched during Cardoso's decade-long watch over his country's foreign policy. To bring the South American space into being a new style of diplomacy was launched and entrenched in Brazil, one that departed from a traditional fear that the country's unique history on the continent as a monarchy and its linguistic profile as a Portuguese-speaking nation would leave it open to charges of imperialism and expansionism from the other South American states. Cardoso's foreign policy clearly positioned Brazil as a leader and coalition builder, but in a manner that was obfuscated and shielded within a regionalism-based approach that allowed an avoidance of many of the costs associated with leadership.

The issue of avoiding the costs associated with leadership was seldom made explicit in my interviews with governmental figures because it was such an apparent restraining reality. Nevertheless, it is something that must be constantly remembered as a critical background factor. In simple terms, Brazil could not afford to engage in the sorts of expenditures typically associated with leadership. One of Cardoso's central goals was to restore financial viability to his country. While Brazil may have had foreign reserves of close to US$200 billion and a reputation as an emerging agroindustrial powerhouse when this book went to press in mid-2008, the Cardoso era can almost be characterized as a period of continual economic crisis management. The *real* was under constant international pressure, and the policy decisions of Cardoso's economic team were constantly questioned and, at times, challenged or undermined by international markets and the IMF (Cardoso and Lafer 2007; Cardoso 2006). While the details of these challenges will not be addressed in the following pages, the point to remember is that the direct expenditure of economic resources was not an option for foreign-policy makers during the Cardoso era.

The solution to the resource-scarcity conundrum facing foreign-policy makers during the Cardoso period was to use the opening of the subregional and regional context as a device to capture the influence necessary to guide and direct the continental environment from within while simultaneously creating a degree of insulation from potential hemispheric and global intervention.

This book thus explains how a complex mix of ideas based on a reformulated dependency view of developing-country insertion into the global economy was married to economic initiatives such as region formation on a subregional and continental scale as well as to a program of physical-infrastructure integration. It was also wed to a national autonomy–preserving approach to the security challenges of democratic fragility, simmering intrastate conflict, and the narco-trafficking/insurgency nexus. Ultimately, a rope was woven that Itamaraty sought to use to corral and lead South American support for international initiatives beneficial for Brazil.

The Need for a New Look at Brazilian Foreign Policy

My claim is not that others have failed to provide detailed and theoretically incisive accounts of Brazilian foreign policy. Many historically informed accounts are magisterial in scope and detail, offering keen explanations of how and why a particular foreign-policy strategy was pursued in a given era (Burns 1966; Cervo 2001; Cervo and Bueno 2002; Hurrell 1986; Lafer 2001a; J. Smith 1991; Spektor 2002; Vaz 2002). The great strength of this type of research lies in the attention it gives to primary documentation and a lucid interpretation of the goals and intentions of foreign-policy makers recorded in government archives (Penna Filho 1999).

Yet this reliance on the archived thoughts and debates of Itamaraty also forms the source of one of the greatest weaknesses in research on contemporary Brazilian foreign policy: it acts to limit study of the trade and security issues currently preoccupying policymakers, because the relevant documentation has yet to be made public. Indeed, this fixation on the validity of archival sources seemingly generates a reluctance to engage in the collation and analysis of the diverse information sources necessary to discern the possible motivations and benefits of immediate Itamaraty action. It fails to link such varied topics as the settling of the Ecuador-Peru border conflict and the construction of a continental energy matrix while the underlying policy issues are fresh and current. The formulation of theoretical explanations for contemporary Brazilian foreign policy consequently exhibits a historical lag, relying as it does on precedent sometimes to the exclusion of contemporary evidence that the thrust and context of Itamaraty action has shifted.

The end of the Cold War and the completion of Brazil's democratic transition prompted a revision of the principles guiding the formulation and operation of the country's foreign policy (Hirst and Soares de Lima 2002, 81–83) and a paradigm shift away from the precepts inherent in the dominant archive-based research. The traditional questions of retaining close approximation to or distinct autonomy from the United States were set aside in favor of a more pragmatic approach seeking to finally build on Brazil's internal potential through active and positive regional engagement.

In this vein Itamaraty's diplomats responded to the changing global environment in the late 1980s and early 1990s by devoting considerable effort to studying Brazil's place in the new international circumstances and publishing the findings of their seminars and discussions in books and academic journals (Amorim 1991a; Barbosa 1994; Fonseca and Nabuco de Castro 1994; Lafer

1990; Lafer 1992a). While these works offer valuable insight into how senior figures within Itamaraty viewed the new international order, concerns that strategic decisions should be closely guarded meant that the contributors offered little substantive or clear insight into the thrust of Brazil's new foreign policy. Instead, oblique glimpses of the larger picture of how diplomats hoped to affect national development and retain autonomy were offered through discussions of Brazil as a "global trader" (Barbosa and César 1994b; Thorstensen 1993), concerns that the country might be excluded from the international system (Abdenur 1994a), and political and economic reorientation toward South America and the Southern Cone (Barbosa 1994; Barbosa and César 1994a).

The possibility that Itamaraty was reorienting Brazil's foreign policy to draw on the country's geographic reality is noted in a 1996 article by Antônio Carlos Lessa. Although Lessa's examination of the strategic triangle being formulated by Itamaraty offers insight into the emerging relations between Brazil, the Southern Cone, the United States, and the European Union (EU), the discussion of the larger strategic formulation of Brazilian foreign policy returns us to the criticism that theorizing remained dependent on the archival approach, resulted in an analysis strongly redolent of pre-1990 conceptions of international order (Lessa 1996, 30). This same handicap marks Cervo's (2002) use of the dynamics in the structuralist core-periphery model to criticize Cardoso for capitulating to international capital and Darc Costa's (2003) somewhat utopian vision of Brazil as a natural continental leader.

Yet the content of Cervo's and Costa's analyses also points in a different direction, one suggesting that an attempt was being made to construct a new method of inserting Brazil into the international system, especially through the creative use of regionalism. Bernal-Meza (2002, 61) is more positive than Cervo and more realistic than Costa, going as far as to mention in passing that Itamaraty was attempting to develop some sort of leadership profile during the Cardoso administration. The question that remains unanswered is why Itamaraty was trying to construct a leadership profile on the continent and how this task was being undertaken.

Here the character of much of the literature on Brazilian foreign policy during the Cardoso era again becomes important. The first impression given by the limited English-language literature is that Itamaraty was almost exclusively concerned with the evolution of the Mercado Comum do Sul (Portuguese Mercosul and Spanish Mercosur both mean Common Market of the South), other international trade arrangements, and bilateral relations with the United States (Sorger and Dymond 1997; Flôres 1997; Hirst 2004). Indeed, discussion of Brazilian foreign policy is largely subsumed in examinations of the economic dynamics of Mercosul (Hirst 1992; Soares de Lima 1999; Pereira 1999; Grugel and Medeiros 1999; Bernier and Roy 1999; Cason 2000; Costa 2000; Costa 2001; Phillips 2001; Cason 2002). Discussions of other areas of foreign policy such as security (Perruci 1995; Wrobel 1996; Hurrell 1998a; Hurrell 1998b) and the growing problem of narco-trafficking (Mora 1996; Procópio Filho and Vaz 1997) receive considerably less attention. The result is a body of literature in English that largely sidesteps the influence that Brazil has had on contemporary South American and hemispheric affairs beyond the potential redirection of trade caused by the advent and prospect of an expanded Mercosul.

Coverage of the entire gamut of foreign-policy issues is significantly better in literature published in Brazil. There, attention is given to a range of issues such as regional energy matrices (Holanda 2001), regional security (Miyamoto 2000), and bilateral relations with Andean as well as Southern Cone countries. Yet these scholars also appear reluctant to engage deeply with the question of what role Brazil is playing in the evolution of South American and broader inter-American affairs (Vizentini 2003; H. Oliveira 2005; Pinheiro 2004). In part this reluctance appears rooted in the nature of the publications and the style of research found in many journal articles and academic monographs. One leading source of academic analysis on contemporary Brazilian foreign-policy issues is *Carta Internacional*, a monthly publication containing short, issue-specific articles produced by the University of São Paulo's Center for Research on International Relations, or 'O Núcleo de Pesquisa em Relações Internacionais da Universidade de São Paulo' (NUPRI). Although the academic journals *Política Externa*, *Revista Brasileira de Política Internacional*, and *Contexto Internacional* offer lengthier and more-detailed articles, the abiding problem is a failure to tease out the consistent themes that transcend specific events and tactics in Brazilian foreign policy and to offer a coherent picture of the overarching strategy being pursued by Itamaraty.

This book provides the basis for a comprehensive understanding of the motivation and operation of Brazilian foreign policy. In it I integrate analysis of the economic, security, and ideational aspects of Brazilian foreign policy to provide a cogent picture of the grand strategy of leadership guiding Itamaraty's pursuit of intra–South American relations during the Cardoso era. This research agenda is immediately problematic because the primary Itamaraty documentation remains classified. During one research trip for this book I was denied access to declassified material because the documents were apparently infested with a toxic fungus caused by a flood in Itamaraty Palace Anexo

II. Thus, instead of relying on comprehensive archival access, in the following pages I have turned my attention to the collation and analysis of news reports, official statements, documents, and actions through seeking the patterns and trends made evident by the actual conduct of Brazilian foreign policy.

Interviews also formed an important part of my research process. Of the fifty-eight interviews I conducted for this book, twenty-seven were with Brazilian diplomats, eighteen with officials in other Brazilian government departments and agencies, eight with officials from Brazilian interest groups and international organizations, and five with diplomats and officials from other countries. Very few of the subjects interviewed had the authority to make public statements and were thus willing to speak only on condition of anonymity. For diplomats in the very strict hierarchy of Itamaraty this was a particular concern. Thus, only diplomats of ambassador rank or higher—Fernando Henrique Cardoso, Luiz Felipe Lampreia, Celso Lafer, Osmar Chohfi, and Marco Aurélio Garcia—have comments directly attributed to them. The empirical contribution that emerges is an explication of the strategy guiding Brazilian foreign policy that demonstrates how seemingly independent actions in issue areas such as infrastructure, security, and economic integration combine to advance leadership of a regional project informed by the principles of consensual hegemony.

Consensual Hegemony and Brazilian Leadership

Leadership is fundamentally about getting others to do something they might not otherwise choose to do; it implies the deployment of power and the possession of purpose (Ikenberry 1996, 388). To understand how the Brazilian leadership project operates we need a method of discerning the sustained and subtle application of power. I call my approach "consensual hegemony" (Burges 2008).

One place to look in the literature of international relations and international political economy is at the concept of hegemony. But use of the term *hegemony* in association with Brazil's foreign policy is controversial. Indeed, middle- and low-ranking diplomats I interviewed frequently reacted with unease and even revulsion to any linkage of Brazil and vague notions of leadership or hegemony, one going as far as to leave a joint interview to avoid being associated with the discussion. Senior diplomats were more sanguine, but exceptionally careful with the language they used to discuss the topic.

This near-automatic rejection of a potentially useful label for Brazil in a regional or subregional context is unfortunate because it closes down avenues for characterizing and understanding foreign-policy actions. At the root of this reaction is an approach to hegemony that almost directly equates it with imposition and coercion and adheres strictly to the security or coercive approach to the concept, which sees the struggle for power as in effect a zero-sum game (Soares de Lima 1986; Chohfi 2002; Krasner 1976; Knorr 1975; Gilpin 1981). Even the collected-goods or benevolent approach to hegemony places a strain on the denizens of Itamaraty because it explicitly highlights the self-interested nature of maintaining and establishing a particular system (Webb and Krasner 1989; Snidal 1985; Keohane 1984; Keohane and Nye 2001).

Interestingly, ranking diplomats grudgingly accept that Brazil has the capacity and propensity to lead, although not in an impositional sense (Chohfi 2002; Lafer 2007; Cardoso and Lafer 2007; M. Garcia 2007). Tracing discussions of hegemony back through the international-relations literature leads to Charles Kindleberger's (1973) work on the onset and severity of the Great Depression, an event that he attributes to an unwillingness by any major state to assume the costs of maintaining and leading the international system.

Coercion, in short, is not the operative element. Rather, the operative element is the willingness of a leading state to coordinate and underwrite the establishment and maintenance of a system, a point that is echoed in treatments of hegemony in a nuclear age (Keohane 1984; Keohane and Nye 2001; Nye 2002). This leaves the question of why a state would choose to accept the costs of leading, which Susan Strange (1994) answers with the idea of structural power.

A state that has the power to lead the system totally—a hegemonic state—also sets the rules of the game; it embeds its interests and priorities in the very structure of the system until another state is able to devise and implement an alternate arrangement. The implication is thus that, while in the initial stages the hegemonic or leading state must absorb the costs of establishing the system, once it is established that state does not need to retain its absolute dominance and ability to carry the costs of maintenance. Instead it needs only the ability to block changes to the system, which is a less-costly proposition in terms of resource expenditure. Moreover, through a careful phrasing of the dictates of the system and a reasonably inclusive approach to its creation the (pre)dominant state can effectively distribute some of the costs of system maintenance by convincing other states that it is also in their own interests to prevent substantive change.

Implicit in the idea of structural power is a quasi-Gramscian approach to hegemony that sees the concept as being most fully exercised when a coercive apparatus becomes virtually unnecessary. The work of maintaining and advancing the system is shared by the other states because the system is framed in a way that includes them and offers them opportunity for advancement (Arrighi 1993, 149–150; Cafruny 1990, 104; Bieler and Morton 2001, 20). While latent threats of coercion may remain (R. Cox 1996, 127), they are subsumed under a co-optive approach that frames disciplinary action in terms of protecting the common interests of all, not solely those of the hegemon (Augelli and Murphy 1993, 128).

More significant for our discussion of Brazil, the implication here is that it is ideas, a sense of a common project with benefits for all, that form the basis of the hegemonic project. In effect, a sort of consensual hegemony emerges, with the would-be consensual hegemon—in this case Brazil—introducing an approach to organizing transnational economic, political, and social relations. This is followed shortly thereafter by a consultation process designed explicitly to include, at least on a prima facie basis, the aims and aspirations of the other countries that will help establish and operate the hegemony through their compliance.

The critical point in consensual hegemony is its Gramscian leanings, that it is an organizing system and not necessarily an overtly direct power relationship of imposition. A state with the power to establish the overarching system or hegemony is the nominal hegemon, an actor which states can choose to accept as predominant for strategic reasons even if it does not have overwhelming dominance (Pedersen 2002). Consensual hegemony is not about the framing of an explicit power relationship by reaching an agreement that one state will be labeled as the dominant one. Rather, it focuses on the articulation and construction of a project, in the Brazilian case, on various regional initiatives in South America.

The role of the hegemon is thus to provide the initial impetus to start the hegemonic process and encourage other countries to participate in the formation of the hegemony. Emphasis is on an inclusive style of leadership; the coercive element shifts from unambiguous and active sanctions to the implicit costs that may result from nonparticipation in the project. Success in the formation of a consensual hegemony explicitly requires the active and willing engagement of other states, which, while requiring the hegemon to absorb some of the costs of leadership to launch the project, also in effect distributes the cost of maintaining the system across all the participating actors. Of course, the solidity and permanence of the system then come to rest on the extent to which the nominally subordinate actors continue to see their interests reflected in the hegemony.

It is this last factor which forms the crux of the challenge facing the Brazilian leadership project outlined in these pages: How might Itamaraty convince the other South American countries to subscribe to the Brazilian vision of continental hegemony without incurring the economic and security costs of leadership for Brazil? This latter aspect is particularly important if we recall that during the 1990s and first years of the 2000s Brazil was in a very tenuous economic state that precluded any suggestion of meaningful resource transfers to other countries as part of a foreign-policy strategy.

The Regional Tool

The central device used by Itamaraty to advance its leadership project in a consensually hegemonic vein is the creation of regional arrangements. Academic study of the new regionalism is clear on the point that regions are state-led, constructed processes that are continually responding to changing global circumstances. A particular concern of regionalism in the South has been to create a sense of collective strength, which can be harnessed in response to the new pressures created by the acceleration of globalization (Hettne and Söderbaum 2000; Gamble and Payne 1996b; Grugel and Hout 1999b; Amin 1999). The obvious leap here is that states band together to form regions to balance the pressures exerted by traditional hegemons or regionally dominant actors (Mansfield and Milner 1999, 609; Pedersen 2002). But a converse relationship is also quietly suggested in this same literature, that states might band together to collectively provide the goods necessary to maintain an existing order. In the context of Brazil's consensually hegemonic leadership strategy this aspect is particularly useful because it positions the region as a device that the leading or predominant state can use to distribute the costs of creating and maintaining the structure it wishes to see directing regional affairs.

Establishment of a region also introduces a useful implicitly coercive element. The decision to create a region or advance a regional project has the potential to impose costs on other countries in the area. Participation in a regional agreement will ostensibly advance the interests and position of the participating states, giving them an advantage over nonparticipating states; nonparticipation in a new regional project or the failure to continue engaging in the extension of a regional project anchored on a regionally predominant state thus contains an element of passive-aggressive coercion and threatens the interests of nonparticipating states by excluding them from the expanded opportunities of the region (Mattli 1999). The corollary is that the predominant state deploying the region as a passive-aggressive coercive instrument must ensure that the regional grouping offers sufficient payoffs to make nonmembership more costly than membership. In the context of the distributed-cost approach to leadership embedded in consensual hegemony this entails a delicate calculus on the ideational, economic, and security levels. A key element in balancing this equation is the notion of regional cohesion, the ability to build the regional project in a way that embraces and includes the members' competing interests in a constructive manner (Hurrell 1995, 44–45).

In practical terms, a demand push—the incitement of domestic political pressure by the dominant state in the other countries for continued participation—for regional membership is needed. Such pressure entails a multilevel approach that appeals to both national leaders and ministerial policy prerogatives as well as to the generation of the sort of business and civil society pressures captured in the idea of a 'commercial fifth column' (Hirschman 1945). The success of the region will ultimately come to rest on the extent to which harmony is achieved in the four key dynamics of culture, security, economic policy, and politics (Hettne 1999, 11–13). Although framing this idea in slightly different terms, this book tells the story of how Brazilian foreign-policy makers during the 1992–2002 period sought to bring about harmony in these dynamics to create a subregional and regional system that would allow Brazil to be first a continental and then an international leader without assuming the full costs of leadership.

Structure of the Book

The book is broken into seven chapters. The first chapter is a historical review of Brazilian foreign policy in South America and traces events from Rio Branco's tenure as head of Itamaraty until the early 1990s. Here my intent is to establish the gradual pattern of change in Brazilian foreign policy and to contextualize the emergence of a consensually hegemonic style of leadership during the Collor/Franco administration and the historical evolution of the regionalist impulse in Brazil's diplomatic strategy. Perhaps the most significant theme in this chapter is the persistence of a quiet leadership impulse in Brazil's foreign policy, a tendency frequently masked behind the language of consensus creation and conciliation that nevertheless fails to hide a clear tendency for Itamaraty to actively pursue policies designed to protect Brazil's national autonomy.

The second chapter draws out and highlights leadership strategies in Brazil's foreign policy during the period in question, making it clear that Itamaraty was trying to lead Brazil's South American neighbors in specific regionalist projects. Here consensual hegemony opens space for understanding how elements other than direct coercion might be consistently and effectively deployed by a diplomatically creative state to pursue a concerted foreign-policy agenda centered on regionalist projects.

The next three chapters combine to offer a detailed treatment of various interlocking aspects of Brazil's intracontinental relations. Given the grounding of Brazilian leadership in a notion of consensual hegemony an immediate problem is the surprising lack of attention given to disaggregating hegemony into manageable component parts in international relations and international political economy literature. Anthony Payne (1994) has noted that scholars have all but failed to offer a description of the anatomy of hegemony beyond stating that it involves possessing a surfeit of power. As he notes, blunt suggestions of total power or dominance are not particularly useful when we turn our attention to the multifaceted and varied realms in which power can be exercised and seek to understand the method of its application. In an effort to provide a descriptive shape to hegemony Payne (1994, 154) points explicitly to Susan Strange's four-sided pyramidal model of structural power as perhaps the clearest description of the component parts of hegemony and their interrelationship. I take Strange's pyramidal model as a starting point for breaking hegemony into its component parts and modify it to focus on three specific areas that require leadership if hegemony is to form: ideas, economics, and security.

Where neorealists see power as being dependent on military might, with such "low-politics" issues as economics and diplomacy playing only a supporting role, Strange (1994, 27) argues that there are four equally important and mutually dependent aspects to structural power: finance, production, security, and ideas. These four aspects are arranged in a pyramidal configuration, meaning that each is "supported, joined up to and held up by the other three" (Strange 1994, 37). Significantly, the interdependent nature of these four elements also means that there is a certain degree of cross-fertilization, that power in one dimension grows from power and position in the other three. This results in the analytical cross-fertilization that will be discussed in the empirical chapters in this book.

The change I introduce to Strange's model is a merging of the economically oriented sides of production and finance into one facet. While Strange sets out a clear logic of separating the economic realm into two sections, the notion of financial power and productive power as different in Latin America in general, and in Brazil in particular, is not quite as self-evident. Despite the persistent holdover of the debt crisis, the link between access to credit and the expansion of production is muddied by widespread business attitudes that make firms reluctant to take on debt to expand production in the manner seen in North America and Western Europe. During the period of study of this book the culture was more one of an expansion of firm activity through the reinvestment of profits. More to the point, the link between production and finance held over from the corporatist-capitalist model is tight to the point where it is not necessarily useful for the sort of analysis presented here to explicitly separate the two facets. The resulting three-sided pyramid—ideas, economics, security—thus provides a guiding structure for three of the chapters on ideas, economics, and security in this book.

Attention is first turned to the ideational underpinning of the leadership project (Chapter 3). I draw on Strange's (1991, 37) suggestion that ideas provide an intellectual currency that can be used to bind countries with a shared identity and ideology. The negative aspect of power inherent in the ideas dimension—withholding or controlling the flow of knowledge to restrict development in the economic and security dimensions of structural power—is left as a subtext. In terms of the overarching leadership project, the ideas dimension assumes a great deal of significance because it provides the currency for the leadership project and forms the foundational basis of the regionalist projects that Itamaraty sought to create and spread throughout South America through a process that more often relied on sustained discussions and consensus creation than on the offering of rents or the application of direct coercion. At the center of this ideational dimension lies the articulation of South America as a distinct geoeconomic and geopolitical space. The notion of South America as a viable regional unit is then wound with a particular understanding of democracy, development, and globalization and how the turn to regionalism will advance the shared continental goals of stable democratic governance and sustained economic development.

Strange's finance and production aspects of structural power are collapsed into a single economic facet of hegemony in Chapter 4. Inspiration for this change comes from the emphasis in structuralist and neostructuralist theory on the economic marginalization of Latin America in the global political economy and the extent to which a concomitant lack of control over finance and production has marked regional development. Here attention will be turned directly to the economic fundament of Brazilian regional projects. I will analyze aspects of Itamaraty-orchestrated leadership in Mercosul before discussing how ostensibly technocratic projects such as the development of physical infrastructure networks have been used to create the underlying conditions necessary to support a regional project in the continent. Indeed, it is in the economic aspect that the oblique nature of Brazilian leadership at times emerges most clearly, with Itamaraty's strategies serving to provide the public goods necessary to encourage other South American states to participate in the regional projects without actually incurring for Brazil the sort of costs of leading suggested by mainstream approaches to hegemony.

Strange (1994, 45) is quite pointed about the need to include security, the subject of Chapter 6, in her model of structural power: "security . . . is the most basic of basic human needs. If someone kills you, you immediately have no further needs." While the primacy of physical survival is certainly not irrelevant to discussion of foreign policy in South America, the historical rarity of serious war and of persistent interstate military aggression in South America calls for a wider consideration of security. Chapter 5 therefore takes a broader view of security. In it I draw on the importance of maintaining national autonomy in the face of sustained attempts at external intervention in the region to discuss Brazil's role in efforts to secure the continent's democracies, settle outstanding territorial disputes, and address new security issues such as narco-trafficking, terrorism, and insurgency. Consideration of Brazilian leadership in the security dimension also serves to return us ultimately to the limits of the leadership style underpinning Itamaraty's regionalist strategy. That strategy has led to effective, cohesive, and regionalized , anti-drug-smuggling and counter-insurgency programs stumbling on an unwillingness to absorb the associated economic and political costs or to undertake the necessary degree of intervention in the international affairs of neighboring countries.

Before drawing conclusions, I first turn my attention in Chapter 6 to the foreign-policy continuities of the Cardoso era during the first four years of the presidency of Luiz Inácio Lula da Silva, universally known as Lula. The transition from the urbane, center-right presidency of Cardoso to the leftist Partido dos Trabalhadores (PT—Workers' Party) of Lula represents far more than a shift along the political spectrum. It brought a dramatic change in the sort of people running the Brazilian state and giving political direction to Itamaraty. Consequently, the sixth chapter will offer a brief exploration of the extent to which the foreign-policy strategy and trajectory established during the Cardoso era subscribed to the Itamaraty dictum that direction changes in Brazilian foreign policy move with glacial velocity. Indeed, as will be suggested with the preliminary evidence available, the only markedly substantial shift that took place between the two presidencies was that the reality of the strategy of consensual hegemony—a clear desire to position Brazil as a regional, continental, and southern leader—became overt in Brazilian foreign-policy discourse during Lula's first term, even if such forthrightness did cause great discomfort among many of the country's diplomats, and that the emphasis shifted from economic to political factors.

1

The Historical Path
of Brazilian Foreign Policy

The notion of an integrated South American political and economic space that formed the core of the leadership project advanced by Itamaraty during the Cardoso era was not a sudden invention. Indeed, an abiding characteristic of Brazilian foreign-policy makers is their slow rate of change and careful consideration before action. Historical context is thus critical for understanding the evolution and nature of policies pursued by Itamaraty during the period in question. As this chapter will describe, the historical trajectory of Brazil's foreign policy both reached a point of crisis and provided recourse to a possible resolution when the Cold War ended in 1989 and the advent of the North American Free Trade Agreement (NAFTA) raised the possibility of a realignment of hemispheric relations that might marginalize Brazil (Abdenur 1994a; Almeida 1993; Amorim 1991a; Barbosa 1994; Lafer 1990; Lafer and Fonseca 1994). The outcome of much discussion within Itamaraty was a return to suggestions of South American regionalism, which had previously been advanced with little success, especially by Rio Branco and Juscelino Kubitschek.

The primary task of this chapter, then, is to trace the development of Brazilian foreign policy in the Americas from Rio Branco's tenure as foreign minister to the beginning of the Fernando Henrique Cardoso presidency. In broad terms this narrative may be divided into three main phases: close approximation to the United States; a "quest for autonomy"; and finally the articulation of a regionally based, cooperatively independent foreign policy.

Attention will first be turned to Rio Branco and his elaboration of a foreign policy of approximation to the United States. An outline of the gradual decline in effectiveness of the Baron's precepts leads to the next section, which begins with the presidency of Juscelino Kubitschek and proceeds to discuss the rise of a foreign policy of autonomy in the 1960s and 1970s. The 1980s brings a change in focus to Brazilian foreign policy and a marked improvement in international relations in the Southern Cone. Here the discussion will center on measures to improve regional cooperation in the economic and security dimensions, programs which eventually assumed a reactive character in response to changes in the hemispheric and global political economy. Ultimately, the reactive turn to regionalism resulted in the creation of Mercosul and efforts to expand the bloc to encompass the bulk of South America and cement the major change in Brazilian foreign-policy thinking in the 1980s: the turn to continental leadership and use of the region as the context for advancing and achieving national development.

A Policy of Approximation

The roots of contemporary Brazilian foreign policy can be traced to the beginning of the twentieth century and Rio Branco's decade-long tenure as foreign minister. It was during this period that Itamaraty began to assume a reputation for professionalism, preparation, and apoliticism—at least with respect to domestic political debates (Vieira 2001). It was also during this period that a series of fundamental precepts for the conceptualization of Brazilian foreign policy were first elaborated (Almeida 1993, 93). At the heart of this emerging policy program was a desire for Brazil to be a leader among states and a shaper of the emerging world order. This ambition was reflected during the Baron's lifetime in the pride Brazilians took in the 1906 Rio de Janeiro Pan American Summit (J. Smith 1991, 53–57), participation in the 1907 Hague Conference, and later inclusion in the Versailles Treaty negotiations and on the Executive Council of the League of Nations (J. Smith 1991, 126–133; Bueno 2002a, 222–233).

Yet there remained the persistent problem of Brazil's actual power not matching its perceived potential, leaving the country vulnerable to a coordinated attack by its Spanish-speaking neighbors or marauding European powers. The solution pursued by Rio Branco was two-pronged. On the continental level he successfully settled Brazil's remaining undefined borders through a process of negotiation and arbitration (Ricupero 2000), taking great care to ensure that he did not create ill-will or leave his country open to the charge of imperial expansionism (Burns 1966, 38–48). Residual concerns that the demarcation of the national territory would be but the first step in a drawn-out process of conquest were subsumed by the second prong of the Baron's strategy: close alliance with the United States to improve Brazil's position in the region and to protect against foreign incursion (J. Smith 1991, 62–67).

Perhaps a greater threat than an alliance of the fractious Spanish-speaking

South American republics was an opportunistic raid by a resource-hungry European power. With an extensive coastline and meager navy, Brazil was essentially defenseless against a concerted and well-armed invasion. Rio Branco's solution was to form a strategic alliance by wrapping his country in the mantle of the Monroe Doctrine; he actively informed the world that Brazil accepted the Americas as the exclusive preserve of U.S. influence and assured Washington that it could count on Brazilian support in international fora (Burns 1966, chapters 2 and 3). Twenty-five years of diplomatic postings in Europe and the United States had allowed the Baron to conduct a comparative analysis of the new and old worlds, leading him to conclude that the United States was ascendant and that North America would become the locus of international power in the twentieth century.   While this pathbreaking analysis came as a shock to the many Brazilians enmeshed in a historical tradition of political and cultural affinity with Europe, the economics of Brazil's international relations had long since centered on the United States. Where the nineteenth century had been marked by the export of primary products to Europe, by the beginning of the twentieth century the United States had emerged as the major market for coffee and rubber (Evans 1979, chapter 2), commodities which made up to 72.5 percent of national exports (Bueno 2002a, 202). Indeed, the perennial focus of United States–Brazil relations was discussions about military assistance programs, tariff rates, coffee prices, and shipping regimes to get Brazilian agricultural products into the North American market (J. Smith 1991, 67–76).

The United States was not interested simply in the goodwill of its large South American neighbor. Rio Branco was clearly aware that the favor and support of the U.S. government depended on his country's ability to provide meaningful assistance in hemispheric affairs. And it is here that the subtlety of Brazilian foreign policy during the Baron's tenure can be found, highlighted most keenly by his success in parlaying approximation to the United States into a nascent subregional leadership role. In an era of slow ocean transport and unreliable telecommunications, Rio Branco recognized that Washington would need an interlocutor in South America if the precepts of the Monroe Doctrine were to remain workable, a role which Rio Branco was happy to see filled by Brazil.

Although the Baron did want peaceful relations with the rest of South America, he was clear that Brazil should have a preeminent role, a position that would emulate U.S. leadership in Central America and the Caribbean (Bueno, 2002b, 164–165; J. Smith 1991, 65). A balancing act was thus introduced into Brazilian foreign policy, one which sought to ensure that Brazil remained the international and institutional leader in the region, but which did not pursue this goal through a policy of open or mindless obstructionism.

Lauro Müller, the Baron's successor, continued this policy and maintained Brazil's nascent continental preeminence by thwarting development of Argentina or Chile as a rival for regional leadership through a non-Brazilian version of Rio Branco's proposed 1904 ABC alliance (Argentina, Brazil, Chile). Subsequent proposals for ABC cooperation were at first defused by the Brazilian foreign minister's suggestion that the whole alphabet be brought in and the rest of South America included (J. Smith 1991, 94–95). Later Chilean efforts to revive the ABC by converting the cancelled 1914 Santiago Pan American Conference into the formative meeting of a tripartite alliance were given polite attention but effectively quashed when the treaty failed to pass the Argentine and Brazilian congresses (J. Smith 1991, 100–102).

The persistent stresses of decades of uncertainty about Brazilian access to the U.S. market and the shifting intensity of military assistance did not begin to form cracks in the policy of approximation until well into the first Getúlio Vargas period (1930–1945). After the Brazilian economy was devastated by the collapse of coffee exports during the Great Depression—GDP contracted 18.7 percent in 1930 and 11.75 percent in 1931—Vargas reached the conclusion that Brazil would have to undergo a process of national development and industrialization, which would require access to new markets, a diversification of exports, and the acquisition of new technologies (J. Smith 1991, 100–102). The result was the first major change in foreign policy since Rio Branco had held office and the rise of a *desenvolvimentista* (developmental) foreign policy (Bueno 2002a, 234–239). While the relationship with the United States remained important, Itamaraty began to work assiduously at opening new markets and investment sources in Europe, experiencing particular success with Germany (Hurrell 1986, 29; Machado da Silva 2000, 101–104; Barreto 2001, 111–117).

Seeking to create an industrialized economy, Vargas attached special significance to the acquisition of steel-production technologies and received competing offers of help from Germany and the United States. Unfortunately, solid commitments remained more elusive than grandiloquent but ultimately empty statements of support.

The distance between words and actions was partially attributable to the U.S. State Department's awareness that Vargas would continue to favor the existing policy of approximation despite a rhetoric of realignment. Indeed, the appraisal made by Itamaraty was that the national interest continued to be best served by fulfilling the role of interlocutor between the United States and South America and resisting the temptation to opportunistically realign with the European powers. This became evident after the onset of World War II when the Brazilian government at first offered substantial "nonaligned" assistance before joining the war in 1942 as the conflict's sole South American combatant.

In the postwar years Brazil remained a staunch ally of the United States, playing an important role in the establishment of the Organization of American States (OAS) and convincing the South American countries to support the Inter-American Reciprocal Assistance Treaty, which was signed at a 1947 conference in Rio de Janeiro (Bueno 2002a, 271; Cervo 1997, 8). Brazilian president Eurico Gaspar Dutra not unreasonably expected some reward for his country's loyalty during and after the war, preferably in the form of Marshall Plan–style assistance with industrialization (Mace 1999, 25). But as Amado Luiz Cervo (2001, 99) notes, the role for Latin America in U.S. foreign policy was changing from active ally to supplier of raw materials and ready supporter of U.S. proposals in international fora. Indeed, the U.S. State Department and intelligence services were soon more concerned with the reliability of the Brazilian government in the event of a war with the Communist bloc (United States 1953, paragraph 9). Moreover, concerns about the political orientation of other Latin American countries began to erode the special treatment afforded to Brazil. Where President Woodrow Wilson actively worked to include Brazilian representatives in the major post–World War I fora, the aftermath of the Second World War saw Brazil excluded from such formative discussions as those held at Bretton Woods. This marginalization was repeated in the United Nations, where energetic Brazilian efforts to help create the body resulted in the consolation prize of perennially providing the annual opening address to the General Assembly, not the desired permanent seat on the United Nations Security Council (UNSC). More galling than this exclusion was Washington's postwar accommodation of Argentina, a policy which restricted flows of military and economic assistance to Brazil and had the potential to dramatically alter the balance of power in the River Plate basin (Hilton 1981).

Turning to South America

Slowly the U.S. policy of benign neglect made it clear that little external assistance would be forthcoming for Brazilian national development. Disappointment that Brazil's loyalty during the Second World War was not rewarded turned to disenchantment as the United States not only began to turn its attention to the policy of containing Communism in Southeast Asia and Europe, but also continued to pursue a policy in South America that effectively downgraded Brazil's privileged role in U.S.–Latin American relations. The outcome was an increasingly independent foreign-policy stance from the short-lived Vargas government (1951–1954). After Vice-Pres. Richard Nixon's disastrous, protest-riddled tour of Latin America in 1958, Brazilian president Juscelino Kubitschek launched the Operação Pan Americana (OPA—Pan American Operation), a proposal which sought to bring about national development through regional cooperation (Cervo 1997, 10).

Three aspects of OPA are of particular importance for the argument here. First, it was cast as a specifically regional project. Whereas in the Baron's era vague notions of regional cooperation were bandied about as possible routes for the quiet ascendancy of an autonomous and independent Brazil, OPA was predicated on the assumption that national development would be impossible without substantial regional cooperation. Second, the project actively sought U.S. support for the region's development goals. Drawing on the U.S. obsession with preventing the spread of Communism in the Americas, Kubitschek argued that political stability could best be assured by facilitating economic development (Penna Filho 2002, 5–6). Finally, OPA represented a major effort to once again act as a sort of U.S. plenipotentiary and smoothe the fractious relations between the widespread popular sentiment on the Latin American street and official Washington that had marred Nixon's tour (Bueno 2002a, 290–295).

The importance of OPA lay not in an immediate transformation of U.S.–Latin American relations—Eisenhower declined to participate in the project in any meaningful way, although Kennedy did use substantial elements of it as inspiration for the Alliance for Progress—but in the changes it induced in Brazilian foreign policy. Although it combined with the structuralist economic theory of the Santiago-based U.N. Economic Commission for Latin America to prompt the 1960 creation of the Associação Latino-Americana de Livre-Comércio (ALALC—Latin American Free-Trade Association), which collapsed and became the Associação Latino-Americana de Integração (ALADI—Latin American Integration Association) in 1980, it did not result in the sort of open and fluid free-trade area that Kubitschek might have hoped for. Moreover, Washington's reluctance to actively engage the OPA initiative prompted a rethinking of Brazil's reliance on the United States and a search for new markets, aid sources, and military linkages (Martins Filho 2007), particularly in recovering Western Europe. This shift in orientation away from near-dependence on the munificence of the U.S. government marked the beginning of *política externa independente* (independent foreign policy), a new direction that made an important break from the grand strategy outlined by Rio Branco in the early 1900s (Penna Filho 2002, 12–14).

Kubitschek's successor, Jânio Quadros (1961), was forthright in articulating a new foreign policy for Brazil, one which aimed to accelerate economic development and project a greater sense of diplomatic independence. The tone of Quadros' new foreign policy was confrontational, pitting Brazil against the United States and underlining the need for unity among developing countries. Forceful rhetoric aside, Quadros' talk of an independent foreign policy during his curtailed presidency was more important for the precedent that it set for policymakers in the 1970s than for its immediate impact on Brazil's international relations (Hurrell 1986, 57–61; U.S. CIA 1961). Indeed, the institution of the Castello Branco military government in 1964 saw a dramatic realignment with the United States, returning to Rio Branco's logic of trading Brazilian hemispheric support for U.S. military and development assistance. On the military front this shift in orientation was clear. Where U.S. military assistance to Brazil between 1950 and 1963 had been U.S.$150.6 million, the three years between 1964 and 1967 saw a total inflow of U.S.$67.1 million.

Underpinning the renewed approximation with the United States orchestrated by Castello Branco was the articulation of the geopolitical approach to international relations, a conceptualization which divided the world into three main concentric circles. The first circle existed on a continental level, calling for Brazil to position itself as the dominant arbiter within South America. This circle was enclosed within the next circle, which covered the Americas, with the United States as the principal actor. Finally, at the top was a more globalized circle encompassing Europe and the Americas, which was again dominated by the United States. Special status for Brazil was seen as emanating from the country's role as the interlocutor between the United States on the hemispheric as well as the global stage and South America on the continental level (Golbery 1967; Child 1979, 90–92).

The 1964–1967 period saw Brazil adopt what amounted to a policy of dependency-theory–style subimperialism, filling the role of intermediate actor between the developing and the developed countries (Reis da Silva 2000). This revival of 1900s-era foreign policy was not particularly successful and did little to improve intraregional relations; in fact, it represented a significant step back from the more cooperatively oriented foreign policy envisioned in Kubitschek's OPA (Hurrell 1986, 81–84).

A Policy of Independence

By the end of the Castello Branco period an old sentiment had begun to resurface, namely, that the United States had benefited greatly from activities and diplomatic initiatives that had proven costly to Brazil. The failure of the White House to show its thanks through a meaningful expansion of aid and development flows—military aid fell to just U.S.$4.3 million in 1970—revived the disenchantment that had led to the *política externa independente* and significantly weakened enthusiasm for the existing close relationship during the 1967–1969 Costa e Silva presidency (Hurrell 1986, 89–128). Indeed, the logic behind a dependence on U.S. economic and military aid was becoming increasingly questionable in the late 1960s, particularly as the Brazilian economic miracle picked up speed at the turn of the decade and other global markets and investment sources emerged.

The years between 1968 and 1973 witnessed unprecedented economic growth in Brazil. Average annual GDP rises of 10 percent in this period were in part fueled by an almost unlimited supply of foreign credit, financing that was available at what amounted to negative real interest rates (Bacha and Malan 1989, 123). But, as Peter Evans has noted, national income stratification meant that much of the country's new wealth was predominantly spent on luxury goods, not investment in a sustainable productive structure. The resultant shift from classical dependency to associated-dependent development—industrialization driven by a socially controlling alliance between the state, local capital, and foreign capital, prompted by a surge in demand for domestically produced consumable and nondurable goods—changed the nature of Brazil's import-substitution model. Machinery, equipment, fuels, and intermediate inputs were switched for the basic commodities that had previously been imported (Evans 1979, 97–98).

The accompanying boom in the production and export of manufactured goods corresponded with the height of the military government, giving the nationalist Médici presidency (1969–1974) a high degree of optimism and reviving public perceptions that Brazil might be on its way to becoming a world power (Hurrell 1986, 150; Souto 2001, 45). This in turn raised concern within the military that excessive reliance on the United States for training and equipment was undermining Brazil's strategic autonomy, particularly with respect to the country's ability to position itself and act as the dominant player in South America and a potent force in the South Atlantic (Martins Filho 2007).

Internal economic growth in Brazil and an expansion of international trade and economic ties were accompanied by a marked deepening of relations with Bolivia and Paraguay as part of a policy to increase Brazil's influence in the continent. Throughout the early 1970s the Brazilian presence in Bolivia expanded rapidly, particularly through large investments in mineral, oil, and gas extraction. Brasília's influence in Paraguay grew through the granting of preferential access to the port of Paranagua and the rapid increase in the number of Brasiguayos—by 1973 over 40,000 Brazilians were working Paraguayan land (Hurrell 1986, 190–192; Warren 1985; Lewis 1993).

This slow outward and absorptive expansion combined with the remnants of Castello Branco's renewal of the policy of approximation to the United States to reawaken fears of Brazilian imperialism in the rest of South America, most especially in Argentina. Matters were not helped by Itamaraty's brusque approach to the development of the giant Itaipú hydroelectric complex. Despite the potential downstream implications the dam had for planned Argentine hydroelectric projects, Brazilian negotiators remained stubbornly resolute that the location and design was a bilateral matter that would be discussed only with partner country Paraguay; this reinforced the impression of subregional hegemonism and added more pressure on already fragile Brazil-Argentina relations (Soares de Lima 1986, chapter 6).

Yet the antagonistic appearance of Brazilian foreign policy during the Médici presidency was misleading. Rather than focusing on regional domination, the emphasis was squarely on national development and the expansion as well as diversification of international linkages (Souto 2001). Increased flows of Brazilian investment into Bolivia and intransigence on the Itaipú issue were part of a larger program designed to reduce national dependence on a few narrow sources of energy (Hurrell 1986, 319–323; Becker and Egler 1992, 50). Massive increases in domestic arms production, first pursued to make up for the shortfall in U.S. military support, became simply another export commodity (Perruci 1995), one which would make an increasingly important contribution to the steadily worsening balance-of-payments situation of the second half of the 1970s. Brazilian policymakers were concerned solely with the internal impact policies would have on the quest for great-power status, not with the construction of regional partnerships. The Médici foreign policy, to borrow Hurrell's phrasing, was a "quest for autonomy" that rejected notions of automatic alignment. Moreover, this policy tack explicitly viewed development, the primary national interest, as a project best pursued alone.

The autonomous tone of Médici's foreign policy was continued by Ernesto Geisel, but with a twist that sought to downplay ideological overtones and seek wide-ranging international linkages to support the country's political and economic interests. While this policy of responsible 'pragmatism' in effect continued the distancing of Brazil from the United States, most notably by cancelling the 1952 military cooperation agreement, there was a concomitant attempt to soften the autonomous overtones inherent in the previous foreign policy while simultaneously retaining the maximum possible diplomatic flexibility in order to advance Brazil's national interest (Hurrell 1986, 197).

Efforts to negotiate the Amazon Cooperation Treaty reflected this change. The ultimate concern was not so much with absorbing neighboring economies as with creating a framework within which the Brazilian government could pursue the sort of positive bilateral relations needed to develop Amazônia. Indeed, the final version of the treaty reflects a specific desire to not impinge on the freedom of action of member states; it focuses instead on the creation of new opportunities through coordinated action on key regional issues.

The final text of the agreement notwithstanding, initial Itamaraty proposals for the border areas of the region—duty-free zones, development of complementary regional economic structures, infrastructure integration—recalled the Médici policy of subimperial economic penetration (Ferris 1981, 162). This suggests that, while Brazilian diplomats were seeking to maximize their influence in the Amazon basin, they remained cognizant of their limited capacity to directly pressure other states into action.

Geisel's continuation of policies designed to bind neighboring countries to Brazil recognized this limitation when he expanded investment in Bolivia, Paraguay, and Uruguay (Hurrell 1986, 165; Souto 2001, 55–57; Marini 1972). Indeed, some urgency was given to this policy when the Peronist candidate—who opposed Itamaraty's regional policy and hinted at a revival of the viceroyalty of La Plata with Buenos Aires as the capital—won Argentina's 1973 presidential election. As had occurred in the past, increasingly heated verbal exchanges were accompanied by a heightening of military preparedness and capacity.

But there were two important differences in this instance. First, both countries were in the early stages of a nuclear-development program, allegedly for peaceful uses, with Argentina being slightly more advanced than Brazil. Second, industrialization with the concomitant rise of a domestic arms industry and the changed international scenario meant that Brazil no longer had to rely on the United States for military and diplomatic support (Martins Filho 2007). Conventional arms could and were domestically manufactured; nuclear technology was obtained from West Germany without the need to adhere to the restrictions attached to U.S. atomic assistance (Soares de Lima 1986, chapters 2 and 3; Arroio 1995; Perruci 1995; Wrobel 1996).

While it was the subsequent Figueiredo presidency that brought the initial resurgence of regional-integration policies in the Southern Cone, these developments were made possible by the cantankerous tone of the Geisel presidency (Hilton 1985; Spektor 2002). As was outlined earlier in this chapter, an explicit goal of Rio Branco's foreign policy of approximation to the United States was the neutralization of the Argentine threat. For over seventy years Brazilian foreign policy had followed the Baron's precepts, maintaining a policy of official cordiality toward Buenos Aires. While the bilateral relationship experienced significant periods of respect and frank communication, mutual trust was never in abundance.

The Geisel period extended the distrustful aspect of Argentine-Brazilian relations, rupturing the policy of official cordiality and raising the very real possibility of a nuclear arms race in the Southern Cone. The difference with past periods of sour relations was that the Brazilian threat to Argentina no longer hinged on a close unwritten alliance with the United States. Indeed, the active destruction of the special relationship between Brasília and Washington—marked most notably by the cancellation of a long-standing bilateral military agreement in 1977 and the pursuit of nuclear technology despite active U.S. opposition—removed the specter of Brazil as the subimperial agent of U.S. domination in South America. Tensions between Argentina and Brazil reverted to their nineteenth-century form, namely, a struggle for influence and control in the River Plate basin and the South Atlantic. In this context mutual distrust between the two administrations flourished into personal animosity, making the improvement of bilateral relations impossible until a leadership change took place (Spektor 2002).

With the departure of Geisel from office in 1979, a resurgence of underlying shared security concerns in the South Atlantic combined with mutual fear of the outcome of nuclear competition to convince the foreign ministries and armed forces in Argentina and Brazil that the pattern of bilateral relations had to be drastically altered. Stanley Hilton (1985, 51) offers the conclusion that the rapprochement of the early 1980s sprang from the realization in Buenos Aires that without a nuclear advantage Argentina could never hope to effectively challenge the much larger, industrialized Brazil for lasting influence in South America. Adding to this sentiment was a tacit understanding between the two countries that the succession of minor conflicts must be halted before a major conflagration occurred (Selcher 1985, 25).

The change in the tenor of bilateral relations at the turn of the decade was captured by two significant and symbolic acts. After over a decade of intransigence, in 1979 the Brazilian government, recognizing the legitimacy of Argentina's downstream interests, particularly with respect to the planned Corpus Dam on the Argentina-Paraguay border, altered its approach to the Itaipú hydroelectric project. Personal animosity on the presidential level was also quickly dissipated by Figueiredo's 1980 state visit to Buenos Aires for the first summit in over forty years.

The rise of political conviviality was accompanied by a growing recognition of the importance of bilateral economic ties. Despite the tense strategic and political situation, bilateral trade had boomed in the 1970s, rising from a combined total of U.S.$597 million in 1975 to U.S.$1,857 million in 1980. From the Brazilian perspective, this growing trade had become increasingly important because its composition was shifting away from a focus on agricultural and primary products to manufactured goods, which accounted for 67 percent of exports to Argentina by 1984 (Manzetti 1990, 113; Soares Carbonar 1990).

Returning to the Southern Cone

The dramatic improvement in bilateral political relations between 1980 and 1982 took place against the backdrop of a global recession. A marked tightening of international credit supplies, particularly the open-market loans which had been used to underwrite the Brazilian economy during the latter half of the 1970s, combined with a drop in international trade to present each country with severe economic challenges. Both Argentina and Brazil were under increasing pressure to slash imports and increase exports in order to raise the foreign exchange needed to service debt obligations and meet International Monetary Fund (IMF) rescue requirements.

Unfortunately, in response to the pressures of widespread recession the global economy was experiencing a period of increased protectionism, a trend which both countries mirrored by raising their tariff levels to force a decline in imports. The impact on bilateral trade was predictable—by 1983 it had fallen to 53.4 percent of its 1980 level, recovering to 71.7 percent of the 1980 level by 1985 (Manzetti 1990, 113; Bacha and Malan 1989).

Concomitant with the protectionist policy–induced drop in trade between Argentina and Brazil was a growing move toward fortress-style economic regionalism. Indeed, within the hemisphere the Brian Mulroney government in Canada responded to recession-caused tensions at the beginning of the decade by proposing the creation of the United States–Canada Free Trade Agreement, an exercise in defensive regionalism which found parallels in both Europe and Southeast Asia (Gilpin 1987, chapter 10; Hirst 1992, 147; Vaz 1999, 17–20). The fear in both Argentina and Brazil was that the pressures of the debt crisis and the unrealized potential of each country would lead to a position of global economic and political marginalization (Barbosa 1994; Abdenur 1994a).

At the inauguration of President Sarney in March 1985, which formally ended military rule in Brazil, Argentine president Alfonsín proposed that the two countries enter into a bilateral economic-integration agreement. Impetus was given to negotiations by the signing of the 30 November 1985 Acta de Iguazú, which committed both countries to greater economic cooperation and integration. By 30 July 1986 negotiations had been completed, allowing Sarney and Alfonsín to sign the twelve protocols which formed the heart of the Programa de Integração e Cooperação Econômica (PICE—Program of Economic Integration and Cooperation). The agreement was ideally timed, allowing cooperation in the achievement of three interrelated goals, namely, reducing dependence on volatile global markets, jointly increasing domestic economic growth, and stabilizing bilateral trade flows (Manzetti 1990, 115).

But the importance of the agreement extended beyond the realm of economics. Agreements such as PICE were part of a larger Alfonsín strategy to prevent a resurgence of authoritarianism in the Southern Cone through a sort of collective democratic security (Fournier 1999; Dávila-Villers 1992). While the maintenance of the democratization process was certainly important to Brazil (Sodré 1987), the country's zeal in actively spreading the political system was somewhat less than that found in Argentina. Itamaraty was more interested in PICE's potential to eliminate tensions on Brazil's southern border and permanently exorcise the prospect of serious conflict with Argentina. Eventual cooperation with Argentina in the formation of the South Pacific Zone of Peace further settled tensions in the River Plate basin and created a framework that it was hoped would liberate the region from the constant implicit threat of armed conflict inherent in the Cold War (T. Costa 1996). The combination of these two developments created a much-improved security climate for Brazil, allowing resources to be diverted toward the Amazon areas (Hirst 1992, 142; Forhmann 2000). But perhaps most important, Argentina's request that

PICE be signed and Uruguay's subsequent accession to the agreement served as implicit confirmation of Brazilian preeminence in the River Plate basin.

Itamaraty's success in achieving a degree of preeminence for Brazil in the 1980s should not be confused with ambitions for continental dominance, a role that Brazil has consistently refused. Indeed, such a status would have required far greater resources than the embattled Brazilian economy was capable of mobilizing in the 1980s or early 1990s (Selcher 1986). But this does not mean that the Foreign Ministry was not seeking to increase its influence in Latin America, particularly in the context of the rising importance of the United States in overcoming the Latin American debt crisis. PICE offered an ideal opportunity to extend the policy of economic penetration that had marked relations with Bolivia and Paraguay since the early 1970s. Unlike previous failed attempts at Latin American integration, such as ALALC and bilateral economic cooperation, the twelve protocols underlying PICE were predicated on a gradualist approach to integration, one which promised to give affected industries a chance to adapt to the reality of coping with foreign competition. Specific long-term goals focusing on the development and industrialization of the member countries were enshrined in the protocols. Provision was also made for a compensation mechanism to redress persistent trade distortions and significant bilateral commercial deficits (Baumann and Lerda 1987b, 20–21).

While PICE did not quite live up to the expectation of creating a common economic area with truly integrated national economies (indeed, the state of transnational infrastructure linkages made such a task very difficult), the intent underlying the protocols remained firmly in place. The importance of PICE to the larger picture of bilateral political relations was such that, rather than downgrading the agreement at each setback, the participating governments responded by setting more ambitious goals, almost biding their time until circumstances were more propitious for a deeper integration.

The PICE process formalized a realignment of Brazilian foreign policy to a position that privileged relations with Argentina. Although the debt crisis of the 1980s had caused a resurgence of amicable relations between the Brazilian and U.S. governments, Itamaraty was keenly aware that a significant part of Washington's sudden interest in the region had less to do with altruistic aid to hemispheric friends than with ensuring that a regionwide debt default did not cause the collapse of the U.S. banking system (Bacha and Malan 1989).

Accession to Argentina's proposal for integration and the subsequent signature of the PICE protocols was thus a sign that the Brazilian government was increasingly turning to the regional level as the lever for achieving national development and increased influence on the continental and international levels. The challenge within this new approach was to ensure that the emerging ties to the comparatively smaller regional partners could be fashioned in a manner that did not act as an undue constraint on the policies and actions of the much larger Brazil. PICE thus proved a harbinger of the strategy that would be deployed to increase influence throughout Latin America. Although it codified the idea of economic integration in the Southern Cone, PICE was not accompanied by the creation of any sort of substantive administrative or disciplinary framework. Disagreements and conflicts would have to be worked out in discussions between the signatory governments.

The absence of a supranational governing body set a significant precedent for the future formation of Mercosul (Vigevani and Oliveira 2007), fulfilling Brazil's preference for institutional informality in South America and ensuring that a measure of sovereignty need not be surrendered in order to increase its influence over its partner countries (Marques 1991; Zelner 1991; Amorim 1991b; Cleaver 1991). Indeed, given the vast disparity in size between the PICE participants and the diversified pattern of Brazil's international trade, any increase in economic interaction between the three countries was almost certainly bound to make Argentina and Uruguay disproportionately more dependent on access to Brazil (Zirker 1994). Moreover, there was no formal mechanism for the other signatory countries to seek redress when the Brazilian government took a somewhat self-serving approach to the integration process by maintaining a series of import restrictions (Corrêa 1999a, 13). Mindful that the resultant trade imbalance might unsettle the agreement, Itamaraty encouraged a process of trade diversion, expanding its purchase of raw materials from Argentina to balance the looming trade deficit (Lampreia 2002; Manzetti 1990, 122).

A similar institutional pattern to that found in PICE was evident in Brazil's participation in the Contadora Support Group. With the group's activities in Central America declining in the mid-1980s as the United States assumed a more positive role in the area, a decision was made to transform the organism into a permanent mechanism for consultation and joint action by forming what is now known as the Grupo do Rio (Rio Group) (Yopo 1991). As with PICE, the Rio Group was created without a central bureaucratic structure, revolving instead around a process of informal consultation as well as presidential and ministerial meetings without the constraint of specified thematic concentration (Guimarães Reis 1990). Decisions and joint declarations were to be the result of discussions leading to a consensus position, which would be projected on behalf of the member countries by the Group's president pro tempore. As the largest participant—the Rio Group does not include the United States—Brazil's position would thus have to be incorporated into any Rio Group position. Moreover, Brazilian diplomats spoke of creating consensus on issues (Chohfi 2002), suggesting that the Rio Group and its informal discussion process were envisioned as a tool which might be used by Itamaraty to patiently generate agreement throughout the region. As will be further discussed, the Rio Group proved to be particularly valuable in instances when resources needed to be mobilized to provide an alternative approach to U.S. policies in areas such as hemispheric integration and democracy protection.

The other interesting point about the Contadora Support Group is that its efforts to find a regionally based resolution to the persistent conflicts in Central America were quietly resisted by the Reagan White House (P. Smith 2000, 213–215). Contadora and the subsequent Rio Group can thus be viewed as part of a concerted effort to provide an indigenous alternative to Washington's dominance in Latin America through a concentration of the capabilities of the member states to create homegrown solutions to regional problems (Martins Filho 2007). That the United States was concerned about a loss of influence in Latin America is made clear by George Bush's 1990 Enterprise for the Americas Initiative (EAI). What was in doubt was U.S. willingness to devote solid resources to renewing and strengthening its ties within the hemisphere.

In an effort to extol the virtues of the EAI, Roger B. Porter (1990) set out Bush's strategy for restarting regional growth and development after the repeated financial crises and U.S. neglect of the region during the lost decade of the 1980s. Erecting the new cooperative edifice on the three pillars of what would become known as the core of the Washington Consensus—trade, investment, and debt reduction—Porter's invitation quickly became remarkable not as an offer of fungible assistance—of the total $1.5 billion in development funds, the United States was prepared to commit only $500 million over five years—but for the extent to which it relied on the ability of Latin American countries to adopt a policy vision offered by the Bush administration as a panacea. The history of the Reagan/Bush era in the region was sidestepped (Muñoz 1996, 30), allowing democracy to be strongly advocated and, more significant, paired with a dramatic opening of national economies as the key to economic recovery.

In what might almost be seen as an editorial rebuttal of Porter's text, the next issue of the *Journal of Interamerican Studies and World Affairs* printed an article by Sidney Weintraub (1991, 11–12) that made pointed use of the conditional tense when discussing what impact the EAI would have on inter-

American relations and Latin American economic recovery. Yet despite the somewhat incredulous tone used by Weintraub to address the proposition that Latin America would be drawn in by the thin bait of financial aid and heavy doses of policy prescription, the overall impression of some Brazilian observers was that the chimera of open access to the huge U.S. market might well be enough to reaffirm Washington's hemispheric dominance (dos Santos 1989). This in turn placed serious pressure on Brazilian efforts to build a quiet measure of leadership in South America (Lafer et al. 1993), particularly with the handicap of the economic crises faced by the Collor/Franco government

Cold War's End and Turn to Mercosul

The clear emphasis on trade in Bush's EAI highlights the extent to which the White House was attempting to hedge its bets against a collapse of the Uruguay round of the General Agreement on Tariffs and Trade (GATT) and seeking to reposition itself to face the possibility of competing blocs in Europe and Southeast Asia by capturing hemispheric markets. Similar concerns marked strategic thinking in many Latin American economies, particularly those in the Southern Cone (Amorim 1991a). As PICE had yet to even suggest itself as a dynamic alternative to European, North American, and Southeast Asian markets, the prospect that the world would subdivide into a series of megablocs held the threat of heightened economic marginalization for Latin America. Bush's vague invitation was thus extremely appealing to countries such as Argentina and Chile.

This alternative was not, however, especially palatable to Brazil's Foreign Ministry. While expanded access to the U.S. market would certainly have been welcome, Itamaraty's reaction to the EAI demonstrated a high degree of skepticism that the necessary liberalization of U.S. trade provisions would be forthcoming. These concerns were amplified by the perception that the U.S. lifeline during the financial crisis of the mid-1980s had created a negative bilateral relationship, particularly with respect to intellectual-property rights and access to the technology that the region would need to continue its industrialization process (L. Fonseca 1989; Amorim 2003a). Moreover, doubt was cast on the effectiveness, not to mention the seriousness, of the EAI's U.S.$300 million per year investment pool to address the shortcomings of the region's economic infrastructure. The risk for Brazil's new policy of development based on regional cooperation was that these two vague commitments from Washington would dissipate the sort of unity that had begun to emerge in the Contadora and Rio

Group process. With this in mind, Collor used a July 1990 visit to Argentina to discuss the prospect for a cooperative response to EAI, setting the stage for the treaty that would form Mercosul (Vaz 2002, 102–104; Bernal-Meza 1999).

Collor's visit to Argentina took place against the backdrop of the economic crisis of the lost decade of the 1980s and the collapse of the debt-funded, protectionist development model, which had been in place throughout the military regime (Rezende 1998, 563–564). Drawing on the mounting sense of frustration with Brazil's continuing economic troubles, Collor campaigned on a platform of change, promising to reform the country's economy and bring fresh thinking to bear on national problems. Claims to originality aside, the policy package offered by Collor subscribed to the neoliberal tenets sweeping through Latin America, a stance being mirrored by Argentine president Carlos Menem.

The core of the Latin American neoliberal project revolved around a retraction of the state from the national economy, with an emphasis on fiscal discipline, tax reform, monetary reform, financial liberalization, privatization, and, most important for the formation of economic regions, the dismantling of protectionist policies (Rosenthal 1997, 193–194). Collor was particularly assiduous at reducing import tariffs, precipitating a decrease of 50 percent in the average tariff level by 1994 as well as the abolition of a range of nontariff barriers (Amann and Baer 2002, 947–948). While this rapid shift to neoliberal policies placed Brazilian industry under tremendous pressure from imports that had previously been excluded by high tariff rates, it also opened space for a deepening of the PICE accords, which had effectively been nullified by protectionist trade measures.

The policy climate was thus ripe for the ambitious outcome of the July 1990 Argentina-Brazil Summit. At the meeting the presidents signed the Act of Buenos Aires, which drew on the shift to greater economic liberalization in the Southern Cone by proposing that the two countries complete the formation of a common market by 31 December 1994 (Cruz et al. 1993). Although the agreement initially was intended to encompass Argentina and Brazil, Uruguay soon made a pointed request for inclusion in an effort to maintain the preferential market access that it had obtained through the PICE process and protect its democratic transition. As the strategic thinking underlying the formation of the bloc was developed it became clear that Chilean membership in the new arrangement would provide an added economic gravitas, which led Chile to be included in the initial stages of negotiations to form the bloc. On a subcontinental level, the elaboration of a regionally based bloc would allow the major South American economies to jointly pursue a development strategy that would facilitate a collective defense of democracy and prevent economic marginalization by the United States (L. Fonseca 1989; Abdenur 1994b).

Mercosul was conceptualized by Brazilian policymakers as an intermediate stop on the road to fully integrating the country into the international economy as a global trader (Vaz 2002, 113) and allowing national industry a phased introduction to the rigors of completely open competition. Efforts were thus turned to creating a customs union, which would operate behind a common external tariff (CET) of 35 percent in order to encourage firms to use the milder pressures of regional competition as preparation for expanded market liberalization.

Although the 1991 Treaty of Asunción called for eventual provision of such deep integration measures as macroeconomic policy coordination, meaningful institutional consolidation of the bloc remained elusive. Dispute settlement and the discussion of new issues thus remained the preserve of political discussions between bloc-member ministers and presidents rather than supranational institutions tasked with some level of regional governance.

This halfway ground between the deep integration of the EU and the strictly trade-related contractual approach of NAFTA suited Brazilian interests and allowed pursuit of an integrationist model without a need to surrender more than vaguely symbolic autonomy (Vigevani and Oliveira 2007; Bernier and Roy 1999). On an economic level the CET was an essential provision because it ensured that Brazilian manufacturers of capital and consumer goods would be protected from potentially cheaper extrabloc competitors (Flôres 1997). Rio Branco–era concerns of an anti-Brazil alliance were echoed on the political level, where weak bloc-level institutions protected Brazil from being subordinated to the collective will of the three significantly smaller partner states. In terms of the larger South American project Mercosul offered a combination of light protectionism from extracontinental forces and access to the large Brazilian market. Indeed, Brazilian diplomats were clear in 1993 that they saw Mercosul as a precursor to a South American free-trade area, a goal that could speedily be pursued through closer association with the Comunidad Andina (CAN—Andean Community) (Pereira 1999, 15).

Although the CET did promise important short- and medium-term economic benefit for the Brazilian economy, the combination of weak institutions and mild protection was not as attractive as Itamaraty might have hoped, causing Chile to withdraw late in the negotiation process. Chile's economic resurgence in the 1980s was in part predicated on a highly diversified pattern of international trade bolstered by a low, non-negotiable fixed tariff of 11 percent. With Brazil setting the CET at a significantly higher 35 percent, the difference between the two positions ultimately became irreconcilable. In part the Chilean government's distaste for the high tariff wall was that it would require a fundamental realignment of the economy from its global economic orientation to the uncertain Brazilian market, implying a degree of dependency which made little sense for the country. As the Chile-Brazil axis of this incarnation of the ABC alliance began to collapse, Argentina's Foreign Ministry was busy negotiating a deep integration agreement with the Rodríguez government in Paraguay and expanding contacts with Uruguay. Facing potential isolation in the Southern Cone, Itamaraty rapidly changed tacks and offered Paraguay membership in the proposed bloc. In what might best be seen as a reflection of Brazil's deep penetration of the fabric of the Paraguayan economy, Asunción quickly transmogrified its talks with Buenos Aires into accession to the nearly complete Mercosul treaty. The end result was thus a commitment between the governments of Argentina, Brazil, Paraguay, and Uruguay to form a common market and customs union (Vaz 2002, chapter 2).

Regionalism in the Southern Cone

As a reaction to Bush's EAI, Brazilian economic integration initiatives were not entirely welcomed in Washington (Perry 2000). The concern was that the drive during the Collor presidency to make Brazil a *demandeur* in international trade talks would result in a viable alternative to hemispheric economic liberalization that might not allow the rapid entry of foreign investment desired by the United States (Amorim 2003a, 2).

Indeed, Itamaraty was keenly aware that it was following a different approach to the post–Cold War neoliberal order from that favored by its North American counterpart (Barbosa 1996; Barbosa and César 1994b). Tensions inherent in the two mildly differing approaches began to make themselves felt in the new Mercosul bloc (Cunningham 1999), with the United States exerting pressure on the other three members in an attempt to isolate the Brazilian stance on new trade issues, particularly in the area of services (Florêncio 1992). Itamaraty's response was to emphasize the foreign-policy changes that had taken place in the 1980s, stressing the belief that Brazil's national development would be possible only through cooperation and positive interaction with neighboring countries (Lafer 2000). As foreign minister Celso Lafer explained in 1992, "il faut faire la politique de sa géographie" [the country must pursue the politics of its geography], suggesting that Brazilian foreign policy should concentrate on maximizing opportunities on a regional level (Lafer 1992a; Abdenur 1994a, 45). In operational terms this strategy sought to break with the autarchic nature of interstate relations in the continent and return to the Castello-Branco idea of *fronteiras vivas*, "living borders" transforming borders from zones of separation into zones of cooperation (Lafer 1992a, 103). Economic integration as a route to both sustainable development and democratic consolidation was the order of the day (Lafer 1992b, 566).

The difference between U.S. and Brazilian foreign economic visions arose over what was entailed in economic integration, how fast it should take place, and what role it would play in the development of the region. Unlike many of its South American neighbors, Brazil had experienced substantial industrialization during its import-substituting years; it had created a viable manufacturing base, which, given the correct encouragement, should be able to compete globally. Mercosul was thus conceptualized as part of a phased introduction into the global economy and provided a circumstance in which expanded intrabloc competition would encourage gains in efficiency and quality. The tariff barrier surrounding the bloc was envisioned in much the same manner as training wheels on a child's bicycle: a temporary safety device allowing Brazilian business the opportunity to develop the skills necessary for competition in the global economy. Policymakers were also aware that, if national firms were to acquire the skills and capabilities necessary to become international players, access to new sources of technology and managerial know-how would be necessary (Lafer 1996; Amorim 2003a; Cardoso and Lafer 2007). Here the large and growing captive market of Mercosul was used as a carrot to entice foreign direct investment and the importing of new productive techniques (Amann 1999; Amann and Nixon 1999; Bonelli 1999; Ferraz et al. 1999). While there is some question about the extent to which foreign direct investment (FDI) flows resulted in the creation of genuinely new enterprises as opposed to a transfer of ownership (Hausmann and Fernández-Arias 2000), there is strong evidence that the inflow of foreign currency and ownership dramatically helped the balance-of-payments situation, particularly during the Cardoso government's privatization process, and resulted in qualitative changes in the efficiency and market orientation of Brazilian firms (Schwartz 1998; Rocha 2002).

Ideally, Itamaraty saw Mercosul expanding to include the rest of South America and offering neighboring countries the opportunity to participate in a process of phased integration that would ease the transition to full global insertion and protect member states from unilateral action by other large economies (Barbosa 1994). From a purely business-oriented perspective, such an initiative would offer Brazilian firms access to a larger captive market and increase the incentive for multinational companies to invest in relatively advanced Brazil as a production base for the Latin American region. Indeed, in a 2000 interview Cardoso strongly advanced the view that his country's future lay in closer ties to its South American neighbors. This vision of the continental economy would see Brazil becoming the industrial powerhouse, Argentina the breadbasket, Chile a ready source of capital (Foreign Broadcast Information Service *Latin American Report* [hereafter FBIS-LAT] 2000–0202), and, one would presume, the rest of the area a market.

The undertones of Marxist quasi-economic imperialism in this vision perhaps played a part in dissuading other countries from signing on to the Mercosul project. Further efforts to entice Chile and Bolivia into the bloc were only partially successful, resulting in their status as associate members.

The Andean Community was more forthright in its rejection. While Chile's concern lay primarily with tariff differentials, the Andean nations were concerned that their national industries would be swamped by Brazilian competition. Any agreement or merger between the two blocs was thus predicated on Mercosul's granting CAN an extended list of concessions and favorable treatment, something Itamaraty officials were adamant Brazil would not allow.

Leadership in a Consensual Hegemonic Mold

Yet the expansion of the regionalist principle underlying Mercosul to include all of South America remained a core goal in Itamaraty's emerging foreign-policy program, particularly after the United States entered into and concluded free-trade negotiations with Mexico. As Luiz Felipe Lampreia (2002), explains: "NAFTA signaled that Mexico, although obviously very Latin American in its cultural history and heritage, opted for being part of North America rather than Latin American in economic terms." NAFTA would also mean that Mexico would be in a position to overturn the tradition established by Rio Branco and supplant Brazil as the interlocutor between the United States and Latin America. The effect, as Celso Lafer describes it, was to create within Itamaraty a "perception that both Central America and Mexico tended more and more to gravitate around the U.S.'s strength of attraction" (Lafer 2007). The response to these changing circumstances elaborated by the then–foreign minister, Fernando Henrique Cardoso, was to reconceptualize the political and economic geography of the hemisphere and look to the continent (Barbosa 1993b; Amorim 1994; Amorim 2003a; Barbosa 2007; Lafer 2007). Lampreia explains that Latin America as an organizing principle was set aside, replaced by the notion of South America: "South America is an entity that can be very clearly described in terms of its geography, of its membership, of its, let us say, belonging as a group of countries. It is virtually [an island] if you see the Panama Canal as a cut in the Isthmus—South America is practically an island and therefore conforms to a very logical and very clear geographical entity which should be the basis for our functioning" (Lampreia 2002).

Brazilian diplomacy consequently underwent a quiet but critical shift (Cervo 1997, 15–17). Whereas the previous years had seen Itamaraty seeking influence throughout the whole of Latin America, as was the case with Brazilian participation in the Contadora Group, the construction of a political concept South America, most notably through the suggestion of a South American Free Trade Area (SAFTA), meant a more localized approach focusing on the country's ten immediate neighbors.

The new political importance given to the continent is made clear in a 15 February 1993 internal Itamaraty memorandum laying the diplomatic groundwork for an ALADI meeting in Uruguay (Barbosa 1993a). As part of its preparation for the implementation of NAFTA, Mexico was seeking a modification to Article 44 of the 1980 Treaty of Montevideo (TM-80), which required an equal extension of most-favored-nation status to all ALADI members. From a commercial perspective, the memo is clear that it was in Brazil's interest to block the request. What is interesting about the document is that the obvious economic considerations—that NAFTA would give preferential market access to U.S. firms at the expense of Brazilian businesses—are overshadowed by a new political dynamic. Blind opposition to any alteration of the treaty text is replaced by measured facilitation, in part to maintain relations with Mexico, but perhaps more important, to demonstrate to the organization's other members that Brazil would not implacably seek to impose its interests on the collective (Cardoso 1995; Cardoso 2000a; Cardoso and Lafer 2007). As the memorandum's author, Rubens Antonio Barbosa, puts it, "I consider the decision we take on this issue to be one of the most important in the realm of regional foreign policy in recent years. I am convinced that Brazil's position—of weakness or strength, of leadership or subordination—will be reflected in our attitude to South America" (Barbosa 1993a, 9). A crucial aspect of Brazil's foreign policy thus became one of maintaining and developing the 1980s trend of building and solidifying positive relations with neighboring countries. Within this context, ALADI became useful because it provided Itamaraty with another quasi-juridical-diplomatic talking point that could be used to deepen existing integration agreements and expand cooperation in such soft-power fields as science, technology, and infrastructure. Overarching this strategic imperative of being seen to pursue a constructive foreign policy was the question of leadership, namely, whether Brazil or a NAFTA-enhanced Mexico would emerge as the stronger force in South America. Barbosa's response to this central challenge was that by suggesting and facilitating a TM-80 waiver Brazil could assert and partially consolidate the leadership role in the continent that it was seeking (Barbosa 1993a; Barbosa 1994, 105).

By 1993 Itamaraty was already facing a challenge to the consensual hegemonic project it was attempting to lead in South America. Responding to the aftereffects of Ross Perot's remarkably successful and isolationist 1992 presidential campaign, Vice-Pres. Al Gore used a visit to Mexico to propose that the 1994 Miami Summit of the Americas mark the beginning of negotiations for a Free Trade Area of the Americas (FTAA). A series of bilateral and multilateral meetings were convened by the United States to plan the agenda for the Summit and set the parameters for the trade discussions.

The reaction at Itamaraty was that the Brazilian economy was not prepared for the shock of full exposure to the pressures of U.S. competition, particularly the sort of rapid and sweeping economic opening envisioned in the initial U.S. proposal. Moreover, Brazilian diplomats reasoned that this analysis applied to many other economies in the region. Attention was thus turned to the Rio Group, using it as a forum to disseminate and articulate an alternate approach to hemispheric integration which, although not blocking the Clinton administration's initiative, did seek to slow its evolution to a pace that would allow Brazil to counteract the powerful appeal of open access to the U.S. market. As will be explained in more detail in the next chapter, the ability of Brazilian diplomats to recruit support from Rio Group partners to reshape the agenda for the 1994 Miami Summit of the Americas was greatly abetted by the strong-arm negotiating tactics employed by the U.S. trade representative, Charlene Barshevsky.

In short, the successful efforts of Brazilian diplomats were predicated on a fortuitous coincidence of interests and their ability to make this congruity apparent to their South American counterparts, not on the inherent attractiveness of an alliance with Brazil. Continental leadership, then, was a problematic proposition, particularly when we consider the requirement that a leader supplies public goods and assumes the costs of their provision. As was the case in 1993, Brazil manifestly lacked the economic resources to fulfill this role—it was during this same time period that the *real* plan was being formulated and applied to rescue the Brazilian economy—nor would its neighbors countenance policies directed toward this goal (Lampreia 2002). Yet, as has been noted, a clear goal of Brazil's foreign policy was to be a leading state within South America.

The proposition that Brazil had leadership ambitions was often obliquely acknowledged but formally disavowed during my interviews with Cardoso-era junior and mid-level Brazilian diplomats. Senior figures in office, such as Itamaraty secretary-general Osmar Chohfi, were slightly more direct in 2002: "Of course, when we say that we don't want to be the leader, we don't want to impose—it depends on what the concept of leadership is. We are very well prepared to give momentum and to present ideas.... The idea is to strengthen our own positions and to have a better possibility of negotiating something that is favorable for everybody, but good for us too" (Chohfi 2002).

Once out of office, Cardoso was even more explicit, noting that from the first days of his presidency "it was clear at the time that Brazil had the leadership" (Cardoso and Lafer 2007). The utility of having an ambiguous attitude toward actively accepting the mantle of leadership will be more fully elaborated later. Of more pressing importance here is the idea of how Brazil could conceptualize its leadership and have it accepted. For Celso Lafer it all depended on what Brazil wanted to do: "The idea with President Cardoso was to see that there was a reciprocity of interests, to make the best economy of our geography" (Lafer 2007).

Brazilian leadership thus emerges as being about generating mutually improved circumstances. Moreover, the concept of leadership was not one of domination, but rather of coordination, gradual alignment of potentially competing interests, of working to create joint solutions to common problems and challenges. It was a softer approach that eschewed force and open coercion in favor of a more subtle dynamic in keeping with the notion of consensual hegemony outlined in the Introduction.

Conclusion

In the abstract, the concept of leadership as a means of facilitating a mutually beneficial end result as opposed to national advancement through the domination of others retains an idealistic attractiveness. The imposition of reality, however, begs the question of how Brazilian foreign-policy makers could implement this vision. The 1980s and early 1990s saw a marked departure from the slow and methodical process of policy change, a departure forced on a reluctant Foreign Ministry by the rapid pace of change which accompanied the end of the Cold War and the exigencies of the debt crisis. From this relatively short period of ad hoc policy reactions to external events a new foreign-policy strategy emerged in Brazil, one centered on the use of regional structures as devices for pursuing the creation of a consensual hegemony in South America.

Three main regional arrangements subsequently served as crucial tools in the implementation of Brazil's foreign policy. The first two, Mercosul and the Rio Group, have been introduced, while the third is an offshoot of unsuccessful efforts to form a South American Free Trade Area and an exemplary case of the use of soft power and the creation of consensus: the continental infrastructure-integration initiative launched at the 2000 Brasília Summit of South American Presidents, directed by the newly formed Iniciativa para a Integração da Infra-estrutura Regional Sul Americana (IIRSA—Regional Infrastructure Integration in South America). The character of Brazilian leadership and the question of how these regional structures were used to advance Brazilian leadership during the Cardoso era form the subject of the following chapters.

2

Leadership in Brazilian Foreign Policy

As outlined in the previous chapter, Brazil's diplomatic history is marked by consistent efforts to avoid any suggestion that the country was seeking a leadership role in the region. The idea that Brazil was looking to lead in South America was resisted by many of the diplomats I interviewed. Most, keeping strictly to the Itamaraty diplomatic tradition of shying away from explicit pursuit or acknowledgment of a leadership role for Brazil, recalled Rio Branco–era fears that perceptions of Brazilian imperialism might lead to a coalition of Spanish-speaking republics that would launch a coordinated attack against the country's sparsely protected borders. This fear prompted a foreign policy emphasizing multilateralism and equality among nations (Burns 1966). In effect, official Itamaraty discourse during the period of interest to us equated leadership with notions of overt and active coercive domination (Lampreia 2002; Chohfi 2002), a position that I will argue was at odds with the reality of Brazilian–South American relations during the Cardoso era and the general style of leading seen in Brazil's foreign policy.

The real issue, which will become increasingly evident throughout the rest of the book, was not so much the exercise of leadership as the perception of this leadership and the careful masking of it behind consensus creation and inclusion. Looking back on his time as foreign minister and an extremely internationally engaged president, Cardoso remarked bluntly about the constant disavowal of Brazilian leadership: "This was our rhetoric. Behind it was the idea that leaders don't need to say they are taking leadership" (Cardoso and Lafer 2007). This logic was embedded in the thinking of senior career figures at Itamaraty, one noting after his retirement that "I like to say that you don't claim leadership. You act. You exert your leadership" (Barbosa 2007).

The nature and style of Brazilian leadership underpinning these statements will be set out in this chapter to illustrate the techniques put into operation in discussions of the ideational, economic, and security aspects of the consensual hegemonic project. Proof of the existence and effectiveness of Itamaraty's leadership style will come through a discussion of the extent to which other South American countries not only cooperated with Brazil, but also adopted and assimilated policies and positions that originated within the Brazilian foreign policy–making system. Indeed, the attempt at consensually constructing a regionalist project would not have been possible without some leadership to instigate the necessary discussion and cooperation. This indicates that the regional foreign policy pursued during the Cardoso era required Brazil to assume an active leadership role.

Before turning to an examination of the nature of Brazilian leadership in South America during the Cardoso era I will briefly focus on a theoretical discussion of the concept. Here two approaches to leadership will emerge, one distinguishing between the implicitly coercive conceptualization (Kindleberger 1973; Gilpin 1981; Keohane 1984; Strange 1994), and the softer form derived from the consensual hegemony approach employed in this book. I will then set out the broad parameters of Brazilian leadership before detailing specific instances. Attention will first be turned to the strong attempts to generate consensus before the 1994 Miami Summit of the Americas and the launch of the Free Trade Area of the Americas. Next, the latently coercive impulse behind Brazil's consensual leadership style emerges more clearly from analysis of its efforts to secure interregional agreements between Mercosul and the Andean Community as well as the European Union. Finally, discussion of IIRSA, a program to advance the consolidation of a South American region by constructing integrated infrastructural matrices, offers an example of how Brazil sought to disperse and avoid the costs associated with consensual leadership.

Leading and Leadership

The concept of leadership in international relations and international political economy has received little sustained study (Ikenberry 1996, 386). In part this is because the subject has been subsumed in larger debates examining questions of domination, hegemony, and power. This oversight is particularly strange given that the question of leadership lies at the heart of key texts of all stripes on hegemony in international relations. Within the realist, neorealist, and neoliberal institutionalist canon the emphasis is generally on a coercive style of leadership, one that requires the leading actor to absorb the costs of maintaining the system. Although some neoliberal institutionalists and structuralists do acknowledge that the formation of regimes can play an important role in defraying the costs of leadership by collectivizing responsibilities, the leading state is still left with the task of underwriting the leadership or systemic project.

The main shortcoming in much of the literature is thus an implicitly mono-lithic approach to leadership that equates it with domination and coercion almost solely in terms of the interests of the leading state. Emphasis has been on the ability of a state to shape the nature of the international system for its own ends as if this were a proposition with isolated benefits, thereby creating a widespread sense that leadership is marked by an exclusionary character that privileges the stronger. The significant interjection Ikenberry offers to the de-bate is that the end of the Cold War opened up space for new approaches to leading, especially for states that could not hope to exercise the domination as-sociated with realist conceptions of hegemony. He places particular emphasis on the changed nature of leadership, which marked a shift from the coercive connotations of gunboat diplomacy to the inclusive intimations of coalition building and consensus generation (Ikenberry 1996).

The suggestion that emerges is that change in the new order is not likely to come through the force of arms—the transformative end-of-war events that marked previous changes in the international order—but rather, through the processes of dialogue and negotiation that mark a Gramscian approach to he-gemony (R. Cox 1983; Femia 1987; Fontana 1993). Gramsci casts hegemony in terms closer to Strange's (1994) vision of structural power as making up a system of overarching beliefs and practices that work subconsciously to delimit the range of actions that can be contemplated, let alone pursued, by a state. While Gramsci (1957, 161) does not discard the use of force in the formation of a hegemonic project, his clear suggestion is that hegemony is greatly weakened if it depends on coercion instead of consent for its legitimacy. The question of leadership can thus be seen as relating to a state's ability to conceptualize a po-tentially hegemonic project—that is, a vision of world or regional order—and persuade other countries to embrace the project; this approach provides some solidity to notions of soft power and ideational diffusion.

Its effectiveness as the leader of a hegemonic project depends on the ability of a state to persuade other states that all share a particular set of interests and aspirations and to recruit their support and active participation in the new project; successful leadership in its ultimate expression is not based on the capacity to forcibly suppress dissent (wield the threatening stick) or provide payoffs (the carrot). From the Gramscian conceptualization of hegemony we can thus derive an approach to leadership that allows us to determine if a state is attempting to act as a leader and whether or not it is experiencing any success.

The first element is the elaboration and dissemination of a vision of how a particular set of relations should be ordered, be it on the local, national, regional, or international level. In the Brazilian case under discussion here the project is a South American region. Second is a willingness to initiate the student-teacher dialectic process, relinquishing some measure of control over the original ideas in order to begin the process that will allow competing goals and aspirations to be absorbed into the project. Success comes in the third stage, when other states not only actively embrace the dissemination of new ideas from the leading state, but also autonomously engage in the further development and application of these ideas. This form of leadership not only avoids the costs that preoccupy Gilpin (1981) in his theory of hegemonic decline, but also allows a diplomatically skilled state to lead despite an otherwise apparent deficiency of power resources. Indeed, the strength of a leadership style informed by a Gramscian approach to hegemony lies in the extent to which the substance of the project is willingly adopted by the encompassed states. The central facts of the leading state's conduct thus center on creating consensus through consistent, clear, and open communication that seeks to include divergent positions in a manner that strengthens the overall structure.

Establishing Brazil's Leadership

The disjuncture between the reality of Brazilian diplomatic activity and the impression that foreign-policy makers wished to create pervaded much of the Cardoso era, with a willingness to publicly acknowledge Brazil's emerging role as a consensual leader coming only after the 2000 Brasília Summit of South American Presidents. The discomfort Brazilian diplomats displayed with the concept of leadership during interviews for this book can be attributed to many of the factors set out in the previous section, namely, that the act of leading is often seen as being predicated on coercion or a project of domination (Chohfi 2002). When I confronted him with the idea of consensual leadership, Cardoso's foreign minister, Luiz Felipe Lampreia, responded with a tentative agreement before offering the qualification that leadership means military power and a willingness to intervene and accept the expanded costs of leadership, two items that the Brazilian populace would not support (Lampreia 2002).

The strictures of political office removed, Cardoso and Lafer were considerably more direct during interviews. Indeed, Cardoso was clear that securing

Brazil's leadership in South America was a central objective of his first official bilateral presidential meeting with Argentina's Menem: "When we arrived there at the first meeting I took control of the situation. My preoccupation was not to jeopardize Menem's position and not to produce a counter-reaction from Menem. I was very pleased at the end because this had been successful. Menem was there and Menem was happy and it was also clear that we were taking the leadership in the game. It was like that up to the end with Argentina. Very close relations. Very good relations. But we had the last word" (Cardoso and Lafer 2007). The notable point in Cardoso's reminiscence is not so much the clear statement that he sought to lead Argentina, an ambition which he also extended to the other South American countries, but that he sought to do it in a quiet, very understated manner. This played directly into the dominant fear within Itamaraty that any overt attempt to act as a leader in the continent would be construed as a disguised instance of neoimperialistic domination.

As one Brazilian government official involved in international affairs has noted, Brazil has a significant amount of power in the continent. In the cases of smaller countries such as Paraguay and Bolivia this disparity in relative power is great enough that the Brazilian ambassador can, and has, given direct policy instructions to presidents as well as senior government and military officials in other countries. For Cardoso this meant that Brazil had to exercise patience with the other bloc members and follow the suggestions German chancellor Helmut Kohl put to him in 1995. The story Kohl recounted was one of setting aside historical tensions and the capacity to act from a position of power in order to create something larger that would entrench the national interest regionally on a lasting, self-sustaining basis. From this Cardoso (2006, 617–619) extracted the guiding principle of conducting Brazilian leadership in a manner that did not seek to gain commercial advantage on the basis of "an eye for an eye," a principle that would become increasingly important throughout the devaluation crises of 1999 and 2002.

The point that a retired leading Brazilian ambassador made in our interview is that "Brazil does not seek leadership. By its sheer weight, by its industrial power, by agricultural power, Brazil has a voice, and others react to this" (Barbosa 2007). Significantly, the ambassador continued to make it clear that this leadership was not driven or underpinned by a coercive imperative: "We will be the leader if we are prepared to take responsibility and to put forward policies that the others will follow or not."

In operational terms, during the Cardoso era these underlying realities of Brazilian leadership suggested that a critical problem facing Itamaraty was the global shift in the styles and implications of leadership posited by Ikenberry. Lampreia (2000a) implicitly took these issues up in an interview given shortly before the 2000 Brasília Presidential Summit. After offering the clear statement that "Brazil has no wish to assume regional leadership nor does it want to be a candidate for the position of South American leader," Lampreia immediately proceeded to point out that "Brazil is not a country exactly equal to the others," and that it had no "intention [of using] South America to build up its leadership but only of using its critical mass to strengthen the idea of South American integration."

Embedded within these comments is an implicit reconceptualization of the role of a leader and potential motivations along the lines suggested by Barbosa. Suggestions that Brazil intended to use its "critical mass"—that is, ideational creativity, market size, and security capacity—to strengthen the idea of South America as a viable geoeconomic space and as an effective geopolitical actor constitute an almost explicit statement that the country wished to lead the other South American countries in the construction of a continental project. The difference comes in the approach to leading this project. As one interviewed diplomat noted, the language of leadership and hegemony was very unhelpful to Itamaraty because it carried connotations of coercion and domination that overshadowed policies designed to function through consensus and dialogue. The focus before the 2000 Brasília Summit was instead on using the space available for consensual leadership and taking great care to reassure the other South American countries that Brazilian leadership was neither inevitable nor permanent, and certainly not the precursor to the emergence of a new subregional power.

A more explicit approach to Brazilian leadership, paralleling the comments by Barbosa, was offered by Itamaraty secretary-general Osmar Chohfi (2002), who observed: "When we say that we don't want to be the leader, we don't want to impose, it depends on what the concept of leadership is. We are very well prepared to give momentum . . . and to present ideas." Subsequent remarks by Chohfi emphasize the extent to which Itamaraty wished to collaborate with Brazil's South American neighbors to articulate a common project that, while obviously good for Brazil, would bring substantial benefits to all. As Celso Lafer (2007) remarked of Itamaraty's work leading up to the IIRSA infrastructure-integration program launched at the 2000 Brasília Summit: "Itamaraty was cautious because of this concern with leadership, with creating jealousy or issues. . . . Itamaraty took great care to exercise a constructive role without creating susceptibilities." The need for the type of consensual leadership acknowledged by Chohfi and Lafer was highlighted as critical by other Brazilian diplomats whom I interviewed, who noted that many other South American countries lacked the institutional capacity necessary to formulate and advance the sort of overarching regional vision set out at the 2000 Brasília Summit.

The approach to leadership adopted by Itamaraty is more in keeping with that found in Gramsci's student-teacher dialectic than with that of a realist's domineering state. Within this framework Brazil emerges as the instigating actor, the framer of the hegemonic project—Barbosa's presenter of policy options—which is then presented to the other states for discussion and further elaboration. In itself this is not an entirely new role, being but a repetition of the sort of past efforts at pan-Americanism pursued by Pres. Juscelino Kubitschek in the late 1950s. The change comes in the approach taken to the goal of continental integration: eschewing the relatively easy path of securing agreement for grandiose ideals and weak treaties and adopting a commitment to articulating a clear strategy and the making of sometimes difficult political choices.

One diplomat I interviewed sought to downplay Brazilian leadership on the grounds that a leader must provide solutions to problems; this suggests that Brazil would have trouble fulfilling this role due to its unwillingness to forcibly implement policies beyond its own borders. A similar theme was repeated by a ranking Itamaraty official, who pointed out to me that the spillover effects of insurgency and narco-trafficking in Colombia called for a degree of interventionist leadership inconsistent with Brazil's diplomatic tradition. While it would be stretching the point to suggest that Brazilian diplomats have a program of actively coercing other countries into adopting particular policies, comments from a NAFTA-member foreign trade official on events at two consecutive FTAA negotiating sessions strongly indicate that Itamaraty was willing to cajole its partners, in this instance nudging an errant Argentine minister back toward the Brazilian-led Mercosul position on the separation of labor and environmental provisions from trade questions. Indeed, Itamaraty's willingness to exercise a consensual leadership style was apparent in FTAA negotiating sessions, where the Brazilian contingent consistently had a selection of alternate texts prepared whenever it appeared that discussion on a particular treaty provision had reached an impasse.

It is in the nexus of quiet cajoling—reminding partners of previous agreements—and the proposition of draft treaty language that the operational basis of Brazilian leadership can be found, hidden within a discourse of consensus creation. By consistently offering draft language for discussion, whether it be an entirely new integration proposal such as IIRSA or contentious sections of the FTAA treaty, Itamaraty found an opportunity to frame the terms of discussion by implicitly setting the content of the debate. By encouraging negotiations to reach a consensus version of the idea originally presented by Brazilian diplomats, Itamaraty was in effect able to diffuse ownership of the final decision across all of the participating countries, thereby masking a leadership role that might otherwise be attributable to Brazil. When Itamaraty encountered difficulty initiating consensus-building discussion processes, an oblique approach discarded the multilateral tactic in favor of the sort of bilateral negotiations that create implicit pressure for other countries to join in or risk exclusion from a possible new reality—a process that amounts to an indirect and passive form of coercion.

Three interlocking elements were central to the "inoffensive" style of leadership pursued by Itamaraty. First, commands and edicts were studiously avoided, strong preference instead being given to invitations to adopt joint positions or attend summit meetings. The leadership function here was that of coordinator, using the position of instigator and organizer as a device to shape the positions and strategies of Brazil's South American and Mercosul partners with regard to shared challenges and opportunities. Backing up these common stances and adding to Brazil's credibility as a potential leader was the tactical aspect of ideational leadership, namely, the conceptualization of new initiatives and the creation of alternative projects. Indeed, this last aspect proved particularly important in the FTAA process, which was to be the dominant hemispheric question during the Cardoso era. Underpinning these elements was the indirect and passive form of coercion inherent in Brazil's desire to be inclusive and consensual: a corresponding willingness existed to pursue policies unilaterally that might ultimately impose costs resulting from exclusion on countries reluctant to join the consensus.

Creating Consensus—Miami 1994

In the early 1990s integration plans were bubbling up in the Americas. Brazilian proposals to expand Mercosul into a SAFTA were precipitated by concerns that NAFTA might cause Mexico to displace Brazil as the preeminent South American state (Barbosa 1993a). In the United States the Clinton White House was becoming increasingly worried that the rancorous journey of the NAFTA treaty through Congress might harm hemispheric relations and result in restricted access to regional markets, particularly in the face of a quiet diplomatic challenge from Brazil (*Financial Times* 2 July 1994).

To repair the damage of the NAFTA debate and forestall the emergence of Brazil as a competing leader, the White House decided in 1993 to propose that a 1994 Presidential Summit launch negotiations for a free-trade area of the Americas. The Brazilian response to the U.S. proposal was cautious, reflecting a concern within Itamaraty that the national economy was still reeling from the twin shocks of the rapid opening that took place under Collor and the fragile macroeconomic situation that Cardoso was attempting to remedy with the *real* plan. Thus, it was reasoned, more liberalization of the sort implicit in an FTAA might prove unduly damaging. Moreover, the analysis within Itamaraty was that if Brazil needed a period of adjustment, then the same was probably true for other South American economies.

The Brazilian position was thus a lengthier approach than that advanced by the United States and advocated a preliminary step of freezing existing tariffs before gradually rolling them back. In the interim created by the tariff negotiations Itamaraty hoped that regional arrangements such as Mercosul, the Andean Community, and the Caribbean Common Market would solidify and link, providing an intermediate stage in a hemispheric arrangement. It is this last aspect, slower construction of hemispheric trade arrangements, that troubled U.S. negotiators, especially principal Clinton Latin American advisor, Richard Feinberg (1997, chapter 8).

Addressing the FTAA process nearly eight years after the Miami Summit, Chohfi (2002) captured the theme dominating the Brazilian approach to the meeting, namely, that Brazil wanted something greater than simple accession to NAFTA. This stance was underpinned by a belief that not only was it possible to reject the initial U.S offer, but by cooperating the South American countries could negotiate an agreement with the United States that offered benefit for all.

While Brazilian assertions of autonomy were not new, the change that bothered Feinberg was Itamaraty's success at broadening that concept to include the rest of South America and the resultant, almost explicit, connection between Brazilian and South American interests (Simões 2001). Emblematic of this shift was a Heritage Foundation (1994) seminar on the Summit in which Paulo Tarso Flecha da Lima, then Brazil's ambassador in Washington, spoke. Focusing on the ideas of symmetry and asymmetry in the Americas, he discarded specific reference to Brazil in favor of the broader concept of Latin America, with particular emphasis on the need for the United States to deal with the region as an equal, not a subservient, partner. Significantly, this stance found resonance throughout Latin America. Another participant at the seminar, Mexican ambassador Montano, expressed full agreement with his Brazilian colleague and offered the humorous quip that "Brazil is now the secretary pro tempore of the Rio Group, and so they are our bosses at the moment" (Heritage Foundation 1994).

Here the concept of leadership emerges again and forms the core of Feinberg's concern. Montano's suggestion was not that the Rio Group members were being ordered about, but that Itamaraty was making effective use of Brazil's pro tempore presidency of the Rio Group to organize a coordinated approach to the Miami Summit.

The Itamaraty response to the Summit invitation was to take what had been a primarily political organization, the Rio Group, and use it as a device for formulating a common position in an economic negotiation. Preparations began early in 1994 when Itamaraty established an internal task force to examine the FTAA question, resulting in the building-block and "stand still and roll back" strategy (Magalhães 1999, 52–54). Of particular relevance to our discussion of carrotless leadership is the observation from the task force co-chair, Amb. Geraldo Holanda Cavalcanti, that an antagonistic approach to hemispheric free trade would not work because open access to the U.S. market remained a central goal for many Latin American economies. The proposal made by Cavalcanti was that Itamaraty devote its efforts to developing a consensus position through the Rio Group, using the organization to create the collective political density necessary to defuse the almost unilateral tenor of early U.S. proposals while simultaneously deflecting suggestions that Brazil was attempting to derail the entire process.

The Brazilian approach thus came to revolve around the provision of alternatives instead of blindly opposing the Summit. With this in mind, in August 1994 Itamaraty conducted a seminar on the future of hemispheric relations and the potential impact of the Miami Summit. The position that emerged from the discussion was that hemispheric integration should be guided by the sort of slow, achievable goal approach that marked the evolution of Mercosul, not the ambitious and sweeping aspirations characteristic of Latin America's bevy of failed integration treaties. This measured approach would seek a middle ground that acknowledged both the widespread desire in Latin America for access to the U.S. market as well as the domestic political reality that the economic dislocations associated with free trade would provoke popular resistance that might slow the process (Magalhães 1999, 64–68).

By the time the Rio Group presidents arrived in Brasília for their 9–10 September 1994 meeting, Itamaraty had dissected the United States' fourteen hemispheric trade initiatives and formulated a counterproposal for consideration by the other Rio Group states. The outcome of their discussions was a Rio Group draft declaration and action plan. Significantly, these documents sought to disassociate provisions on the environment, labor, and good governance from those concerning trade and pushed for a slower and steadier approach to the negotiation and implementation of an FTAA (Grupo do Rio 1995, 539–601), two positions at the core of the Brazilian vision of hemispheric trade liberalization.

U.S. dissatisfaction with the Rio Group's counterproposal became apparent at the final pre–Miami Summit meetings in Virginia when U.S. negotiators sought to cast Brazil as an obstructionist actor (Feinberg 1997, 140–144). Their disparaging tone was coupled with a negotiating atmosphere that saw the United States attempting to divide Rio Group members and push countries into agreeing with the U.S. language. One side effect of this high-pressure negotiating style that particularly disturbed Brazilian diplomats was the secrecy in which the actual U.S. proposal was cloaked, which, until that point, had never been shown in its entirety to any of the other thirty-three participating countries. Brazilian efforts were consequently devoted to reminding the other Rio Group members that collective action offered the best prospects for a workable final agreement.

To bolster solidarity at the September Brasília meeting, Brazilian diplomats tabled a document that placed the U.S. text of the Miami declaration in one column and the Rio Group wording in an adjacent column. The intent was to remind the Rio Group countries not only that maintaining a collective position would result in a stronger agreement, but also that Brazil wanted the Miami meeting to be more than a photo opportunity (Magalhães 1999, 121–123). This initiative was paralleled by an all-night meeting with U.S. negotiators to explain clause by clause the logic behind the Rio Group's language. By the end of the meeting in Virginia the final text agreed on for signature at the Miami Summit of the Americas comprised roughly 85 percent Rio Group text.

Deployment of the Rio Group as a consensus-generating body required some surrender of ownership and control over the final declaration. But by providing the initial text Itamaraty was able to frame the final product in much the same way that Gramsci sees a teacher setting the implicit boundaries for what a student might contemplate. The power inherent in this style of leadership became apparent in the pre-Summit meetings when Brazilian diplomats were able to maintain Rio Group solidarity in the face of sustained U.S. pressure by highlighting the consensual nature of the document. That Brazil played a leadership role in the process is clear, and was acknowledged at the end of the Miami Summit by President Clinton (Federal News Service 11 December 1994). In keeping with the characteristics of a consensual hegemony-building approach, Brazilian leadership in Miami did not function through coercion or imposition, but through a process of coordination, consultation, and discussion.

Expanding Regionalism

Paralleling the willingness to coordinate, consult, and discuss that marked the Miami Summit of the Americas was an emerging tendency for Itamaraty to pursue a policy of leading by initiating action, priming the pump of the consensus-creation process. Indeed, this aspect of leadership was to prove important in tackling the two main barriers to a South American region.

The first, as outlined above, was the allure of open access to the large U.S. economy, which caused countries in the region to gravitate to the United States on a bilateral basis without necessarily giving full consideration to the benefits of a collective approach to multilateral trade negotiations. A second hurdle was grounded in historical failures (and the Brazilian role in these failures) to achieve greater regional integration under the ALALC and the ALADI processes. Lacking the capacity or political will necessary to force adherence to the continental project or to provide the incentives necessary to buy compliance, Itamaraty adopted an approach to external relations that sought to initiate new agreements with the EU as well as to build trade relations with neighboring countries. The overt intent was not to construct an exclusionary system, but to use the prospect of access to the large Brazilian economy as a lever to forge new trade agreements that would advance the continental project and open up international markets (Abdenur 1997). Ultimately, the intent was to create a situation where other states could not afford to exclude themselves from the process.

While the decision to form Mercosul had precipitated a jump in intraregional trade in the Southern Cone, at the time of the 1994 Miami Summit the treaty had yet to be fully implemented and as such could not begin to provide an attractive alternative to open access to the U.S. market. Prospects for some sort of agreement between the Rio Group and the EU, a potential counterweight to the United States, also appeared to be in doubt after a fractious ministerial meeting in April 1994 (IPS 23 April 1994).

Yet there remained a clear awareness within Itamaraty that Brazilian and Mercosul closeness to the EU might provide a critical counterweight in FTAA negotiations and draw other South American countries to the continental project (BBC AL/2375/L), or at least point out that there was an alternative to the United States. Not surprisingly, then, plans to strengthen the EU-Brazil linkages that might transmute into a wider Mercosul-EU accord were quickly formulated. Within days of the 1994 ministerial meeting Brazilian diplomats expressed a desire for closer political and commercial links with Europe (Lampreia 1999a, 121). This sentiment was almost immediately reciprocated by the EU's commissioner for development, Manuel Marín, who lamented the sense of a growing divide between the two regions (IPS 12 May 1994). By 1995 the potential for a Mercosul-EU agreement had achieved a certain degree of momentum in the Southern Cone, emerging as one theme addressed during Cardoso's speech at the annual Summit of bloc presidents (BBC AL/2375/L). The idea of a Mercosul-EU accord continued to be advanced by Brazilian diplomats in September, most notably when Cardoso sought to draw a parallel between the Franco-German axis in Europe and Argentine-Brazilian relations (AP 21 Sept. 1995).

Impetus was given to interregional relations by the signature of the EU-Brazil Framework Cooperation Agreement in late 1995 (*European Report* 25 Oct. 1995). By December of that year a similar interregional protocol had been agreed on, offering the promise not only of a trade deal, but also of an interregional association covering wider political and economic issues (IPS 13 Dec. 1995).

The decision to enter into talks did not guarantee an agreement. Discussions remained centered on the need to negotiate a free-trade agreement, with efforts being devoted almost exclusively to debating what sectors should be included in an interregional accord. June of 1999 saw some progress on this front when sustained pressure from Brazilian diplomats succeeded in securing French consent to the inclusion of agriculture in trade talks (IPS 22 June 1999), but further details about the exact terms of discussion and consensus on a timeline remained elusive (*Lloyd's List* 29 June 1999).

The significant point about the 1999 Mercosul-EU meetings for my discussion of leadership is that they took place in the midst of the blocwide economic crisis caused by the devaluation of the Brazilian *real*, by suggestions that Mercosul was about to collapse, and by a belief that Brazil should pursue an independent path. Indeed, continued talks for a separate EU-Brazil agreement implied that the economic attraction of South America was not in Mercosul but in the industrialized Brazilian market (*AFX News* 30 Sept. 1999). This external impression was bolstered by continuous overtures to Brazil from the Germans, Spanish, and Portuguese to strengthen Mercosul as a regional political counterpart to the EU and position Brazil as a regional interlocutor (Cardoso and Lafer 2007). Cardoso's response was to redirect these to an economic bolstering of Mercosul by using the Brazilian market as a lever to extract concessions from Europe. French acquiescence to negotiations on farm issues at the June 1999 EU-Mercosul meeting emerges as a case in point, coming after Cardoso issued veiled threats to abandon the EU-Brazil and interregional process if Europe did not allow him to demonstrate Brazil's capacity for leadership, which could bring tangible benefits to all members of the Southern Cone economic bloc (BBC AL/W0586/WL). At one point Cardoso bluntly told France's Chirac: "The only possibility for you, France, is to invest in Brazilian agriculture . . . because you cannot compete in terms of price" (Cardoso and Lafer 2007). Significantly, the costs involved in this attempt at leadership were implied and not actual, allowing Brazil to present itself as investing in the future of Mercosul without any real expenditure, especially since the EU's willingness to discuss agriculture remained quite distinct from actually signing any substantive agreement on the topic. More to the point, it was only Brazil that was able to act as an effective and forceful intermediary between Europe and South America, chiefly through the personal relationships that Cardoso had developed with European counterparts in Germany, the United Kingdom, Spain, Portugal, France, and Italy (Cardoso and Lafer 2007).

Although progress in the EU-Mercosul talks fell short of expectations, with 2000 and 2001 bringing repeated meetings seeking agreement on the terms of discussion (Hoffmann 2002; *European Report* 11 Nov. 2000 and 24 March 2001), the larger point of interest for Itamaraty was the tenor of interregional relations. European interest in Mercosul was not limited to economic questions, but encompassed the goal of seeing similar regional projects formed in other parts of the world to counterbalance U.S. power (Santander 2002, 495).

An important aspect of the 1995 agreement between the EU and Mercosul related to capacity building and technical assistance for strengthening Mercosul (Devlin et al. 2003, 21). Indeed, at this point there was a certain consonance between Brazilian and EU ambitions for Mercosul, with both actors viewing the bloc as the core of a larger South American free-trade area capable of acting in a significant manner on the global stage (Whitehead 1999, 63–64). The difference between the two approaches to the creation of SAFTA was that the EU was restricted to making statements in favor of a continent-wide region— preferring bloc-bloc negotiations to bloc-country talks—while Brazil could actively pursue the concept. Considerable efforts had already been focused in this direction through the elaboration of the 4+1 mechanism that brought Bolivia and Chile into Mercosul as associate members. The next logical step was to pursue a free-trade agreement between the continent's two economic blocs, a prospect enthusiastically embraced by the Comunidad Andina (CAN— Andean Community) in 1997 (*AFP* 22 April 1997).

The initial enthusiasm that led to an April 1998 agreement on the need for a Mercosul-CAN free-trade agreement soon ran into difficulties (IPS 14 April 1998). Within a year the talks had fallen victim to a combination of the economic crisis caused by devaluation of the *real* and disagreement on preferential tariff policies (*AFP* 27 Feb. 1999; BBC AL/W0584/WL). Itamaraty's response to this setback points to the masked coercive possibilities implicit in the continued pursuit of a regional project on a unilateral basis. Withdrawal from negotiations by the other three Mercosul countries was met with formal notification that Brazil would use the attraction of its internal market and continue with the talks on its own (IPS 13 April 1999). Substance was added by Itamaraty's announcement of a ninety-day unilateral extension of the existing bilateral trade agreement with the Andean countries. Yet concomitant care was taken to assure Brazil's bloc partners that independent continuation of the talks was not an attempt to rupture Mercosul. Explicit acknowledgment was given to the difficulties afflicting Mercosul and the impact they had had on the formulation of a joint position, particularly with respect to reconciling the importance given by each country to market access in agriculture and manufactured goods (*AFP* 27 Feb. 1999; BBC AL/W0584/WL).

The consistent Itamaraty message was that Brazil was pursuing a shortcut toward a future interregional deal, words that were cautiously accepted by Argentina with the proviso that a full trade deal with CAN must involve all of Mercosul (*LAWR*-WR-99–15). Indeed, Brazilian officials were careful to point out that they were not seeking a trade deal, but a harmonization of existing arrangements that should lay the groundwork for a future pact between the two blocs (IPS 13 April 1999). The unspoken reality was that such a deal would largely be of Brazilian design and would require the other Mercosul countries to accept participation in the process or risk losing preferential access to Brazil.

The bilateral talks resulted in a one-year agreement between Brazil and CAN that created a preferential tariff system for over 3,000 products. Significantly, Brazil declined CAN requests for a three-year agreement, insisting that the accord should be revisited after one year with a view to including the other Mercosul countries (IPS 05 July 1999). This stipulation also implicitly held forth the possibility of nonrenewal by Brazil.

Although the deal was extended for one year in August 2000, it took another year for Mercosul to resume negotiations, despite Lampreia's 1999 call for a deepening and expansion of the bloc (*LAWR*-RB-00–07), a measure that would be relatively cost-free in terms of gross trade flows. Again, the concerns of Brazil's Mercosul partners were acknowledged when Itamaraty reversed standing policy and agreed to a two-track approach that would see the Andean countries gain access to Argentina and Brazil more quickly than to Paraguay or Uruguay (*Gazeta Mercantil* 20 August 2001).

Talks between the two blocs nevertheless ran into many of the old barriers, with a December 2002 deadline missed because of a combination of internal CAN tariff-harmonization issues and the residual impact of the economic crisis caused by Argentina's economic collapse. As in 1999, Itamaraty continued to work toward a future interregional deal, in this case accepting a Peruvian invitation to pursue a bilateral accord as part of the framework for a continental agreement (*LAWR*-RS-02–10).

Although these negotiations were marked by unilateral tendencies to the extent that Itamaraty was determined that the reticence of Brazil's bloc partners would not prevent an eventual agreement, a central feature was a willingness to welcome the other Mercosul countries back to the negotiating table, but not to restart the talks at the stage where these countries had left the process. A crucial point here is the patient approach to foreign policy within Itamaraty, a strategic stance that some Brazilian diplomats have contrasted with the impetuous and tactical diplomacy of the other Mercosul countries. Direct pressure was not exerted on the other countries. Rather, it was implied, bundled into the knowledge that new rules for intracontinental relations were being formulated without input from the weaker, abstaining regional countries.

The problem that Brazilian diplomats ran into in their attempt to extend the consensual aspect of their leadership in South America was the question of cost. In particular the Andean Community, under pressure from domestic leaders fearing Brazilian competition, wanted rewards for signing an interregional deal and emphasized the need for special concessions in any such agreement and for expanded flows of Brazilian investment. The problem, explained one Brazilian official close to the interregional talks, was that the mind-set in Brazil and Itamaraty during the Cardoso era all but precluded the material expenditure involved in either option, which was not unreasonable given the economic challenges Brazil faced during the first six years of the Cardoso presidency. The issue that became a problem was that the institutional structures in Brazil—primarily the Banco Nacional de Desenvolvimento Econômico e Social (BNDES—National Economic and Social Development Bank) and the ALADI Reciprocal Credit Convention—necessary for the sort of investment programs sought by CAN members were configured in a manner that would not have allowed Brazil to assume the relatively minor financial costs to seal the agreement despite the growing political will in Itamaraty and the presidency (Cardoso and Lafer 2007). In short, the public unwillingness to assume the fiscal costs of leadership highlighted by Lampreia required that an alternative route be found for providing the material payoffs necessary to advance the South American project.

South American Infrastructure Integration

Cardoso's response to the slow pace of interregional talks deviated from the tradition of frustrated acceptance. Instead, Itamaraty was tasked with pursuing a policy of active leadership that sought to add tangible substance to the prevailing rhetoric. In effect the goal was to restart the Gramscian student-teacher dialectic style of leadership seen before the 1994 Miami Summit of the Americas and frame it around the Brazil-led design of the continental integration project to be launched at the 2000 Summit of South American Presidents in Brasília. Indeed, the fact that Itamaraty was able to bring all of the continent's leaders to Brasília for the 31 August–1 September 2000 meeting and achieve strong consensus on and adherence to a plan of action suggests an implicit acceptance of the consensual leadership role that Brazil had been accruing over the previous six years.

Two aspects of the 2000 Brasília Summit of South American Presidents are central to the discussion in this chapter. In historical terms the meeting was the first exclusive gathering of South American presidents, giving symbolic gravitas to South America as a viable geopolitical entity. Second, the document signed by the assembled leaders represented a concrete and realizable vision of a South American region as it incorporated agreements on five key issue areas. The first four areas—the need to protect democracy, encourage trade, combat illicit drugs, and cooperate in the pursuit of the technology needed to compete internationally—restated existing positions formulated in groupings such as Mercosul, the Rio Group, and the OAS.

It was the fifth issue area—physical-infrastructure integration—that represented a new approach to continental integration and formed the substance of Brazilian leadership. The idea presented in Brasília was to construct "axes of development," corridors of energy, transportation, and communications infrastructure connecting the different regions of South America. Critically, the elaboration of the axes was to be based on demand—not central planning or competing national political considerations—in an effort to foster the creation of regionally integrated production chains (Silveira 2001).

Implicit in the program of physical, as opposed to commercial or political, integration advanced at the Brasília Summit was a view of the global system that saw the beneficial insertion of South American countries into the international economy as being dependent on heightened continental cohesion and unity (*Brasília Communiqué*, paragraphs 12 and 13).

The attractiveness of the axes-of-development approach to continental integration was that it provided ostensibly apolitical support for the substantive linkages necessary to implement the South American project. This directly addressed the political and economic bickering that Cardoso had noted in attempts to strengthen Mercosul and engage in interregional negotiations within South America: "To do something based on physical integration is a much more powerful instrument to really connect trade" (Cardoso and Lafer 2007). The potential advantage of the proposed axes of infrastructure is that they circumvented questions about specific industrial sectors by focusing on providing the conditions for economic growth and offering opportunities for grass roots–level economic relationships that transcended national borders (Silveira 2001). Indeed, the section of the *Brasília Communiqué* dealing with infrastructure integration (paragraphs 36–46) focuses on the changes that expanded physical linkages might bring about in intracontinental economic relations by positioning the resulting interdependence as a support strut for continued and deeper cooperation in other issue areas.

Significantly, the Brazilian infrastructure proposal was having a deeper impact on the ideational approach to development and foreign relations in South America. Despite its initial resistance to an idea that was formed by Cardoso and thrust on a dubious Foreign Ministry (Cardoso and Lafer 2007), Itamaraty again exercised a quiet degree of leadership, encouraging a homogenization of different national positions through patient discussion of the formation and direction of IIRSA. Implicit in the IIRSA framework was a shift in national priorities and the inculcation of neighboring countries with the ideational element of the Brazilian vision of a South American region. The unstated element in the push to encourage initiatives toward greater regionalization of national economies was the impact that greater interdependence would have on the Itamaraty goal of advancing South America as an operational concept; this would bind the interests of countries in the continent closer to those of Brazil as elements of national economies became increasingly embedded in the Brazilian market.

While Cardoso was pleased to see a rise in Brazilian foreign direct investment in neighboring countries, his concern was that this would be viewed as an almost imperialistic outright purchase of other regional economies. What he wanted instead was a European-style "true integration in terms of physical integration plus capital fusion," one that would be predicated on the creation of transnational production chains crisscrossing the continent (Cardoso and Lafer 2007). The process was imbued with a self-reinforcing dynamic strongly reminiscent of the mercantilistic notions of a commercial fifth column outlined by Hirschman (1945) in the European context and increased the potency of the ideational aspects of Brazilian foreign policy as linkages between Brazil and the rest of South America grew closer. Elements of this sort of transformation began to appear in the revivification of the Mercosul-CAN negotiations toward the end of the Cardoso presidency (Mercosul/Comunidad Andina 2002) and increases in Brazil's purchases of energy from other countries in the continent.

The substance of Brazilian leadership came to dominate the discussion at the South American Presidents' Summits, with a continuation of infrastructure integration being of particular importance. A version of the Gramscian student-teacher dialectic can be superimposed here, with Itamaraty serving as teacher and introducing physical integration as the subject for discussion to mold the thinking of the other states. Explicit in this Gramscian dynamic is a point at which the teacher in effect becomes the student, learning from the independent thought and exploration of the pupil. But for this transformation to come about—for the follower to autonomously and independently act to protect and advance the leader's project—the substance of the lesson must become embedded in the thought processes of the student, suggesting the need for a period during which the teacher acts to maintain focus on the topic at hand. The central task for Itamaraty was thus maintaining the continent's focus on the subject of infrastructure integration and implementing the plan devised at the Brasília Summit and elaborated by ministers and technocrats at a series of IIRSA meetings.

As preparations for the 26–27 July 2002 Second South American Presidents' Summit in Guayaquil progressed, Brazilian diplomats found that they had to exert some pressure to resist plans that would narrow the focus of the Summit process. Of particular concern were moves by host nation Ecuador as well as Venezuela to turn the meeting into an energy summit (*El País* 27 July 2002). One diplomat described the initial draft proposed by the Ecuadorians as problematic because of its concentration on energy issues, which raised fears that unnecessary repetition of statements agreed on in the *Brasília Communiqué* might cause the process to lose "the punch" needed to drive continental integration (A. Gonçalves 2002). Indeed, at thirty-four paragraphs, the *Declaração sobre a zona de paz sul-americana* that formed the Consensus of Guayaquil was just over half the length of the Brasília text.

Although considerable attention was given to energy issues (paragraphs 16–18 and 20–24), the focus was not on the quasi-nationalist agenda advanced by Venezuela, but on building an integrated South American energy matrix. New clauses in the South American Summit document concerned the area of security, resulting in the assembled presidents declaring the continent a zone of peace as well as adopting several provisions to combat terrorism. In these terms the Guayaquil meeting can be likened to Gramsci's second teacher-student encounter, where the theme of the lesson is restated and elaborated by the students, but is still within the guiding framework established by the teacher.

Conclusion

Throughout this chapter I have argued that Brazilian diplomacy during the Cardoso era demonstrated a style of leadership predicated on consensus creation, the launching of initiatives, and the sharing of new ideas. As I shall argue in the wider book, the goal was to establish South America as a viable geopolitical and geoeconomic regional space, an ambition requiring the active collaboration of the other countries on the continent.

The challenge facing Itamaraty was how Brazil might take on a leadership role without falling prey to accusations of "hegemonism" or imperialism. In part the strategy adopted by Brazilian diplomats rested on the active denial of a desire for leadership, a stance that the evidence presented in this chapter suggests was mildly disingenuous. Throughout discussions during the Miami Summit of the Americas, interregional trade associations between Mercosul and the EU or CAN, and the Brasília and Guayaquil South American Presidents Summits, Brazil was noticeable for its active leadership. Yet this leadership role was distinctly at odds with the coercive precepts and preconceptions that I outlined at the beginning of this chapter, assuming instead a consensual nature that mirrored important aspects of the Gramscian student-teacher dialectic. Here we find an important indicator of both the Brazilian approach to foreign relations and the larger Itamaraty strategy of strengthening South America as a viable international actor.

As is the case with Gramsci's conceptualization of hegemony, Brazilian leadership is predicated on an approach that sees an effective leader as one that does not need to force cooperation. Instead, dialogue and discussion are mixed with a certain degree of cajoling and "leading by doing" to disseminate a project and include others in it, thereby creating a situation in which the leader emerges as more of an instigator and guide than an enforcer and disciplinarian. Perhaps more significant for the larger theoretical discussion of this book, for the type of consensual leadership at times exercised by Itamaraty to function effectively it must pervade the ideational, economic, and security aspects of consensual hegemony. Indeed, events toward the end of the Cardoso administration suggest this linkage most strongly, with widespread acceptance of the IIRSA project being shortly followed by active revivification of Mercosul-CAN talks, which set the stage for a deal between the two in 2003.

3

The Ideas Dimension

In the Introduction I adopted Susan Strange's pyramidal model of structural power as a guide for understanding the different aspects of power involved in leading the construction of a hegemony. The elegance of Strange's model is that it captures the interconnected nature of the various constituent dimensions of structural power, graphically portraying the manner in which each facet simultaneously relies on and bolsters the other aspects.

As will be discussed in Chapters 4 and 5, Brazilian power in the economic and security aspects is far from absolute (Lafer 2000, 221), leaving the question of how Itamaraty could have hoped to construct and lead a viable South American project. The key lies in the subtext concerning the importance of ideas in the construction of Brazil's foreign policy. In his Portuguese memoirs Cardoso (2006, 612) is explicit that, in a time of scarce economic resources, as was the case during his presidency, foreign policy comes to rest increasingly on diplomatic actions focused on the careful selection of objectives and partners. This is not to suggest, however, that Brazilian foreign policy is dependent on the persuasive power of its ideational underpinnings; I will make it clear that dissemination of the ideas at the heart of the continental project elaborated by Itamaraty are conditioned by Brazil's willingness to absorb some of the costs of leadership. Rather, the pyramidal model in the Brazilian case might be described as a geometrically imperfect shape with its pinnacle shifted to one side so that the ideas dimension plays a slightly more important role in ensuring structural stability than in the ideal-type model outlined earlier. As this chapter will demonstrate, three main ideas—democracy, liberal economics, and a clear vision of globalization—emerge as the material taken up in the Gramscian student-teacher dialectic, providing a common frame of reference for and the substance around which the leadership effort is organized.

The purpose of this chapter is to set out the central ideas underpinning the South American project pursued by Brazilian foreign-policy makers during the Cardoso era. At the heart of Brazil's foreign policy lie two intertwined goals broadly shared by the other South American countries, namely, national development and democratic consolidation (Abdenur 1994b, 51; Lafer 2001–2002, 161). Conditioning the policy responses designed to attain these goals are the core values and beliefs forming the basis for the ideational aspect of the Brazilian continental project. As the brief theoretical review in this chapter will explain, notions of self-identity are in part fashioned through interaction with the larger international context, working to construct a particular vision of how the global system operates and what role a particular state plays within it. In the Brazilian case, during the Cardoso era notions of self-identity revolved around the physical size of the country—its continental dimensions—and the notion of South America as distinct regional space (Lafer 2007). Indeed, subsequent chapters in this book will reveal the construction of South America and the South Americanness of Brazil as a central element of the ideas aspect of consensual hegemony underpinning the leadership project.

The idea of South America as a distinct region is in turn embedded within a larger worldview that owes much to the version of dependency theory that Cardoso helped articulate as a leading sociologist in the 1960s and 1970s (Goertzl 1999, chapters 2 and 3). A clear suggestion in this chapter is that the precepts of dependency theory shaped Brazilian foreign policy during the Cardoso era, providing added impetus to notions of an asymmetric world order that permeated Itamaraty before Cardoso's tenure as foreign minister in 1992–1993. Indeed, at this point it is important to be clear that Cardoso did not reject his earlier writings during the 1994 presidential campaign (Cardoso 2006, chapter 10; dos Santos and Randall 1998, 53). Although slightly ambiguous language was subsequently employed to assuage international capital markets—at one point Cardoso likened the creation of dependency to the academic preparation of Mary Shelley's Dr. Frankenstein (Cardoso 1995, 8)—the precepts of dependency theory clearly informed his approach to the changing international political economy of the post–Cold War era. Indeed, he has acknowledged this a number of times (Cardoso and Toledo 1998, 172–173; Cardoso and Lafer 2007).

In a move paralleled inside Itamaraty, the intellectual shift instead involved a revision of the theory to incorporate the new reality of the international economic system. Here a methodological point becomes pertinent. Like most political figures Cardoso did not draft his own speeches, relying instead on a team of writers to prepare many of the texts cited in this chapter. Significantly, the individuals tasked with preparing the various public statements were diplomats seconded to the presidency, suggesting an internalization of the dependency theory worldview within Itamaraty as well as very tight presidential control over the intellectual and strategic conceptualization of Brazilian foreign policy (Danese 1999; Lampreia and Cruz 2005; G. Fonseca 2004, 258–259).

In terms of the pyramidal model of hegemony I employ, then, the ideas dimension emerges as the support structure for the economic and security aspects, providing the intellectual direction needed to conceptualize the other elements. As the physical interdependence of the pyramid suggests, policies founded on the ideational base permeate the other two aspects, providing a practical forum where the ideas can be taken up, interpreted, and re-presented in a process that recalls Gramsci's student-teacher dialectic.

The focus of this chapter is thus the substance of the ideas aspect of the South American project pursued by Cardoso's foreign policy, not the manner in which these policies were disseminated throughout the continent. After a brief theoretical exploration of the linkage between ideas and foreign policy formulation, attention will be turned to the reconceptualization of the working definition of Brazilian national identity employed by Itamaraty. This sense of identity then forms a platform for an exploration of the worldview guiding Brazilian foreign policy during the Cardoso era, opening space for consideration of the role of democracy, variations on a liberal economic theme, and globalization in the ideas aspect of the South American project.

The Power of Ideas

Susan Strange (1994, 119) justifies her decision to include a "knowledge" or "ideas" structure in her pyramidal model of structural power by noting that the ability to control and influence knowledge and ideas directly affects what actors believe and understand as being possible. In the realm of foreign policy formulation the power of ideas rests in the ability to erect implicit boundaries around conceivable action, limits that are formed by particular conceptions of the international system and how it operates. Significantly, the beliefs and worldviews that form the substance of ideas are not presented as existing in isolation, but emerge from notions of self-conception and identity. Ideas are consequently something internalized and institutionalized, forming guides for the continuation of habitual action instead of the more wrenching innovation and reconceptualization involved in shifting the ideational basis underlying the policy process (Goldstein and Keohane 1993, 5–9).

This conceptualization of ideas is very close to that of the consensual approach to hegemony, where a particular pattern of thinking and convictions become subconsciously embedded in an actor's psyche, working to automatically proscribe or validate particular courses of action. Yet this revision is not completely satisfying because it functions mainly as another limitation on state action, albeit one derived from a shared attitude. No attention is given to how this belief system is formed, and, more significant for the work presented here, little discussion is devoted to how a would-be leading state might lever the ideational dimension in order to compensate for a lack of overall dominating power.

Moreover, implicit in the attainment of Strange's structural power—one state is dominant in all four aspects of structural power—is the realist suggestion that states in the international system operate on an exclusively self-interested basis, constantly seeking power over other states. One of the great benefits of structural power is that it embeds in the system the advancement of the interests and priorities of the dominant state long after that state has declined in power (Strange 1994, 24–29), providing great incentive for a state to exercise power when it can. A measure of support for this suggestion comes from discussions of the bureaucratic deployment of ideas, in which it is argued that the choice of a particular ideational approach in the policymaking process is not automatic and is likely to serve a specific interest. In short, the suggestion is that the ideas employed in the policymaking process—beliefs, worldviews, and self-identity—are formulated to service a specific goal (Goldstein and Keohane 1993, 11).

The social-constructivist school of international relations takes up the constructed nature of ideas, arguing that assumptions about an anarchical international system operating in a self-help manner are problematic because they take as given the manner in which states interact. As Wendt notes in his critique of realist-style approaches (1992, 402), "self-help is an institution, not a constitutive feature of anarchy." This suggests that actors in the international system have consciously decided to withhold trust and base decision-making processes on worst-case scenarios.

Two important points for our discussion of ideas follow from this argument. The first is a rough translation to international relations of the constructivist tradition in sociology that reality is made by its actors to meet specific goals and aspirations (Berger and Luckman 1966). In the realm of international relations and international political economy this means that the nature of interstate relations is not caused by the system's anarchic character, but is instead constructed and shaped by the historical pattern of interaction as states, at least subconsciously, seek to embed a pattern of rules and norms favorable to the most influential actors.

The acknowledgment of questions about structure-agency and the persistence of a particular and evolving dependency worldview were made explicit during my interview with Cardoso and his second foreign minister, Celso Lafer:

> LAFER: On the issue of dependency the guiding line of the president is that the international scene, the international functioning of the economy, conditions but does not determine what a country can do.
> CARDOSO: Yes.
> LAFER: His whole effort as president and as an intellectual was to examine what were the alternatives for Brazil. During his presidency and the handling of foreign policy this was the rule of thumb. We are not conditioned. We are not determined. We have a certain amount of freedom. How do we explore this space of freedom?
> CARDOSO: There politics is important. Not just economic determinism, or structure. We have some possibility in terms of different policies. That is the basic point and it never changed in my mind. [*Dependency and Development in Latin America*] is not a book to reprise imperialist theory, but to explain how it is possible to move in spite of it. (Cardoso and Lafer 2007)

Conditioning this interaction is the second contribution, which asks whether foreign policy identities and interests are exogenous or endogenous to the international system. Wendt (1992, 402–406) concludes, in essence, that the substance of foreign policy emerges from domestic society, which constructs its external identity and priorities through a comparison with other actors in the international system.

In this light a government's foreign policy emerges as the result of a dialectical process involving both internal and external influences. Here a space is opened for the wider, but not necessarily systemic, dissemination of an ideational project. With internal conceptions of self-identity conditioned by interaction with the external, expansion of patterns of cooperation and solidarity on a regional basis creates an opportunity to generate the consensus necessary for the erection of a consensual hegemony. The possibility of nonconflictual formulation of hegemonic structures is thus opened, with collective action and solidarity providing the density of influence that an alternate conception of the system would need in order to cause change in the overarching hegemony.

Several elements emerge from this theoretical discussion as being critical to the elaboration of the ideas aspect of leadership and consensual hegemony. If we draw on the reflexive nature of self-conception and worldview outlined above, it becomes evident that a clear conceptualization of national identity must be developed, a notion of identity that can be expanded to the regional space in the broader discussion of a South American project. Undergirding this sense of self and region must be a clear conceptualization of how the international system operates and the place that a particular actor occupies within that order. Significantly, notions of identity and worldview inform and guide policy, providing an analytical avenue for understanding the dissemination of the ideas dimension throughout the other three aspects of Strange's pyramidal model. Indeed, the notions of identity and worldview provide the material addressed in the Gramscian student-teacher dialectic, the route used to disseminate the intellectual basis and ownership of the regionalist projects throughout South America.

Brazil's International Identity

The suggestion that a national identity is constructed in relation to both domestic and international reality finds resonance in the development of Brazil's foreign policy. Celso Lafer (1990, 33), twice Brazil's foreign minister, goes as far as to highlight the formation of national identity as being a central factor in international relations because of the manner in which conceptions of "self" and of "other" affect the formulation of policy and national insertion into the international system. This centrality of identity in the internal intellectual approach to foreign-policy making at Itamaraty offers some explanation for Rio Branco's iconic status as the "patron saint of Brazilian diplomacy." Indeed, efforts to refine conceptions of the national identity, particularly the Argentina-Brazil-Chile alliance policies he pursued in the Southern Cone subregion, often draw on his legacy.

During the early 1990s reference to Rio Branco's subregional strategies re-emerged in Itamaraty as diplomats searched for a new paradigm for understanding the changes that had been caused by the end of the Cold War (Lafer and Fonseca 1994, 54–55; Lafer et al. 1993, 272; Barbosa 2007). The interesting development at this point was that the existing and widely used terminology of international identity was deliberately thrown into flux; sharp distinctions between "developed" and "developing" were replaced by the broader notion of "Western" in a philosophical and humanistic sense, identifying Brazil with

Western notions of democracy and economic liberalism (Aleixo 1989, 29). Moreover, the dissolution of ideology as an effective currency in international relations was accompanied by a decline in charity to developing countries, what was described as a transition from "trade as aid" to "trade not aid" (Feinberg 1997, 35). This shift in the approach to national identification was precipitated by what Celso Amorim (1991a, 26, 30) identifies as an unprecedented disconnection between international politics and economics, a change that ended the tactic of using the promise of political alignment as currency for the recruitment of economic assistance. In effect, the reflexive nature of identity formation outlined above was coming into play, resulting in a reappraisal of national conceptions of identity as a new worldview began to dominate approaches to the international system.

A crucial policy outcome of the shift in Itamaraty's notions of Brazilian self-identity caused by the end of the Cold War was an acceleration away from a protectionist import-substitution industrialization model to a more liberal approach to economics and international trade that focused on gaining international market access and adopting measures to ensure national competitiveness despite the challenge created by the repeated economic crises of the 1990s (Cardoso and Toledo 1998, 301–303). While the Brazilian variant of liberalism will receive more attention later in this chapter, the important point for our immediate discussion is that it precipitated a revision within Itamaraty of Brazil's regional and international identity. The concern was that the collapse of Cold War political alliances would cause a surge in competition for the investment and technology needed for economic advancement. Another factor was the rise of regionalism, particularly the prospect of the three competing megablocs of Europe, NAFTA, and the Asian Pacific (Barbosa 1994, 103, 107–108; Almeida 1993; Lampreia 1996a, 42–44). At issue was how Brazil might combat heightened protectionist barriers to its exports and ensure continued inflows of the capital and technology needed for national development. The answer, as Pres. Fernando Collor made clear at the signing of the Mercosul treaty in 1991, was a turn to regionalism and South America (Collor 1991a).

As was detailed in Chapter 1, Mercosul represented a consolidation of the Argentine-Brazilian political and economic approximation effected by the PICE accords, which drew the two buffer states of Paraguay and Uruguay into the process. The point that was not discussed earlier was the extent to which the advent of Mercosul represented a fundamental shift in Brazil's self-identity as employed by Itamaraty. Mercosul brought obvious economic benefits (discussed in the next chapter), but Celso Amorim also points to the political effects of the bloc, positioning it as the nucleus for an expanded South American region (Amorim 2003a, 12). In effect, the definition of Brazilian identity employed by Itamaraty was undergoing a mild geographical retraction from the third worldism of the 1970s to focus on the continental level as a platform for enhanced international insertion. The suggestion made by Itamaraty secretary-general Roberto Abdenur (1994b, 55) was that Brazil should pursue a foreign policy matching the country's dimensions. Abdenur's argument drew on a brief point foreign minister Celso Lafer made to the Chamber of Deputies in 1992, namely, that integration should be pursued because Brazil's circumstance was Latin America (Lafer 1992c), a proposition that recalled Golbery's geopolitical vision of Latin America as Brazil's natural sphere of influence. Lafer (1994, 25) continued to develop this theme, leading to a suggestion in 1994 that foreshadowed the *Brasília Communiqué* issued at the 2000 Summit of South American Presidents: in Brazil's case a foreign policy informed by a country's geography called for borders that acted as "frontiers of cooperation," not "frontiers of separation." Indeed, the reconceptualization that Lafer initiated provided critical foundation stones for the South American idea that Ambassador Rubens Barbosa was advocating and Cardoso was seeking to elaborate further as foreign minister and then president. The centrality of Lafer's role in this intellectual genesis was clearly signaled when he, along with Hélio Jaguaribe, was charged by Cardoso with running a detailed academic seminar aiming to quell voices within Itamaraty questioning the wisdom of the South American concept during early discussions about the 2000 Brasília Summit of South American Presidents (Cardoso and Lafer 2007; Lafer 2007; Barbosa 2007).

The argument offered by Lafer draws on the same ideational premise that Feinberg was attempting to use in the early 1990s to revive a hemispheric movement in U.S. foreign policy, namely, that Latin America was an artificial construct imposed for analytical convenience (Feinberg 1997, chapter 1; Cardoso 2006, 88). It was not that Cardoso was attempting to discard the idea of South America as a binding concept; rather, he was reframing the terms of reference: "When I was appointed foreign minister I made a speech. My idea—yours [Lafer], too—was that we have to play a game composed of variable geometry. . . . Let's look at both Latin America and South America" (Cardoso and Lafer 2007). Pursuit of this shift, initiated under Lafer's first period as foreign minister, pushed farther during Cardoso's ministry, and consolidated during his presidency, was welcomed by key players in Itamaraty: "Latin America was yesterday's outmoded concept. From Fernando Henrique on, and I helped with this conceptual change, we were aiming at 'South America.' South American integration in trade, energy, physical integration, whatever. We speak about South America, and this started with Fernando Henrique" (Barbosa 2007). While this intellectual and conceptual shift was actively taking place within Itamaraty during the 1990s, it largely remained an internal discussion due to the financial and political restrictions imposed on Brazilian diplomacy by the rigors of repeated financial crises, including the surprise devaluation of the *real* in 1999.

Very active public presentation of the idea of "South America" as a guiding priority had to wait until 2000 and was floated in its most comprehensive and sweeping forms by Celso Lafer in the lead-up to the Brasília Summit of South American Presidents. In an article published in English (2000) and an extended essay in Portuguese (2001), Lafer sought to refine and subdivide the concept of Latin America, drawing on ties of history, geography, and international political relations to establish South America as the most apt reference point for both Brazil and the other countries of the continent. The picture painted by Lafer (2000, 216–217) is of a foreign policy consciously seeking to create a continent of friends and neighbors who act in good faith to resolve regional disputes without conflict.

The point that Cardoso noted in the early 1990s was that countries of continental dimensions, such as Brazil, have a tendency to look inward rather than outward. This is an untenable action in the context of the new pressures created by the post–Cold War surge in globalization, requiring the sort of shift in attitude that he encouraged to seek new realities by exploiting the possibilities inherent in the regional context demonstrated by the European example (Cardoso and Toledo 1998, 91, 127–128). Indeed, the suggestion that intracontinental interdependence and mutual assistance formed a central element of Brazilian foreign policy during the Cardoso era provides the ideational explanation for the policies discussed in Chapters 4 and 5 here as well as the leadership style outlined in Chapter 2 (Barros 1995; Cardoso and Lafer 2007).

Significantly, the very elements that had historically been used to differentiate Brazil from its neighbors—language, political history, and size—were sidelined in an attempt to buttress economic and political approximation with a sense of cultural affinity (Fundação Alexandre de Gusmáo [hereafter FUNAG] 1997). Perhaps the most amusing manifestation of the attempt to construct and disseminate the emotive and cultural notions of South Americanness came with Cardoso's 2000 musings on the continent's "elective affinity," as demonstrated in shared forms of irony, ways of walking, and general deportment at the beach (Cardoso 2000h). On a more serious level Lafer (2000, 218–219) points to other core identity characteristics of Brazil as being key to the successful construction of a shared continental identity, with respect for national sovereignty and a formal policy of treating smaller neighboring countries as equals providing a foundation for regional cooperation.

Of course, these touted cultural affinities buttressed the more pressing reality, namely, that the closest viable markets for many states in Brazil were their immediate neighboring country. In areas such as the Amazon and western Brazil geographical and logistical practicalities meant that São Paulo and Rio de Janeiro might just as well be in Europe (Cardoso and Toledo 1998, 130–131).

The reconceptualization of Itamaraty's working definition of Brazilian national identity, driven by the foreign-policy review Cardoso instigated (Brazil 1993), was not a capricious undertaking, but part of the larger strategy of adapting to the new post–Cold War reality by in effect seeking to construct a leadership project that drew on a sense of solidarity and cooperation with neighboring countries facing similar developmental challenges (Barbosa 1996, 75; Barbosa 2001; Sardenberg 1998, 15–16). Two articles by Rubens Barbosa are particularly informative here. The first reiterates the political nature of Mercosul and SAFTA, framing South America as the context for Brazilian foreign policy (Barbosa 1994); the second highlights the shift away from decades of protectionist policy toward an identity as a "global trader" (Barbosa and César 1994b).

Again, the policy problem driving a reevaluation of the ideational element of Brazilian foreign policy was the search for a response to changing global circumstances and the reflexive relationship between policy goals and identity. The worldview alluded to earlier in this chapter once again became important. The double transition from authoritarianism to democracy and from protectionist to open-market economics implicit in Barbosa's articles is suggestive of an absorption of the internationally hegemonic liberal ideology that was spreading in the late 1980s and early 1990s, particularly during the Collor presidency (Lafer et al. 1993, 272–273), recalling Aleixo's (1989) observation that Brazil was adopting an identity guided by broadly Western philosophical and humanistic traditions.

Yet there was recognition within Itamaraty and by Cardoso as president that untrammeled acceptance of the global zeitgeist could marginalize Brazil economically and politically in the international system (Cardoso and Lafer 2007). As will become apparent in Chapter 5, although vociferous acceptance and defense of the need for democratic governance was sincere, Brazilian diplomatic discourse was framed in terms that continued to privilege the concept of sovereignty in an attempt to ensure that regime type and economic orthodoxy did not emerge as new tools of subtle control wielded by globally dominant states (G. Fonseca 2004, 282–289). Emphasis was instead placed on encouraging conditions that would allow democracy to become an internally sustainable reality. In a similar manner, the elaboration of "South American" instead of "Latin American" as an identifying label emerged as a device to frame continental regional projects, a rhetorical shift that formed a major recurring theme in the speeches Lafer (2002a) made during his second period as foreign minister. The intent was then to deploy the collectively expanded power of the region as a buttress to support the sense of policy autonomy needed to modify and dilute the proscriptive nature of the near-global hegemonic Washington Consensus economic program and formulate policy that would serve the developmental needs of the country.

I am suggesting that the economic aspects of foreign policy pursued during the Cardoso era incorporated important elements of the neoliberal ideology, but not in the more orthodox manner seen in Chile. As I will argue in the remainder of this chapter, an unwillingness to adhere strictly to the Washington Consensus was grounded in the worldview employed by foreign-policy makers, an approach to the international system that developed during the Cardoso era into a revised and updated version of dependency theory.

The Brazilian Worldview

Suggestions that Itamaraty's worldview in the post–Cold War years was at least implicitly influenced by dependency theory emerged in the propositions advanced to describe the new world order. A central theme in the discourse emanating from Brazilian diplomats was the structuralist notion of asymmetry in international political and economic relations, the idea that all states were not endowed with the same capacity to compete in an increasingly vibrant global market. The apparent pattern of global ideational homogeneity added to these tensions by initiating and embedding a viewpoint in Itamaraty that saw countervailing centripetal and centrifugal forces on states (Lafer 2001b, 56; Barbosa 1994, 101–103; Thorstensen 1993). While growing consensus on the economic and political themes of free markets and democracy acted as a centripetal force drawing previously distrustful states together, the collapse of Cold War brakes on national, religious, and ethnic tensions acted in a centrifugal manner to push peoples apart. Spin was added to these two forces by rapid advances in technology as well as the revival of regionalism with the negotiation of the

NAFTA treaty and agreement to form the European Union. Access to the new technology and membership in the burgeoning regional groups in effect formed the new dividing line between those countries positioned to progress and those in danger of stagnation or marginalization (Lafer 1990; Jaguaribe 1994, 70).

In foreign-policy terms the question facing Itamaraty traced back to the long-standing goal of national development (Lampreia and Cruz 2005; Perruci 1995): How might the country be inserted into the new international order in a manner that would avoid perpetual marginalization? Addressing this challenge during his first tenure as foreign minister, Lafer (1992a) noted that the Brazilian response must come from a clear conception of national identity, an intellectual construction rooted in the technological, economic, and social divide between developed and developing countries. Here the earlier allusions to a shift away from "third worldist" rhetoric became evident, with the at once fully industrialized and underdeveloped nature of the Brazilian economy resulting in an analysis positioning technological capacity as a central variable in international insertion. In effect, the ability to access or develop new technology and production methods was placed beside the control of capital and production processes in the dependency framework to form the worldview guiding Brazilian foreign policy during the Cardoso era (Cardoso and Toledo 1998, chapter 21).

With Cardoso's appointment as foreign minister by Itamar Franco in 1992 and his service as president from 1995 to 2002, the dependency influence on the worldview and beliefs driving Brazil's foreign policy became increasingly apparent, albeit in a significantly revised form (Cardoso and Toledo 1998, 172–173). The importance afforded to national identity by Lafer as well as Wendt's suggestion that there is a dialectic relationship between domestic self-image and a state's foreign-policy expression found a certain consonance with both dependency theory and the consensual hegemonic character of foreign-policy making during the Cardoso presidency (Cardoso 2001, 5; Cardoso 1996c, 253–254).

The sort of social construction and substate transnational interaction hinted at in the constructivist approach to international relations finds resonance in the dependency proposition that economic relationships are intrinsically social relationships. This suggests that they are inherently mutable. But for change or transformation to take place the existing pattern of domination and subordination must be altered; the subaltern, recalling Lafer's sustained effort to create South America as a central identifying idea in Brazilian foreign policy (Lafer 2002a), must reshape its self-image and alter its insertion into the hegemonic system (Cardoso and Faletto 1979, 13–15).

Cardoso's important contribution to the ideational base of his country's foreign policy came from a revision of his version of dependency theory, which tightened the connections between identity and worldview being conceptualized by Itamaraty. In this vein, Cardoso (1993, 275–277) notes that the spread of democracy and the increasing importance of technology or knowledge-centered industry radically reformed the dynamics of the core-periphery relationship, resulting in a "democratic-technological" revolution. In the language of dependency theory, a comparative advantage based on an abundance of arable land and a low-cost, unskilled workforce held little currency in a 1990s information economy, having been displaced by a requirement for sustained investment in the human and scientific capital needed for advanced production techniques (Ocampo and Martin 2003).

In keeping with the reflexive nature of ideas and identity being discussed in this chapter, changed international circumstances, in short, required a revision of the state and the role it should play in the domestic economy and its role as an intermediary at the global level (Cardoso and Lafer 2007; Flecha de Lima 1994). Indeed, it is in the combination of the internal and the external, the political and the economic that we find the key to ideational innovation in Brazilian foreign policy. Explicit in the revision of dependency theory led by Cardoso was a call for new approaches to economic development that rejected protectionist impulses in favor of liberalization and opening to the global economy, with the state acting to level the playing field by using institutions such as BNDES to even out the disparity in national and international rates for export financing (Cardoso and Toledo 1998, 303–304; Lafer 2001c). Certainly, there was an element of pragmatism here. Cardoso recognized that even through collective action South America could not hope to match the industrial and technological capacities of the developed world by pursuing a policy of autarchy. But there was also an underpinning to the policies of liberalization and economic opening that related to the national identifying features of democratic governance and the decision to label Brazil as "South American" instead of "Latin American." The influence of policy prerogatives on the ideational dimension was also apparent in the manner in which Cardoso explicitly linked the importance for Brazil of preserving democracy to the changed nature of the global economy: "Remember that in the 1990s we had to face two main problems: consolidate democracy and become integrated at the global level" (Cardoso and Lafer 2007). In short, there was a very keen sense in both Planalto and Itamaraty that consolidation and promotion of the appropriate regime type—democracy—was as important as the adoption of market-friendly economic policies for Brazilian attempts to achieve a beneficial insertion into the asymmetric international system. Any strategy of using the regional context as a lever for enhanced international insertion thus relied on the construction of an ideational package building around these principles, but in a manner sensitive to the peccadilloes of neighboring countries.

Democratic Foundations of Development

On a moral level Cardoso (2000d) was clear that the only valid regime type was democracy. Yet it is also evident from his writings on authoritarianism and democracy in Latin America that moral preferences do not carry sufficient weight to guarantee the presence or persistence of a particular regime type. For democracy to become an entrenched reality it must serve as an expression of the social and economic demands of society and act as a broker to ensure that balance is achieved in the advancement of competing interests (Cardoso 2007; Moore 1966; Rueschemeyer et al. 1992). As will be discussed more extensively in Chapter 5, democracy is valuable in itself because it brings a measure of regional security by encouraging the transparency and confidence-building measures that reduce conflict-causing tensions and misunderstandings (Lampreia 2000c). It creates conditions propitious for national development, the attraction of foreign direct investment, and integration into the global economy (Barbosa 1996, 76; Lampreia 1996a, 47).

But this regional effect is a downstream result of the domestic changes that can be wrought by democratic governance. Keeping in mind that the core goal of the hegemonic project articulated by Itamaraty is improved insertion of the region into the international system, the ideational power of democracy is found in its capacity to alter the national political economy so that domestic actors are able to exploit opportunities presented by globalization and negate the economic basis for challenges from autocratic enclaves (Cardoso and Toledo 1998, 288–298). Democracy thus emerges simultaneously as a reflection of a changed socioeconomic reality and as the instrument that brings about change in the existing socioeconomic reality.

The socioeconomic approach to regime type and democracy is strongly reflected in the model of associated-dependent development Cardoso uses to explain the coup that deposed Pres. João Goulart in 1964 (Cardoso 1973). Kubitschek's policy of rapid industrialization in the 1950s brought large inflows of FDI from a range of multinational corporations, ultimately resulting in changes to domestic power structures. The traditional agrarian elite lost position to populist politicians who drew support from an increasingly urbanized, wage-earning populace. Opposition came from antipopulist sectors in the technocracy and the military, whose interests most closely aligned with those of the multinational corporations; this created a need to dismantle the instruments of pressure that the popular sectors were using to push for income redistribution and expanded welfare programs (Cardoso 1973, 146–147). In dependency-style language, perpetuation of the existing pattern of capitalist accumulation required the institution of a regime capable of repressing dissent and forcing compliance with the productive requisites of the multinational corporations (Gordon 2001, 11).

Building on the associated-dependent development model, Cardoso argues in a subsequent essay (1979) that South American authoritarian regimes are fundamentally capitalist in nature, and that the actors governing these countries make use of state enterprises to entrench their power by pursuing specific modes of development. The causal link suggested by this argument is not that authoritarianism breeds dependency, but that the authoritarian regime emerges as an intermediary for the domestic representatives of international capital. This ensures that conditions within a country remain propitious for continued capital accumulation. In effect, the state emerges as an entrepreneurial actor entering into agreements with international economic actors, thereby entrenching and perpetuating the relationship of dependency. Although Cardoso (1979) is clear that such a strategy might be followed just as effectively by a democratic regime, the repressive nature of an authoritarian regime makes it easier for those governing the country to suppress dissent and establish capital-friendly patterns of social control. In either case the crucial point is that the state becomes the central actor in the national economy, in effect determining what sectors will be pursued and how the country will be inserted into the international economic system (Lafer 1996, 63).

By the 1980s the nature of the overarching global capitalist structure had begun the transformation noted earlier, creating fissures in the associated-dependent development model that provided an unforeseen opportunity for dissent within the authoritarian regime. As Brazil's military government consolidated and the economy industrialized, the space separating state and civil society grew, opening new ground in which democratic aspirations could develop (Cardoso 1989, 310–311). Running parallel to the political changes within Brazil was the rising interdependence of global production systems, suggesting that attempts at autarchic development of complete national industries were becoming increasingly impracticable and calling into question Itamaraty's operating definition of "Brazil" (Cardoso 2001, 244–245; Cardoso 2001, 261–262).

The combination of technological advances and the decentralization of production caused by the rise of multinational corporations created a boom in commerce that escaped the control of not only the state, but also the elite, which had sought to use the instruments of the state to maintain privilege and prerogative. Moreover, the expansion of multinational corporation (MNC) activity was accompanied by a concomitant "democratization" of capital, with new ventures increasingly relying on the entrepreneurial impulse of individuals instead of a creeping expansion of elite activity. In Cardoso's words, "contemporary capitalism presupposes a 'specific socialization' that turns mere accumulation into a part of a broader civilization process" (2001, 236).

Thus, the same networks that helped form the associated-dependent development model pushed a reaffirmation of the principles of free markets and political liberalism, leaving the state with no viable autonomous solution to the challenges of globalization (Cardoso and Toledo 1998, 86–87). Although the state remained central in the business of formally negotiating regional and multilateral trade agreements, a parallel process of interfirm and firm-state interaction was changing the state's role in the strategic developmental direction of the national economy (Cardoso 2001, 238; Cardoso 1997c; Cardoso 1997b). Facilitation replaced direction, with the state needing to abandon its role as a substitute for civil society in order to pursue the social policies that would better prepare the population for the new international economic reality. In turn this would create conditions for growth in the new economic model (Cardoso 2001, 243; Cardoso 2001, 254; Cardoso, 2000d).

The democratic impulse that would see the state retract its tentacles from civil society and become a responsive rather than a commanding entity was, in Cardoso's view, heightened by the political and economic changes that accompanied the end of the Cold War in 1989 (Cardoso 1990–2001; Font 2003; Font and Spanakos 2004). During the associated-dependent development era multinational corporations were in part attracted by the prospect of cheap, unskilled labor and abundant raw materials. The economic logic of authoritarianism thus rested in part on the ability to control these factors and furnish them to international capital in a dependent relationship. Leaps in science and technology in the 1980s worked in precisely the manner predicted by the Comisión Económica para América Latina (CEPAL—Economic Commission for Latin

America) structuralist theorists (Kay 1989, chapter 2), driving down the importance of labor and raw material as input factors in the production process. The suggestion that emerges from statements made by Cardoso and leading Brazilian diplomats in the 1990s is that this "democratic-technological" revolution attacked the economic basis for the bureaucratic-authoritarian models that had dominated the region by inserting knowledge as the crucial value-adding factor (Cardoso 1996d–2001; Cardoso 1993–2001; Jaguaribe 1994, 70). With the new economic model based on decentralized forms of management and decision making that transgressed national frontiers, propositions that a small elite might continue to wield the instruments of the state to direct the economy for their own benefit foundered on the polyarchic reality of the emerging international political economy (Cardoso 1993–2001, 275; Hilton and Cardoso 1996).

The suggestion that emerges in the dependency-inspired worldview is that the globalized information economy was simply too complex for authoritarian patterns of centralized policymaking, so the intricacies of diffuse, transnationalized production strategies escaped the predictive capacities of the state. In this context democracy became an essential form of governance for states hoping to integrate successfully into the global economy. In strategic terms emphasis needed to be placed not only on providing the population with the skills and aptitudes necessary to continue attracting FDI, but also on ensuring that national regulatory and legal structures were sufficient for internationally oriented firms (Cardoso 1993–2001, 276–279; Faria and Graeff 1999, 1–5; United Nations Conference on Trade and Development [hereafter UNCTAD] 2000). Representative democracy provided an avenue for a continuous rhythm of feedback from society, allowing the state to adjust policies to meet the changing needs of the growing domestic entrepreneurial sector, national partners with international capital, and the population at large (Cardoso 1999d).

Additional pressure for democratization came from what Cardoso terms the "atomization of property," caused by the growth in pension and investment funds, which diluted ownership of firms domestically and across national borders. The effect was to weaken and depersonalize relations between employers and employees, driving yet another wedge into the corporatist model that underpinned the authoritarian regime (Cardoso 1996b–2001, 258–259). Diffusion of the centers of capital and labor control across the national boundary offered the prospect of a permanent dismantling of the clientelistic patterns of government behavior that had previously supported authoritarianism. In this respect integration into global markets emerged as a safety check protecting what was still a relatively young democratization project in Brazil (Sorger and Dymond 1997).

The importance of democracy as a guiding belief weaves through the other ideational elements of Brazilian foreign policy, providing the stability and transparency necessary to allow Brazil to lead a consensual hegemonic project, and thereby support a cooperative approach to global issues. A willingness to construct the regulatory patterns and juridical structures associated with the vision of democracy pursued during the Cardoso presidency also provided the certainty of outcomes sought by domestic, regional, and international business actors seeking to integrate Brazil and South America into global production systems (Cardoso and Lafer 2007) (discussed in more detail in Chapter 4). Adopting democracy as a core value also helped provide the regional stability necessary for economic interpenetration (Lampreia 1997; Lampreia 1998c), resulting in the nascent security community discussed in Chapter 5.

We thus find an almost circular ideational process at work here, with moves to deepen democracy being founded on economic liberalization policies, which were in turn grounded in democratization; all reflected a changed set of core domestic political values precipitated by an alteration in the operating conception of the global system. But, as will be set out in the next two sections, economic liberalization should not be confused with outright adoption of neoliberal policies (Cardoso and Lafer 2007). The cooperation and interdependence that grew from the political economy of democracy implicit in the Cardoso-era beliefs and worldview acted on a global level to open a space for the South not only to critique and potentially reshape globalization processes, but also to formulate policy approaches that differed from those mandated by international financial agencies and capital markets (Prado 2005; Cardoso 2006, chapters 4 and 5).

Brazilian (Neo)liberalism

The economic and political programs that Cardoso led during his presidency were underpinned by the *real* plan that he directed as finance minister in 1993 and 1994 (Prado 2005; Cardoso 2006, chapter 4). Ultimately, the *real* plan came under criticism for making Brazil dangerously dependent on sustained inflows of foreign capital in order to roll over existing debt obligations (Rocha 2002; Bresser-Pereira 2002). But in the short and medium term the effective linking of the new currency, the *real*, to the U.S. dollar dramatically reduced inflationary tensions and brought exchange rate stability. Perhaps the most important outcome of the *real* plan was the restoration of confidence and predictability, allowing businesses and individuals to resume the investment and savings activities essential to economic growth as well as signaling to global markets that Brazil was serious about stability (Morton 2000; Perry 2000).

The transparent manner in which Cardoso pursued monetary reform had as much to do with the return of investor and citizen confidence as did the arcana of economic theory (Kingstone 2000; Prado 2005). This transparency carried over into the larger field of economic-policy making where Cardoso (2000c) began not only to outline a new vision of a fiscally responsible state in an interdependent global economy, but also to actively encourage consultations with civil society and business groups, thereby providing a domestic foundation for the worldview and identity being elaborated in Itamaraty (Lafer 2002b, 92; Cardoso 2006, 616).

The central programmatic idea driving Cardoso's economic policy was that the state should no longer be a murky actor attempting to command the economy. It should instead assume the role of transparent regulator and facilitator, guiding the invisible hand in order to prevent market failures and ensure that all segments of society might become active participants in the economy (Cardoso 1990–2001, 243). The state should also be actively involved in breaking down international barriers to the socioeconomic and democratic development of each state (Cardoso 2006, 602).

A clear implication here is that there remained a need for an active state (Cardoso 1996c–2001, 254), a proposition at odds with the neoliberal label sometimes attributed to Cardoso, a moniker he rejects with some annoyance and explicitly attributes to the widely quoted, but fabricated, statement: "Forget everything I wrote in the past. The world has changed, and today's reality is different" (Cardoso 2006, 206; Cardoso and Toledo 1998, 289). On an ideational level the result was an approach to economic policy that melded with the transformative conceptualization of democracy outlined above, providing an interpretation of the Washington Consensus that allowed a fiscally responsible policy response to the developmentalist worldview of an asymmetric international economy (Cardoso 2000f).

Brazilian foreign policy in the Cardoso era was marked by a circular conceptualization of Latin American development challenges: states forgo investment in human capital in order to meet foreign-debt obligations, which in turn requires sustained economic growth that is not possible without investment in human capital. The crux of this fiscal dilemma is the inability of the state to raise sufficient tax revenue to both engage in investment and purchase the foreign exchange for debt payments (Cardoso 1990–2001, 241–243; Schwartz 1998). With international capital markets reluctant to continue lending to developing markets in the midst of the international recession and crises of the 1990s, the solution became recruitment of the FDI that would bring the technology necessary to make national industry more competitive (Cardoso 1990–2001, 242; Cardoso 2000f; Flôres 1997, 619–625; Amorim 1991a, 28–29; Vieira 2001, 2610–262). To encourage this, the state had to implement industrial and technological policies that encouraged both FDI and an expansion of domestic entrepreneurial activity to exploit and build on the transferred technology (Cardoso and Toledo 1998, 295–298). In this context the state assumed a critical welfare and redistributional role, ensuring that traditional landowning and capitalist oligarchies did not block a reformulation and reorientation of the national economy. And it is this last element that emerged as central to the ideational aspect of Cardoso's foreign policy. In an approach that recalls our earlier theoretical discussion, participation in the global economy was viewed as requiring an outward orientation, a willingness to participate in international processes, and an acceptance that policy prerogatives and societal demands would be formed as much by the global context as the domestic (Lafer 2001; Cardoso 1990–2001, 242). The net effect was to reverse the dependency theory–inspired policies of import-substitution industrialization, which resulted in market liberalization and increased vulnerability to the exigencies of the global economy.

In order to integrate Brazil into emerging globalized production processes Cardoso continued the policies of economic opening and privatization started by Collor, fueling suggestions that he was pursuing a neoliberal policy agenda (Cervo 1997; T. Costa 2000; Hilton and Cardoso 1996, 735). Yet ostensible obeisance to tremendous international pressures to follow economic orthodoxy (G. Fonseca 2004, 283) belies a fundamental change in the position that the state was to play in the national economy. While there was certainly an openness to auctioning off state companies when and where appropriate, the attraction extended beyond raising funds to meet the country's debt obligations (Cardoso and Toledo 1998, 298). One motivating factor was a desire to incite transnational joint ventures as well as mergers and acquisitions in order to bring advanced production processes and technology to Brazil (Cardoso and Lafer 2007), although this resulted in branch plant production of licensed products and a retraction in domestic industrial design innovation (Amann 1999; Amann and Nixon 1999; Vieira 2001; Ferraz et al. 1999).

Here the public policy challenge was to ensure that reformulation of the Brazilian economy's international insertion did not result in a simple retooling of existing domestic patterns of socioeconomic domination. In this respect perceptions of the conditions set by international capital for continued investment flows interacted with the expression of democracy as a core value to bolster the democratization project. The tradition of quiet backroom deals that had marked corporatist and authoritarian Brazil were anathema to multinational corporations concerned that the profitability of their investments of capital and technology might suddenly be held hostage by the mysterious internal workings of a clientelistic state. The need Cardoso saw was for the growth of public and regulatory institutions that operated with relative autonomy from daily political pressure (Cardoso and Lafer 2007). Recruitment of foreign capital and technology thus brought pressure for regulatory reform and judicial probity (UNCTAD 2000), providing an external pretext for the dismantling of traditional extrainstitutional domestic power structures founded on the capacity to grant favors and regulatory waivers.

As has been mentioned, the transnationalization of production suggested that notions of autarchy should be abandoned and internationalization embraced. Significantly, this position extended beyond the realm of national manufacturing and service industries to encompass the entire gamut of economic activity (Cardoso 2007). Drawing on the revision of dependency theory, the interdependence of globalization was interpreted as requiring a fundamental reshaping of the national economy's character by actively seeking to pursue the regionally integrated economic space (discussed in Chapter 4) as an avenue for simultaneously providing some shelter to infant industries without running the risks of inefficiency and global uncompetitiveness that came with the protectionist policies of the 1960s and 1970s (Cardoso 1997d; Lafer 2001d; Sardenberg 1998, 14–15).

The obvious implication here is the Washington Consensus position that the state in the new international political economy should embrace the principles of comparative advantage and allow market pressure to bring about national specialization in price-competitive industries. But the view of developmental requisites expressed in Cardoso administration policies diverged from the ideal-type neoliberal paradigm (Cunningham 1999; Perry 2000, 412–413).; Policymakers argued not only that the state should remain involved in strategic industries such as oil extraction, but also that state policies should be directed toward encouraging the development of the human resources capacities needed by new, high-value-added industries (Cardoso 2000b). The intent was not to engage in autarchic economic activity and perpetuate the existence of state enterprises that had helped maintain the military regime, but to encourage international joint ventures with public and private Brazilian firms to further internationalize the national economy.

Accompanying this decision to liberalize approaches to national development was a need to develop international partnerships in order to devise the necessary production and interpersonal networks (Cardoso 1996b–2001, 261–263; Cardoso 2000h; Schwartz 1998). Again, the neoliberal option of rapid economic opening as seen in Chile was eschewed in favor of a more measured approach that sought to prevent Brazil being marginalized internationally as a source of raw materials and cheap, unskilled labor.

In many respects it is at this point that we find the strength in the ideational package offered by the Brazilian hegemonic project, namely, in the decision to use the regional context for advancing an approach to globalization that would ensure an equal insertion of developed and developing countries. The goal was to maintain space for the state to continue guiding national development and assist the population through the implementation of effective social policies (Cardoso 2000e). Rather than depending on free markets to bring sustained economic growth—a formula that was greeted with increasing skepticism throughout the continent during Cardoso's second term—market requisites were seen more as a disciplinary force that would prevent a return to the inefficient state of earlier decades and the reemergence of autocratic movements. The challenge, as will be discussed in the next section, was to pursue this almost heterodox view of economics in the face of fiscal pressures imposed by international capital markets and the trade barriers maintained by the developed countries.

It is at this point that the international view of the Cardoso presidency's economic policies becomes particularly powerful. Rather than relying on the actual or potential capacity of a single economy to mitigate global market pressures, a sense of regional and developmental solidarity was encouraged through the formation of a consensual hegemonic project in the shape of a region, be it Mercosul or a wider South America (Lafer 2001b; Lafer 2001e). Interpenetration on a regional level offered the potential for a political economy that might collaboratively pursue development and use the cooperation necessary for consensual hegemony to collectively exert pressure on the global hegemony; this would bring about alterations in the structure of the global system that would create conditions propitious for national development.

Development and Globalization

Here we turn our attention to the issue of the insertion of a developing economy into the international system. The global scenario described by Brazil's foreign policy during the Cardoso era was essentially one of vigilante capitalism, with international capital markets acting as unelected and largely unaccountable arbiters of what was acceptable in terms of fiscal and social policy in developing countries (Cardoso 1996a). Of central concern to Brazil were the successive financial crises that occurred during the Cardoso era, each of which drained the country of foreign reserves and greatly elevated the cost of meeting international debt obligations (Lampreia 1998c; Corrêa 1999a; Barbosa 2007; Lafer 2007). Failure to adhere to the policy prescriptions of the Washington Consensus, as verified by the IMF, at a minimum raised questions in capital markets that translated into higher borrowing costs. In effect there was a strong impetus for a homogenization of economic policies centered on the short-term repayment of debt, not the creation of long-term sustainable economies (Cardoso 1996d–2001, 245–246). In part Cardoso (2000i) attributes this to technical failures of the economic programs at major international financial agencies. His criticisms range from shortcomings in debt-accounting techniques to accusations of sheer ignorance of the economic realities of Latin American countries (Cardoso 1995, 11). But the larger problem he identifies is one of global governance, specifically the fact that the globalization of economics was not accompanied by a similar change in politics (Cardoso 1999b; Cardoso 2000a; Cardoso 2002).

Suggestions that the structure of the international system did not favor Latin American countries are certainly not new (Prebisch 1951). The difference in this particular instance was that a new asymmetric quality to the global economic system was identified (Cardoso 1999c). Existing structures and practices in the international economy created a situation in which the developed countries not only drove the information economy, but also were its main beneficiaries. The danger for developing countries was that they would become entrenched as consumers of information industries and providers of low-cost resources and labor, activities left to states marginalized from the benefits of globalization (Ocampo and Martin 2003).

In response to the dangers inherent in this situation a loosely Gramscian conception of capitalist hegemony became evident in Brazilian foreign policy. Suggestions that a war of position should be pursued were rapidly discarded by reference to the failed attempts at constructing a new international economic order in the 1970s. Indeed, the tenor of economic policies in Brazil and the continuation of policies designed to embrace globalization served as a clear indication that the reality of capitalism was accepted. The alternative offered by Brazilian foreign policy amounted to a sort of war of movement that accepted the core precepts of the capitalist system, but also subjected it to rigorous debate and criticism in order to incite reform (Cardoso 1999c; Cardoso 2002).

Here the adjective *asymmetric* was deployed to describe the global economic system, but this time focusing on the manner in which the rules governing international trade were applied. Principles of economic development based on comparative advantage were critiqued by highlighting the uneven nature of international trading rules and norms that made it illegal for developing countries to subsidize manufacturing and other value-added industries, but that permitted heavy state subsidy of export-oriented agriculture in developed countries (Cardoso 1997a; Barbosa 1996, 75–76). Rather than calling for abolition of the international trading regimes that prevented state support of industry in countries such as Brazil, Cardoso and Itamaraty instead charged developed countries with hypocrisy and called for trade liberalization in all areas (Lafer 2001f; Barbosa 1994). Significantly, the focus was extended beyond the formal legal prose of various treaties to include the range of nontariff barriers and peripheral issues that were arrayed against expanded developing-country exports. Particular attention was given to combating repeated attempts at including labor and environmental provisions in both the FTAA and the WTO, provisions that foreign-policy makers feared might be manipulated by developed governments to negate the expanded market access being sought in various multilateral fora (Lafer 1996, 61; Cardoso 1998a; Lampreia 1999b).

In some respects the structures underpinning the domestic political aspects of the associated-dependent development model were replicated on the international level. Governmental structures did exist to manage the international economic system, but as was the case in pre-1985 Brazil, they (and their weaknesses) served more to protect and perpetuate the embedded interests of the developed economies at the expense of the developing world. Calls for "more democracy" on the international level thus emerged as an interesting, if somewhat confusing, proposition that translated into an important ideational aspect of Brazil's foreign policy (Cardoso and Toledo 1998, 88–90). The suggestion was not necessarily that some form of internationally representative governing body be formed, but that all participants in multilateral fora such as the IMF and the World Bank have an equal voice. This proposition in effect restated Brazil's long-standing adherence to the principle of multilateralism (Cervo 2002, 10–16), combining it with the notion of solidarity among developing countries.

Implicit in the call for solidarity was the realization that the state retained an important role in the international economic system. Despite globalization, states preserved the ability to restrict the free flow of goods and services over their borders, which meant that any expansion of the international trading system required the agreement of participating states (Cardoso 1997b; Cardoso 2000i; Lampreia 2001). In an effective foreshadowing of the 2003 Cancún WTO ministerial meeting (Narlikar 2004; Narlikar and Tussie 2004; Narlikar and Wilkinson 2004), explicit in the combination of multilateralism and solidarity was the idea that negotiations to expand international trade agreements be used as an opportunity to reshape North-South economic relations (Cardoso 1996d, 247–248; Cardoso 1996a; Cardoso and Soares 1998, 257–263; T. Costa 2001; Abdenur 1994b; Lafer 1996, 52–53). By rejecting bilateral in favor of multilateral agreements developing countries might avoid pressure to sign unfavorable trade deals and could exert collective coercion for institutional change on the developed countries, or at least prevent the entrenchment of further asymmetries in the system (Cardoso 1999a; Cardoso 1999e).

The ideational underpinning of the Brazilian combination of multilateralism and solidarity lies in the change it invoked in relations between developing countries and the global economic system (Cardoso 1999c) and the dialogue and confidence necessary for consensual hegemony it established. Indeed, the expanded South-South cooperation implicit in the idea of solidarity opened new avenues for economic advancement (Cardoso 1996a; Lampreia 1999b; Abdenur 1994a, 40–41; Lafer and Fonseca 1994), suggesting that globalization need not imply subservience to the North and that the South had agency within the existing structure (Cardoso 1996d). At its simplest the effect was to renew confidence in developing countries (FBIS-LAT-98–204)—what Lafer termed "auto-confiança" and Lula later dubbed "auto-estima"—resulting in an attitudinal change that made it possible to realistically envision and advance alternate arrangements for dealing with the pressures of international capital markets and the challenges of national insertion into the global economy. This change led to, in effect, a call to pursue a collective vision and project for global economic participation.

Central to this transformation was the opening of a space where conceptions of self-identity could be maintained and developed. Indeed, the approach to the promotion of democracy adopted by Itamaraty during the Cardoso presidency belies a fundamental concern with allowing the citizenry of individual states the freedom to formulate their own responses to domestic situations that reflected their own conceptions of national identity. The suggestion was that South American states need not parrot notions of identity received from Europe or Latin America, that through solidarity new responses to global challenges might be created in a manner that reflected regional values and priorities (Cardoso 1995; Burges 2005b).

Here Celso Lafer (2000, 207) is again instructive. He notes that a country's foreign policy is a function of its national identity, which is in turn a reflection of the character of its international insertion. The implication is that what a state views as possible and acceptable is conditioned by the collected consensus of the international community, suggesting that a homogenization of identity will necessarily reduce the range of options that might be considered in a given situation. By drawing on the notion of consensual hegemony the preservation and strengthening of identity emerges as yet another route for influencing the operation and evolution of the global governance structures discussed in the previous paragraph; this gave emotional and intellectual density to the regional projects outlined by Brazil.

Solidarity and cooperation emerge repeatedly as the principles cited in foreign-policy statements inciting a discussion about how democracy should be sustained and what economic policies should be pursued, both central considerations in the pursuit of national development. In some respects the realms of ideas and policies begin to blend here. Concepts of solidarity and cooperation within South America created a space where the Gramscian student-teacher dialectic might come into operation and lead to debate and the eventual formulation of a common approach to the shared challenge of national development. As the foregoing discussion of democracy and economic policy suggests, these two broad ideational zones lie at the core of Brazilian approaches to development during the Cardoso era. An explicit aspect of both was the need to internationalize, to ground domestic changes in an international context. This led not only to a revisionist dependency critique of the structure of the international political economy, but also to a renewed call for solidarity and cooperation in the South and, in particular, the construction of South America as an identity.

The obvious suggestion here is that the Cardoso administration was seeking to disseminate a particular ideational vision throughout South America, a task consonant with the leadership project being pursued by Itamaraty. (Indeed, the

extent to which Itamaraty succeeded in inculcating the values and belief preferences in continent-wide agreements is discussed at greater length in Chapter
2, where I argue that Brazil exercised a significant measure of leadership, albeit
one of varying effectiveness.) Of more immediate consequence for the discussion in the next two chapters is the extent to which the worldview articulated
by Itamaraty combined with the concept of South America to provide the ideational basis for Brazil's continental policy. The main strategy deployed in the
formation of the Brazilian leadership project was the construction of open regionalism projects: first in the Southern Cone via Mercosul; then in the wider
continental space through the pursuit of some form of a SAFTA that initially
appeared as a call for an economic agreement, but later became a more subtle
integration program via IIRSA's infrastructure axes.

Conclusion

As Celso Lafer (2002c, 101) noted in his address to a new year of recruits at
Itamaraty on the "Day of the Diplomat" celebrations in 2002, "the power of
diplomacy, in large part, is the power of speech. It is the privileged instrument
of contact with reality at the disposal of a diplomat." Clearly, ideas by themselves are not enough to bring about structural change, hence our borrowing
of Strange's pyramidal model. Indeed, as I argue in this book, ideas need to be
bolstered not only by the willingness to lead, but also by an ability to coordinate responses to security and economic issues. As well, they must absorb some
of the associated costs. What is critical is that the ideas aspect of a consensual
approach to hegemony offers the prospect of positive inclusion for all by the
leader, particularly if the leading state does not possess the dominating preponderance of power needed to enforce compliance. For the ideational aspect of
consensual hegemony to come into play there must be a willingness to include
others in the elaboration of the core principles, and there must be a real sense
that the contributions of all parties are being synthesized as the ideas evolve
and are elaborated.

The process that is in operation here can be understood by drawing on
Gramsci's student-teacher dialectic, with the ideas outlined in this chapter
providing the ideational grounding for the policies pursued in the economic
and security dimensions as well as the justification for Brazilian leadership.
Indeed, the negotiation involved in the economic and security aspects and
the conceptualization of an inclusive leadership style might represent the active implementation of the student-teacher dialectic. Through the process of

discussion and revision inherent in the student-teacher relationship we can also discern the internal-external reflexive process of identity formation outlined at the beginning of this chapter, with different views of how to achieve common security and economic goals emerging as the arena in which the shared identity necessary for the leadership of a consensual hegemony is negotiated.

4

The Economic Dimension

The physics underlying the pyramidal model of hegemony—that each of the sides depends on the support of the others for stability—suggests that the economic dimension of a consensual hegemony must be constructed in a manner that explicitly includes or controls all participating states. The two economic facets of Strange's structural-power pyramid emphasize the use of production and finance as instruments of control, as sources of power for inducing the cooperation or assent of other actors for a particular structuring of the global system. A similar logic applies to the economic dimension of the consensual hegemony, except here the focus is on the inclusive connotations of consensus. Indeed, by building on discussion of the ideas element in the previous chapter the interdependence of each facet of the pyramid becomes increasingly explicit.

In Chapter 3 I argued that the ideational aspect of the hegemonic project advanced by Itamaraty was predicated on a reinterpretation of dependency theory that called for an extension of national economic frontiers to the boundaries of the continent; this larger space was then used as a platform for fashioning a more favorable relationship with the wider international environment. While it would certainly be possible to pursue an Albert Hirschman–style policy of economic penetration to precipitate internal pressure for compliance in nominally subordinate countries (Hirschman 1945), such a course of action would require the expenditure of resources and absorption of costs central to coercive conceptions of hegemony. During the Cardoso era Brazil manifestly lacked these economic resources as the country grappled with a succession of destabilizing crises and sought to entrench sustainable, long-term macroeconomic stability.

In this chapter I explore a different approach, arguing that Brazil's foreign policy during the Cardoso presidency explicitly pursued an inclusive vision for the economic space of South America by using the mechanisms of the "new" regionalism to seek the interdependence implicit in the ideas aspect and essential for the security dimension of the pyramidal model of hegemony. Rather than overt or covert economic domination the goal was integration anchored on the Brazilian market; policymakers sought a situation where transnationalized production chains might develop by exploiting the respective strengths of each participating country (Cardoso and Lafer 2007). Unlike past attempts at integration, which sought to allocate particular industries to each country, the integration movement advanced in Brazilian foreign policy called on firms and governments to seek new opportunities and partnerships within South America as a launching pad for international competition—in effect an attempt to lead the formation of cohesive regionalism. Here the security aspect of our hegemonic model makes its presence felt, as it provided the stability necessary to allow a reconceptualization of the source of two crucial economic inputs: energy supplies and transportation networks.

Although in this chapter I examine Itamaraty's attempts to lead with a policy that would see South America transformed into an integrated economic space, I will not argue that these efforts were entirely successful. Again, the important points for our purposes are the intent and the dynamics of the attempt, each providing insight into how leadership might be conceptualized and pursued. The discussion begins with a brief review of open regionalism to set a theoretical framework for the economic policies pursued by Itamaraty during the Cardoso era.

Significant attention is given to the most profound regional project undertaken by Brazil—Mercosul—with emphasis being placed on the transformations the bloc has precipitated in trade and investment patterns. Indeed, Mercosul provides an instructive example as I discuss the physical and financial construction of a regional bloc and how this process was evolving in the South American context. In this respect the narrative addresses the goal of expanding Mercosul into a continental bloc.

I argue that Brazilian foreign policy was one of facilitating the creation of a larger regional space, not enforcing or mandating regional expansion (Amorim 2003a, 12; Franco 1993). Its focus consequently sidestepped political attempts at negotiating interregional agreements, a subject addressed earlier, to take a broader view of Brazil's foreign economic policy, which encompassed questions of value-added trade flows, physical infrastructure construction, and development financing. Government-led instantaneous integration was sidelined as a primary policy goal, being replaced by a longer-term approach seeking sustained and domestically rooted pressure for the elaboration of South America as an active and viable geoeconomic space.

Attention will first be turned to the theory behind the new regionalism, and the challenges implicit in the formation of a region will be set out. The experience of South America's primary regional example, Mercosul, forms the basis for the next section, where the nature and context of that customs union will be explored. From our discussion of Mercosul the point that will emerge is the importance of physical connections between would-be regional partners. Subsequent sections establish the role of transportation and energy networks in the expansion of trade with Brazil's Mercosul partners. In the final section the lessons of Mercosul become manifest in the redirection of Brazil's foreign policy that led to the launch of IIRSA at the 2000 Summit of South American Presidents in Brasília and an attempt to advance the South America project through a program of physical-infrastructure integration.

Forming the New Regionalism

Only a handful of countries are in a position to fully exploit the opportunities made available by globalization, and these countries are overwhelmingly in the developed "North" (Hettne 1995, 225). Bearing this problematic in mind, it is useful to view the new regionalism as a principally defensive response to the triple impact of the economic crises of the 1980s, the end of the Cold War, and the rising pressures of globalization. The "new" regionalism thus emerges as a strategy pursued by peripheral and semiperipheral states to avoid economic marginalization that calls on states to sacrifice some measure of national sovereignty to create a stronger regional response to global pressures (Grugel and Hout 1999b, 2–6). Although the discussion of the security aspect of the South American regionalist project will make it clear that there was substantial Brazilian resistance to the surrender of sovereignty, the notion of collectivization plays an important role in the economic aspect. A structure is needed to facilitate the economic internationalization and solidarity envisioned by the ideas dimension of our model, a requirement that points to the state-led nature of regionalism (Gamble and Payne 1996b, 2, 17).

The region emerges in this context as a device designed to reconfigure geoeconomic spaces so that international opportunities can be collectively engaged by the participating states (Park 1995, 31). But more important, the region emerges as an artificial construct elaborated at the governmental level to reorder economic relations. Acceptance and success of a regional project should not, therefore, be taken as a given; as one diplomat explained, businessmen will simply not participate in projects that do not make money.

In effect, the formation of a region relies on the presence or development of a shared set of interests and ambitions—a regionalization of economic interests—with bloc resiliency largely depending on the degree of homogenization among participating states (Hettne 1999, 9–15). Two interlocking challenges to region formation emerge from this point—each acknowledged by senior Brazilian foreign-policy makers as creating the vicious circle that confronted Brazil's South American project. Without the active engagement of business the economic success of a regional project will remain at best questionable. And it is this same economic success that provides the political justification for region formation and incites domestic pressure for greater integration.

Here it is useful to draw on Albert Hirschman's argument that World War Two resulted in part from a clash of competing trade policies, with competition for market share resulting in Armageddon. Hirschman's suggestion (1945, 29) is that excessive reliance on a single export market can result in the emergence of a "commercial fifth column," an economic elite that will push its government to adopt policies sympathetic to the dominant export market.

While I will not argue that Brazil was pursuing the sort of mercantilistic power implied in Hirschman's proposition, the suggestion is that the emergence of something similar to a commercial fifth column can prove crucial to the advancement of a regional project. In effect the challenge is to transfer ownership of regional integration from policymakers at the national level to economic actors on the firm and civil society levels, precipitating the domestic political pressure necessary to translate vague agreements into substantive reality. Indeed, this is precisely what Cardoso and leading ambassadors such as Barbosa mean when they talk about the need for transnational production chains and the development of infrastructure axes as opposed to poles (Cardoso and Lafer 2007; Barbosa 2007).

As will be argued below, the foreign policy used by Brazil to pursue the creation of a South American regional space drew on lessons revealed by repeated crises within Mercosul. The result was a turn away from the sort of political discussions outlined in Chapter 2 in favor of the technocratic realm of infrastructure integration. In the case of Mercosul the Argentine-Brazilian political approximation that led to economic-integration agreements prompted a demand for improved transportation networks to facilitate commerce. With growing intrabloc trade volumes came the rise of a Hirschman-style commercial fifth column that had its economic interests tied to perpetuation of the regional bloc. This resulted in direct pressure to resolve the political tensions following the 1999 devaluation of the Brazilian *real* and the 2001 debt default in Argentina. The proposition that emerged from the Mercosul experience was that political will for integration required physical support in the form of expanded infrastructure linkages; this suggested that a technocratic approach to practical integration might succeed on a continental level where political efforts were failing.

Brazil's continental foreign policy consequently experienced a shift away from diplomatic negotiations to the technocratic realm of transnational infrastructure project conceptualization. Again, the impulse behind this policy change recalls Hirschman's commercial fifth column as it sought to create the transportation and energy corridors that would make transnational commerce attractive to business and that in the medium and long term might lead to expanded domestic pressure for increased subregional and continental economic integration.

Mercosul

As discussed in the first chapter, the 1970s and 1980s saw a dramatic change in Southern Cone economic interactions. Despite the alternating hot and cold relations between the Argentine and Brazilian presidencies, bilateral trade flows continued to increase rapidly over the fifteen-year period between 1975 and 1990. Nevertheless, trade flows did not expand at the expected rate in the late 1980s, a shortfall largely attributable to the persistence of protectionist impulses that survived the signing of the PICE agreements (Manzetti 1990).

The onset of the 1990s saw the election of Carlos Menem in Argentina and Fernando Collor in Brazil, bringing a fundamental shift in economic policy that resulted in the adoption of a free-market approach to economic policy that favored trade liberalization. Of particular importance to the South American project that the Cardoso administration would pursue with increasing vigor was the decision by Collor and Menem to revitalize Argentine-Brazilian approximation through the creation of Mercosul (Vaz 2002; Pereira 1999). By the time Cardoso was elected to the presidency Mercosul's open-regionalism project was precipitating the sort of economic changes suggested earlier, auguring a miniaturized Southern Cone version of the projected South American political economy envisioned by a number of highly influential figures within Itamaraty. Key to this process was firm-level reconceptualization of market access, production, and investment decisions, using the regional level as a preparatory base for global insertion.

Mercosul Trade Patterns

Mercosul represented an important departure from the PICE process, aiming as it did for a customs union as a middle ground between the supranational governance of the EU and the contractual model of NAFTA (Bernier and Roy 1999). At the heart of the bloc was a common external tariff set at a maximum of 20 percent for most products, with some imports being subject to levels as high as 35 percent. Internal trade liberalization proceeded at a rapid pace after the bloc-forming Treaty of Asunción was signed in 1991, and 100 percent of the agreed tariffs were eliminated after the December 1994 Protocolo de Ouro Preto.

Although not explicitly addressed here, a crucial structural feature of Mercosul was the absence of supranational institutions with the power to arbitrate in disputes or police the provisions of the treaty. Instead, the bloc was to be run by three main intergovernmental bodies: the Consejo Mercado Común (CMC—Common Market Council), the Grupo Mercado Común (GMC—Common Market Group), and the Comisión de Comercio del Mercosul (CCM—Mercosul Trade Commission). Political direction was given to the bloc by the CMC, which brought together member foreign and economy ministers to make decisions about the integration process. The GMC acted as an eight-member executive agency for the CMC, regularly convening representatives from the respective foreign and economy ministries to implement and oversee the bloc's treaty. Finally, the CCM assumed a more technical role, using ten committees to monitor the bloc's common trade policies.

The lack of a regionally oriented supranational institutional base endowed with power to run the bloc meant that internal economic disputes quickly became points of political contention requiring direct presidential intervention. The result was a highly politicized decision-making process that did little to rein in unilateralism or ensure observance of agreements made in the CMC, GMC, or CCM. Moreover, the shallowness of bloc institutionalization created a feedback mechanism in the bloc's governance structure, with domestic political pressure from economic sectors hurt by trade liberalization pushing for changes in policy on the national and regional levels (Phillips 2004, chapter 5).

While the structures of the bloc and the CET were imperfect—Argentina, Brazil, Paraguay, and Uruguay were allowed to exempt, respectively, 394, 324, 439, and 960 products from the CET—the data in Table 4.1 demonstrates that the creation of Mercosul had a dramatic effect on trade between the four member countries. Where the PICE agreement acted more as a brake on declining economic exchange in the 1980s, Mercosul had an almost immediate positive impact on trade flows. In 1989, three years into the PICE agreements, intrabloc exports stood at U.S.$3.72 billion, up only marginally from the 1986 level of U.S.$2.60 billion. In contrast, the advent of Mercosul precipitated a dramatic leap. One year after the Treaty of Asunción was signed intrabloc exports had increased to U.S.$7.22 billion, reaching a high of U.S.$20.35 billion by 1998.

Table 4.1. Intra-Mercosul Exports (in U.S. dollars)

	Argentina	Brazil	Paraguay	Uruguay	Total
1986	894,662	1,176,333	132,861	394,217	2,598,073
1989	1,427,977	1,379,997	388,074	525,775	3,721,823
1992	2,290,290	4,127,730	242,010	559,491	7,219,521
1993	3,674,292	5,393,879	287,288	675,442	10,030,901
1994	4,803,662	5,921,139	340,104	891,603	11,956,508
1995	6,769,337	6,153,411	465,487	995,338	14,383,573
1996	7,921,823	7,305,195	660,141	1,150,518	17,037,677
1997	9,068,209	9,043,577	586,311	1,355,174	20,053,271
1998	9,420,718	8,877,051	530,790	1,522,719	20,351,278
1999	7,070,507	6,777,755	307,486	1,006,861	15,162,609
2000	8,390,556	7,732,049	553,133	1,022,702	17,698,440
2001	7,428,957	6,363,558	518,633	839,856	15,151,004
2002	5,695,494	3,310,705	552,753	606,800	10,165,752

Source: IADB/INTAL (Institute for the Integration of Latin America and the Caribbean) DataIntal v.4.1. www.iadb.org/intal.

Table 4.2. Mercosul Exports to Brazil (in U.S. dollars)

	Exports from				
	Argentina	Paraguay	Uruguay	Total Intrabloc to Brazil exports	Percentage of total exports to Brazil
1989	1,124,072	328,485	441,406	1,893,963	50.9
1992	1,648,761	169,963	293,808	2,112,532	29.3
1995	5,484,046	383,031	705,326	6,572,403	45.7
1996	6,614,829	520,729	831,680	7,967,238	46.8
1997	7,734,065	457,863	940,110	9,132,038	45.5
1998	7,949,264	349,323	937,637	9,236,224	45.4
1999	5,689,535	234,975	557,109	6,481,619	42.7
2000	6,990,288	336,562	530,023	7,856,873	44.4
2001	6,205,540	277,813	440,697	6,924,050	45.7
2002	4,827,749	352,969	431,782	5,612,500	55.2

Source: IADB/INTAL (Institute for the Integration of Latin America and the Caribbean) DataIntal v.4.1. www.iadb.org/intal.

The explosion in trade within Mercosul was in part explained by a similar leap in the importance of Brazil as an export market for Argentina, Paraguay, and Uruguay (Table 4.2). Although the Brazilian market absorbed just under a third (29.3 percent) of annual intrabloc export flows immediately after the inception of Mercosul in 1992, by 1996 the proportion had risen markedly, reaching a high of 46.8 percent in 1996 before declining slightly after the devaluation of the *real* in 1999, and then rising to 55.2 percent in the wake of Argentina's 2002 currency revaluation.

In effect the size of the Brazilian market was used as an anchor to encourage the expansion of intrabloc economic activity. By 1996 Brazil had supplanted the United States as Argentina's single largest export outlet (Hasmi 2000, 43). Moreover, this change was brought about by a redirection of Argentine industry, which sought to grow by using the shelter of the CET to increase value-added exports to Brazil (Tables 4.3 and 4.4). At the height of the PICE process Brazil was already an important market for Argentine industrialists, absorbing 16.0 percent of value-added exports in 1989. Mercosul greatly amplified this importance. By 1998 Brazil absorbed 52.2 percent of Argentina's manufactured exports. Although the figure dropped precipitously with *real* devaluation in

Table 4.3. Manufactured Exports as a Percentage of Total Exports

	1989	1992	1993	1994	1995	1996	1997	1998	1999	2000	2001	2002
Argentina												
To Brazil	38.7	38.8	41.5	39.9	46.1	44.1	52.4	55.2	48.8	46.2	52.2	47.3
Other	28.4	22.3	28.9	30.2	30.7	27.0	30.1	31.8	29.0	29.1	29.3	26.6
Paraguay												
To Brazil	9.1	8.9	10.7	12.2	6.0	10.1	9.1	10.4	9.1	10.6	6.7	6.2
Other	7.8	14.2	15.0	18.1	13.2	16.2	14.3	13.0	14.8	18.4	15.6	8.5
Uruguay												
To Brazil	51.7	46.5	37.2	36.4	36.8	33.6	37.1	34.6	38.6	38.8	39.0	38.4
Other	60.5	58.9	51.9	51.8	47.6	45.4	43.5	42.7	42.2	45.7	46.9	42.7
Bolivia												
To Brazil	27.4	12.0	29.4	12.9	19.7	24.9	23.0	13.3	16.1	6.1	4.9	1.9
Other	10.8	5.0	13.6	18.6	13.4	20.3	14.5	13.1	38.1	27.0	20.4	15.9
Chile												
To Brazil	15.2	12.2	16.5	24.1	24.9	26.8	30.2	29.6	29.6	28.3	29.3	30.2
Other	14.9	10.9	14.0	14.3	10.9	12.6	13.6	15.7	15.2	14.8	16.2	15.7

Source: IADB/INTAL (Institute for the Integration of Latin America and the Caribbean) DataIntal v.4.1. www.iadb. org/intal.

Table 4.4. Manufactured Exports to Brazil as a Percentage of Total Manufactured Exports

Exporting Countries	1989	1992	1993	1994	1995	1996	1997	1998	1999	2000	2001	2002
Argentina	16.0	23.8	30.9	30.5	39.4	45.5	52.9	52.2	41.1	42.0	41.5	33.4
Bolivia	14.3	4.1	6.0	2.2	2.5	3.4	4.7	2.4	1.2	2.6	5.3	2.9
Chile	6.6	5.1	5.1	8.8	14.6	13.0	12.5	9.9	8.5	10.2	8.8	7.7
Colombia	0.8	1.0	1.2	1.2	2.4	2.6	2.1	2.0	2.2	3.0	2.5	1.6
Ecuador	5.9	2.1	1.8	1.3	2.4	1.6	1.7	1.6	1.7	1.1	0.6	1.1
Paraguay	37.6	16.5	21.1	21.7	21.1	31.1	25.5	27.6	19.5	22.3	12.2	27.2
Peru	1.4	0.9	1.1	1.7	2.3	2.2	1.6	1.2	1.6	1.5	2.5	1.8
Uruguay	23.6	13.8	16.3	18.2	25.8	25.6	29.6	27.6	22.8	19.6	17.8	20.8
Venezuela	2.3	1.9	2.6	2.8	3.1	4.2	4.0	3.6	3.0	4.4	5.5	3.9

Source: IADB/INTAL (Institute for the Integration of Latin America and the Caribbean) DataIntal v.4.1. www.iadb. org/intal.

Table 4.5. Percentage of National Exports to Brazil

	1989	1992	1993	1994	1995	1996	1997	1998	1999	2000	2001	2002
Argentina	11.8	13.7	21.5	23.1	26.2	27.8	30.3	30.1	24.4	26.5	23.3	18.8
Bolivia	5.6	1.7	2.8	3.3	1.7	2.8	2.9	2.4	2.9	11.4	22.1	24.3
Chile	6.4	4.6	4.3	5.2	6.4	6.1	5.6	5.3	4.4	5.3	4.9	4.0
Colombia	0.4	0.8	0.8	0.7	1.1	1.1	1.1	0.9	1.4	2.2	1.4	0.9
Ecuador	0.4	0.4	0.7	0.2	1.2	0.9	0.5	0.8	0.4	0.4	0.3	0.2
Paraguay	32.5	26.3	29.7	32.3	46.7	49.9	40.1	34.4	31.7	38.6	28.1	37.1
Peru	3.5	4.7	3.7	4.2	3.1	4.1	3.8	3.2	2.9	3.3	3.2	2.6
Uruguay	27.6	17.5	22.8	25.9	33.3	34.7	34.8	34.1	24.9	23.1	21.4	23.2
Venezuela	2.0	1.8	2.4	3.4	3.9	3.2	4.2	3.9	4.1	3.6	2.7	2.4

Source: IADB/INTAL (Institute for the Integration of Latin America and the Caribbean) DataIntal v.4.1. www.iadb. org/intal.

1999 and the onset of regional economic crises, Brazil remained a crucial market, absorbing 41.1 percent, 42.0 percent, 41.5 percent, and 33.4 percent of Argentina's manufactured exports between 1999 and 2002, respectively.

While the equivalent figures for Uruguay are not as high, rising from 13.8 percent in 1992 to 27.6 percent in 1998, they do show a marked increase in Brazil's absorption of value-added exports, particularly as Argentina tipped into economic crisis in 2001. Although the Brazilian market absorbed 19.6 percent of Uruguay's foreign manufactures sales in 2000, 17.8 percent in 2001, and 20.8 percent in 2002, the actual proportion of overall exports destined for Brazil (Table 4.5) fell heavily with the *real*'s devaluation, dropping from 34.1 percent in 1998 to 24.9 percent in 1999, declining further to 23.2 percent by 2002.

In the largely agrarian economy of Paraguay, Brazil remained of paramount importance in the 1990s, consistently absorbing well over 30 percent of that country's exports in the 1990s—the exceptions being 1992 (26.3%), 1993 (29.7%) and 2001 (28.1%—reaching a high of 49.9 percent in 1996. (*Oxford Analytica* 4 Dec. 2002; 16 Jan. 2002). Indeed, official statistics tended to understate the central role Brazil and the Mercosul region played in the Paraguayan economy because a substantial portion of economic exchange was illicit in nature (Nickson 1997; Aquino 1997; J. Gonçalves 1995).

Mercosul assumed similar, although less marked, importance for Brazilian exporters. Policymakers in the Secretaria de Comércio Exterior (SECEX— Foreign Trade Secretariat) of the Ministério do Desenvolvimento, Indústria e Comércio Exterior (MDIC—Ministry of Development, Industry, and Foreign Trade) emphasized that Brazil was a "global trader" seeking to diversify its international markets in order to protect against the sort of economic shocks that ricocheted throughout the region after the Mexico crisis of 1994.

Although Mercosul's share of Brazil's industrial exports rose in the 1990s, going from 9.3 percent in 1991 to a high of 22.5 percent in 1997, the proportion of total exports destined for the bloc remained minor in comparison to Argentine, Paraguayan, and Uruguayan exports to Brazil. Perhaps of greater importance was the composition of Brazilian exports to the other members of the bloc. After the first year of the bloc's operation, industrial exports consistently accounted for over 89 percent of Brazil's exports to the other Mercosul members until 2002 (Table 4.6). In this respect Mercosul carried meaningful signs of being an effective application of the ambitions outlined in Chapter 3, namely, the deployment of regionalism as a device to encourage an expansion and strengthening of value-added industries throughout the region.

Optimism about the expansion of value-added trade within Mercosul must, however, be tempered with the realization that regional integration also embedded vulnerability to economic disruption in the two major bloc members. Dramatic evidence of this first came with the devaluation of the Brazilian *real* in 1999. After six years of expansion intrabloc trade flows saw a marked contraction, falling from U.S.$20.35 billion in 1998 to U.S.$15.16 billion in 1999 (see Table 4.1). Of this U.S.$5.19 billion year-on-year drop, U.S.$2.75 billion can be attributed to a reduction in Brazilian imports from other bloc members, which included a U.S.$2.26 billion drop in imports from Argentina. Although substantive on a proportional basis, drops in Paraguayan and Uru-

Table 4.6. Industrial Exports as a Percentage of Total Brazilian Exports

Exporting Countries	1990	1991	1992	1993	1994	1995	1996	1997	1998	1999	2000	2001	2002
To Argentina	73.8	82.9	89.0	87.9	87.8	87.0	89.1	90.0	89.7	90.4	91.7	89.8	85.8
To Bolivia	98.9	98.5	97.9	98.3	98.2	98.1	98.2	97.3	95.8	93.2	89.9	90.4	89.2
To Chile	95.4	94.9	95.3	96.6	94.8	92.8	93.4	94.0	94.5	91.3	90.4	81.6	80.5
To Colombia	90.8	87.1	88.2	92.5	91.9	92.3	93.0	92.3	92.0	93.6	93.2	93.3	93.5
To Ecuador	93.4	99.2	99.4	97.0	95.7	99.0	97.5	95.2	90.2	95.5	93.5	93.0	93.2
To Guyana	99.2	99.7	98.9	99.9	99.9	99.8	100.0	99.5	99.9	99.8	99.9	100.0	99.2
To Paraguay	99.3	98.7	98.1	98.7	98.0	97.9	96.2	96.0	95.4	94.8	95.3	96.8	96.2
To Peru	96.7	97.5	95.1	92.8	97.3	97.9	95.2	97.3	94.0	94.5	96.0	93.5	96.1
To Suriname	98.6	99.3	99.7	100.0	99.6	98.5	97.0	92.7	92.5	98.2	99.6	97.6	91.7
To Uruguay	85.8	83.2	87.9	87.8	88.0	85.6	81.8	81.6	84.0	82.3	83.2	80.3	79.5
To Venezuela	71.3	66.8	85.7	79.9	81.3	81.5	86.9	91.0	92.4	90.2	90.3	94.4	93.7
To Mercosul	83.8	86.4	90.1	89.8	89.7	89.1	89.6	90.1	89.9	90.1	91.4	89.7	86.8
Other	54.2	56.2	58.0	60.8	57.3	55.0	55.3	55.1	57.5	56.9	59.0	56.5	54.7

Source: MDIC.

guayan exports to Brazil did not account for the remaining decline in intrabloc trade (see Tables 4.1 and 4.2). In 1999 year-on-year Paraguayan exports to the bloc fell by U.S.$223 million versus a U.S.$114 million drop in sales to Brazil; at U.S.$516 million the fall in Uruguayan exports to the bloc was greater than the corresponding U.S.$380 million fall in trade to Brazil. While the protectionist Argentine reaction to the 1999 devaluation (discussed in the next section) certainly contributed to the fall in intrabloc trade, the disparity between Brazil-bound and bloc-bound flows suggests that there were wider knock-on effects from the devaluation, providing somewhat perverse evidence that Mercosul was resulting in some sort of integrated regional economic structure, although not necessarily the integrated production chains sought by Brazilian policymakers.

Confirmation of this hypothesis came with the November 2001 debt default in Argentina, which effectively quashed a nascent post–*real* devaluation regional economic recovery and sent intrabloc exports plunging from U.S.$17.7 billion in 2000 to U.S.$10.2 billion in 2002 (see Table 4.1). Significantly, the contagion effect of the 2002 crisis, perhaps felt most severely in Uruguay, extended beyond a simple contraction in Argentine imports. Currency collapse and an imploding domestic banking system in Argentina combined to temporarily stop the flow of capital needed to pay for that country's exports and prevent producers from exploiting suddenly lower production costs. Of the U.S.$4.98 billion drop in intrabloc trade U.S.$1.73 billion can be explained by the fall in Argentine exports, of which U.S.$1.31 billion was a drop in shipments to Brazil.

The proposition that will be elaborated from these events in the next section is not so much that regionally integrated production chains had formed, but that Mercosul was working as a first stage of internationalization for domestic industries by encouraging firms to look beyond national borders for new markets within the bloc. As such, preservation of Mercosul assumed economic importance to match the political imperatives that were a major factor in its formation, prompting practical attempts to strengthen intrabloc linkages as an ongoing response to regional economic crisis.

Reaction to the Real's Devaluation

As the 1990s progressed, the Argentine economy's growing reliance on the Mercosul market became increasingly evident and was apparently noted by Brazil's foreign-policy makers. During the postdevaluation crisis in 1999 a disjuncture emerged between the rhetoric and actions of the Cardoso administration, suggesting a grudging willingness to implement the idea of eschewing the traditional mercantilist tit-for-tat approach to trade disputes and instead absorbing some of the economic costs necessary to ensure the survival of the bloc as a foundation stone for the larger South American project. Indeed, justification of this strategy emerged in the midst of the 1999 dispute when business groups appeared in Argentina and Brazil as lobbyists for a resolution of the dispute, providing nonstate-level support for policies aiming to consolidate the regional project.

The Cardoso administration's decision to accommodate rather than retaliate against Argentina in 1999 was not an isolated event, but instead the continuation of a standing policy. Jeffrey Cason (2002) offers a useful discussion of how the Cardoso government altered restrictive trade policies in the mid-1990s, particularly in the automotive industry and import financing, to maintain the integrity of the bloc by accommodating the economic concerns of the other members. As is made clear in Cason's analysis, the Cardoso foreign economic policy team's first inclination was not to grant Argentina preferential treatment within policies designed to address the mounting balance-of-payment problems created by the success of the *real* plan. Palliative action was instead incited by the crescendo of Argentine complaints, which threatened to rupture the bloc. In the first half of 1995, tensions over Brazil's automotive import quotas and their application to Mercosul members promised a significant rift, with Pres. Carlos Menem suggesting that in light of the tensions any meeting with his Brazilian counterpart would be a wasted effort (Cason 2002, 30–31; *LAWR*-RB-95–06). By December of that year a waiver for Argentina-produced automobiles induced a significant change in tone from Menem, leading him to write that Mercosul was the future for its member states and that preservation and consolidation of the bloc was a priority for his government (FBIS-LAT 95–241).

The stresses placed on the Mercosul agreement by the automotive and import financing measures were minor in comparison to the shocks administered by the 1999 devaluation of the *real*. Argentine industry had pursued a different development path within Mercosul, reorienting production toward the Brazilian market instead of using the open-regionalism project as a platform from which to pursue a broader-based export strategy. After a series of sustained speculative attacks on the Brazilian currency threatened to exhaust the country's foreign reserves, Cardoso took the decision on 13 January 1999 to devalue the *real*. Notably, the decision came as a massive surprise to the other Mercosul countries, all of which had developed a habit of keeping each other quietly appraised of shifts in macroeconomic policy. Cardoso explains that the sudden devaluation was not part of a secret plot to seize market share for Brazil, but an unwanted necessity thrust on him virtually overnight by international markets (Cardoso 2006; Cardoso and Lafer 2007; Cardoso and Winter 2006).

The shock for Argentine business was immediate and acute, and businesspeople feared that they lacked the efficiency to compete in a Brazilian market where the currency differential had suddenly inflated the *real* price of their goods (*OESP* 4 Feb. 1999). Brazilian government acknowledgment of the impact that the devaluation would have on trade within Mercosul came quickly (FBIS-LAT 5 Feb. 1999; 4 Feb. 1999). Within a month of floating the *real* Cardoso signed the declaration of São José de Campos with Menem, acquiescing to Argentine requests that money from the Brazilian BNDES export-financing program Proex be withheld from consumer goods sales aimed at the Mercosul market (Agencia Estado 12 Feb. 1999).

At the heart of the agreement lay a special trade commission comprising representatives from the foreign trade secretariats of each country charged with monitoring bilateral trade to gauge the effects of the devaluation. The consultative institutional framework established by the accord combined with Cardoso's forceful assertion that "we have decided to strengthen our support for and our belief in Mercosul" (FBIS-LAT 12 Feb. 1999) to suggest that measures would be taken to ensure that the new macroeconomic reality in Brazil would not destabilize the bloc. Such assumptions were overly optimistic, and the months following the devaluation were marked by the imposition of a series of unilateral measures by both countries (Phillips 2001, 568–569).

Ambassador José Botafogo Gonçalves, serving at the time as executive secretary of the Câmara de Comércio Exterior (CAMEX— Foreign Trade Council) in the MDIC, tempered potential negative Brazilian reaction to the end of Proex support for consumer goods by noting that 98 percent of the financing from the program had been used for capital goods, items not included in the São José de Campos agreement. Indeed, the bilateral rumbustiousness was foreshadowed by Botafogo's warning that in the wake of the *real*'s devaluation Brazil "would not accept surtaxes, quota systems, or any other type of protectionist measure" (FBIS-LAT 1999–0225).   Subsequent protective measures undertaken by Argentina were quickly condemned by Brazilian trade officials, but there was very little in the way of concrete retaliatory action. Against the backdrop of a ministerial meeting to discuss the effect that the devaluation would have on bilateral agricultural trade, Brazil's minister of agriculture, Francisco Turra, offered his Argentine counterpart a warning: continued imports of wheat from Argentina—a policy begun in the 1980s to address trade imbalances and an important contributor to Argentina's U.S.$2.4 billion agricultural trade surplus with Brazil—were contingent on the Menem administration's withdrawing a charge before the WTO that Brazil was using unfair trade practices to export chicken and pork (FBIS-LAT 1999–0225).

Underlying the cantankerous relations in early 1999 was a clearly stated desire to ensure that the devaluation of the *real* did not result in a trade-balance disruption of sufficient magnitude to sunder Mercosul (*OESP* 4 Feb. 1999; 5 Feb. 1999). Certainly this did not preclude staunch official opposition to temporary measures or revisions of the bloc's terms to ease economic pressures brought about by the devaluation. Indeed, such a position was consistent with

Brazilian trade policy and persisted in the wake of the 2001 economic collapse in Argentina, a stance categorized by Brazilian foreign-trade officials as part of an ongoing effort to manage the evolution of Mercosul. But the emphasis was clearly on ensuring that an intrabloc balance-of-payments crisis did not develop, with Botafogo going as far as to suggest in February 1999 that Brazilian firms might want to consider negotiating voluntary production agreements with their counterparts in the other Mercosul countries (FBIS-LAT 1999–0225).

By April 1999 changes in government policy joined with the blend of officially encouraged private sector measures to alleviate tensions associated with the bilateral trade balance. Officials in both MDIC and the Ministry of Finance announced revisions to the taxes levied on the 300 items Brazil was allowed to exclude from the CET. While initial plans to reduce tariffs on food products, petrochemicals, and fertilizers were sidelined because of producer complaints, a fall in the dollar's value, and a finding that there had not been an excessive increase in the actual price of these products, import duties on a range of consumer electronics and medical products were lowered, leaving Brazil with eighteen free slots on its CET exception list (FBIS- LAT 1999–0405). This decision was followed in short measure by the announcement that Brazil would eliminate the use of Proex financing for automotive exports to Argentina. Despite the persistence of temporary Argentine import barriers that punished Brazilian steel producers more than those from Russia or the Ukraine, foreign minister Lampreia supported the policy change with the simple and somewhat unrevealing explanation that the auto industry—an issue of long-standing bilateral contention—deserved special treatment because it was particularly sensitive to the effects of the *real*'s devaluation (FBIS-LAT 1999–0427).

By adopting a relatively patient and nonretaliatory approach to Argentina's postdevaluation protectionist measures Brazil's foreign-policy makers demonstrated an awareness of the Mercosul-induced economic interdependence discussed in the previous section. Political efforts were thus turned to ensuring that cantankerous rhetoric did not create immutable political pressure for restrictive trade policies with the potential to destroy the bloc. Even after Argentina's trade deficit with Brazil had reverted to a surplus in May 1999, Brazilian ministers continued to follow a policy of complaint without matching retaliation (FBIS-LAT 1999–0512). Increasingly, efforts were turned toward restoring political stability in the bloc. To this end Cardoso made a private visit to Menem, an action interpreted as an attempt to give the departing Argentine president the support needed to pursue policies that would restore a measure of equilibrium not only to Mercosul, but also to the Argentine economy (FBIS-LAT 1999–607).

While the political dynamics of the Cardoso-Menem relationship were certainly important and in keeping with the presidential diplomacy that marked bloc evolution (Malamud 2005), in terms of the argument presented in this chapter the visit was more significant for the evidence it provided of actual integration of regional economic structures. Tangible proof of the "Mercosulization" of bloc business thinking came when representatives from the Congress of Latin American Businessmen in Buenos Aires handed Cardoso a document formally requesting that greater efforts be devoted to consolidating and deepening the bloc, a proposition at odds with the intergovernmental commercial discord discussed during meetings with Menem (FBIS-LAT 1999–0609). Although the immediate effect of the petition did little to derail Argentine measures designed to slow the flow of imports into the country (FBIS-LAT 1999–0616/0621/0716/0725), officials did acknowledge that overall bilateral trade had dropped, not simply exports to Brazil (see Table 4.1).

The Argentine business initiative was complemented by the suggestion from the Association of Brazilian Enterprises for the Integration of the Mercosul that its members directly contact their Argentine counterparts in an effort to understand the issues and pressure their respective governments for a change in policy (FBIS-LAT 1999–0727/0811). By August the mix of sustained pressure from bloc business groups and ministerial as well as presidential negotiations bore fruit with the publication of Argentine Resolution 995, which officially excluded Mercosul countries from the import safeguards imposed by Argentina (FBIS-LAT 199–0812).

The two significant points that emerge from the intra-Mercosul trade dispute after the 1999 devaluation of the *real* both relate to the depth of integration experienced by regional economies. On a political level, ministers recognized that Mercosul had brought a transformation in the operation of their respective economies, suggesting that serious effort should be given to preserving the bloc. The central role of Mercosul in the larger Brazilian foreign-policy objective of a consensual hegemony built around a South American region was reinforced by a willingness to absorb some of the dispute costs by not applying punitive measures permitted under either the ALADI or Mercosul treaties (FBIS-LAT 1999–730). Indeed, Lafer (2007) is explicit that, despite the very challenging domestic economic circumstances Brazil faced during the Cardoso era, there was an "understanding that we would have to anchor the cost" of any potentially successful regional project.

Perhaps more important was the business reaction to rising bilateral tensions in the six months after the devaluation. Insistence that the dispute be quickly contained and resolved demonstrated that a substantial number of Argentine and Brazilian firms had enlarged their strategic view to encompass the regional economic space. This attitudinal shift bolstered the South American project and pointed to Brazilian leadership of a nascent consensual hegemony because it provided nonstate sources of strong political pressure to continue pursuing what had originally been a presidential-level political initiative. This suggests that government efforts to create the necessary conditions for expanded economic integration could be successful. Indications of this transformation were also found in changed patterns of regional foreign direct investment, the subject of the next section.

Intra-Mercosul Investment Flows

An implicit aspect of the internationalization of an economy throughout a regional space is the creation of transnational production chains and corporate ventures, leading to an increase in foreign direct investment flows between bloc member states. The interesting characteristic of Mercosul is that the rise of intrabloc FDI flows was slow in coming, only beginning to pick up after the 1999 devaluation of the *real* and the rapid decline of the Argentine economy in 2001.

Context is critical here. Inflation was a constant specter haunting Brazil's foreign policy and business decision making during at least the first six years of the Cardoso era. While Cardoso himself addresses the criticality of national macroeconomic stability in great detail in a wide range of publications, he reduced his fundamental concern to a simple statement: "Inflation had to be tamed or the state would have collapsed" (Cardoso and Lafer 2007). This concern pervaded all elements of public-policy thinking, as noted by a leading ambassador of the era: "In the first four years Cardoso had to fight four international financial crises that nearly broke the Brazilian economy. . . . So the main concern was domestic" (Barbosa 2007). The result was very high domestic interest rates and a pervading sense that the financial ship of state, while undergoing rapid and comprehensive repair, remained a precarious craft sailing on very perilous seas. For Brazilian business this translated into a risk-averse approach to financing, one that saw them shy away from the sort of debt-heavy leveraged investments seen in North America and Europe, and now in post-Cardoso Brazil.

The economic fragility mitigating against a rise in Brazilian FDI can be explained in part by the international financial dynamics of the *real* plan. The 1994 pegging of the *real* to the U.S. dollar and the active decision to tap international capital markets in order to keep inflation under control resulted in the need for a constant inward flow of foreign currency (Rocha 2002; Branford 2003; Bresser-Pereira 2002). Brazilian efforts were consequently devoted to encouraging strong capital inflows and discouraging outflows (Tarzi 1999, 528; Chudnovsky and López 2000, 65), with serious attention being turned to the continental level only after the aftershocks of the 1999 *real* devaluation had been dealt with. Indeed, one leading study on Latin American multinational corporations notes that in the 1990s official interest in Brazilian-led FDI was so low that the statistics submitted to UNCTAD were sketchy at best, probably understating the actual outflows of capital (Chudnovsky and López 1999, 26). Nevertheless, Brazilian firms remained the dominant Latin American foreign investors until the mid-1990s and increased their activity after the Mercosul treaty was signed in 1991, although not nearly as much as was the case in Argentina or Chile.

In the 1986–1991 period Brazil's global FDI outflows were U.S.$443 million, rising to U.S.$887 million between 1992 and 1997. The level stands in contrast to Argentine outflows, which multiplied fivefold from U.S.$18 million to U.S.$101 million in the same period, and the rise in Chilean outflows from U.S.$27 million to U.S.$910 million (Chudnovsky and López 1999, table 14). The difference in rates of expansion is in part explained by the reality that less than 1 percent of Brazilian firms were engaged in a process of internationalization between 1992 and 1996: the majority of Brazilian investment took place in the petroleum and banking sectors (Bonelli 1998, 235; López 1999, 303). The relative paucity of activity by Brazilian firms in the manufacturing sectors was partly the result of domestic industrial restructuring (Chudnovsky and López 2000, 55). While some large conglomerates rationalized their business model to focus on core activities, others were involved in a spate of mergers and acquisitions that saw many existing manufacturing firms, particularly in the auto parts sector (Siffert Filho and Silva 1999), absorbed by foreign multinationals seeking to either capture market share or acquire efficient production facilities (López 1999). The picture of Brazilian FDI during the first five years of the Cardoso administration thus emerges as one of investment activity by service-sector firms, with many of them choosing to use Mercosul as a device to export from existing production facilities.

The figures cited above refer to global outflows and consequently are not particularly useful in considering the impact that Brazilian foreign direct investment might have had on the South American project pursued during the Cardoso era. Indeed, a disaggregation of investment flows indicates that Brazilian investment in Argentina in the mid-1990s was following a markedly different pattern from that in other locations. Although accounting for only 6.7 percent of Brazilian FDI stock in 1996, a figure which had trebled from 2.1 percent in 1992, Argentina was the third most important destination for Brazilian capital.

Perhaps more significant was the nature of these investments. Capital invested in the Cayman Islands (28.6 percent in 1996, down from 48 percent in 1992) was primarily intended to shelter funds from instability in the Brazilian economy; investments in the United States (25.7 percent in 1992 and 34.0 percent in 1996) were concentrated in the oil industry in support of Petrobrás activities (71 percent) and the financial sector (21 percent). By contrast, 49 percent of the Brazilian capital stock in Argentina was in the manufacturing sector, with an emphasis on steel and metalworking firms. A focus on FDI in the manufacturing sector made Argentina the principal foreign investment site, capturing 25 percent of Brazilian FDI in this area.

Yet the overall emphasis in Brazilian FDI remained decidedly on tertiary industries such as banking and construction, with 30 percent of investment in Argentina destined for the financial sector (López 1999, 320–323). This point was emphasized by Brazil's Central Bank when a more accurate accounting of privately held Brazilian foreign capital stocks was begun in 2001, with the proportion of Brazilian foreign direct investment in the tertiary sector rising from 91 percent after the first survey to 96 percent in 2002 (Banco Central do Brasil 2002).

Brazil's Central Bank was less willing to emphasize the slow rate of growth in the country's foreign capital stock. Official figures from 2001 and 2002 indicate that total Brazilian FDI stocks were, respectively, U.S.$43.641 billion and U.S.$45.366 billion. Indeed, holdings in Argentina and Uruguay actually fell during this period, from U.S.$1.625 billion to U.S.$1.502 billion and U.S.$3.121 billion to U.S.$1.548 billion, respectively (Banco Central do Brasil 2002). The suggestion that the regional project was bringing a true integration of national economies thus becomes problematic, with Brazilian funds accounting for just 2.2 percent of the U.S.$73.4 billion foreign investment in Argentina in 2000 (UNCTAD 2001).

Events after November 2001 complicate the integration proposition further. The economic collapse of Argentina and its contagion in Uruguay should have prompted a round of mergers and acquisitions (M&A), with Brazilian firms using the comparative stability of their country as a platform from which to purchase profitable Argentine and Uruguayan firms made inexpensive by the national financial crisis. Yet for the most part such activity did not take place (the Petrobrás purchase of the Argentine oil company Pérez Companc being an important exception (*Business News Americas* 16 Oct. 2002), suggesting that a barrier might exist to the expected normal operation of market forces.

Significantly, this disjuncture between expected and actual market activity was accompanied by an apparent shift in Brazilian government attitudes toward FDI by domestic firms, particularly within the South American context. Where in 2001 officials were suggesting that Brazilian capital was needed at home, by 2002 a different position was being voiced by officials within Itamaraty, MDIC, and BNDES. As one interviewee explained in 2002, the government was not particularly displeased that businesses were contemplating the expansion of their enterprises into neighboring countries.

A central problem facing Brazilian firms wishing to exploit the opportunities for low-cost expansion into the other Mercosul countries was the high cost of capital. Although Brazil was on a sounder fiscal footing than its neighbors in late 2001 and 2002, international capital market fears of contagion and the effects of a possible Lula presidential victory worked to exert considerable downward pressure on the *real* and dramatically raise the cost of financing Brazilian FDI (*Financial Times* 30 April 2002).

At this point a significant shift in policy took place. In a statement noting that it would be illegal for BNDES to provide direct aid to Argentina, the newly appointed Brazilian ambassador in Buenos Aires, José Botafogo Gonçalves, observed that there was no reason that the bank could not finance Brazilian FDI in that country (*OESP* 11 Jan. 2002). In effect, Botafogo was proposing that the EXIM facility (export-import financing) of BNDES, which will be discussed in greater detail later in this chapter, be used to not only finance the export of Brazilian goods and services, but also to underwrite a process of mergers and acquisitions of Argentine firms.

Although technicians at the BNDES forcefully disavow Itamaraty influence as a factor in the expansion of BNDES-EXIM, they are quick to acknowledge that the idea came in response to an early 2000 request by a group of 180 businessmen called the *Grupo Brasil* (Brazil Group) representing Brazilian businesses operating in Argentina. Indeed, BNDES director Renato Sucupira responded to the growing sentiment that Brazilian business needed to increase its outward orientation through increased FDI by ordering creation of the new facility (*O Globo* 27 Jan. 2000), which was in turn advocated by Cardoso with the proviso that any financing extended under the program be commercially viable (Cardoso and Lafer 2007).

Within this context Botafogo's suggestion emerges as a particularly astute political maneuver. Although the institutional procedures permitting BNDES financing of Brazilian FDI had been completed, the political of assent the powerful administrative structure of the Bank was still required. This was made problematic by a distinctly nationalistic rhetoric in Brazil's presidential election.

Three factors become important here for the larger argument that Brazilian foreign policy was seeking to internationalize the national economy and position Mercosul as the foundation for a larger South American space. Perhaps the most interesting is the sudden change in attitude of the Central Bank to Brazil-originating FDI flows. The decision to begin the collection of detailed FDI statistics in 2001 emerges as contemporaneous with business pressures to make BNDES financing available for FDI in Argentina. This suggests that government policy was starting to respond to pressures for greater integration instead of trying to induce a regional view in economic actors. Indeed, the confluence of these two factors reinforces the point made in the discussion of events after the 1999 devaluation of the *real*, namely, that as the domestic economic situation solidified, the medium- and long-term strategic view of firms in the region was expanding beyond national boundaries to encompass at least the regional, if not the global, market.

Here it is possible to posit an explanation for the problematic observation that Brazilian FDI in Argentina and Uruguay did not expand as a result of exploiting the 2001–2002 crises. Unless a company has enormous cash reserves, M&A activity requires access to affordable capital, which was not readily available in Brazil. The pressure applied on BNDES to make EXIM financing available for FDI suggests that Brazilian firms wished to expand regionally, but were unable to access affordable financing.

In short, the foreign economic policy goal of expanding the strategic vision of business to embrace opportunities beyond the domestic market was proving successful, but was constrained by global economic conditions. The decision to extend BNDES-EXIM financing—the third factor—thus becomes a proactive policy response to facilitate a nonstate-level deepening of the regional project by seeking to provide the financing necessary for greater integration of the participating economies. Indeed, the business facilitation explicit in these policy changes stood in direct contrast to the sometimes rancorous political climate between the bloc presidents. This suggests that at least in some sectors practical "ownership" of Mercosul was slowly shifting from the strictly political territory of the state to the daily economic reality of the firm and creating the fifth-column pressure necessary for leadership of a consensual hegemony.

Building a South American Regional Project

Significantly, efforts to expand Mercosul into a larger South American regional bloc did not experience a great deal of success during the first six years of the Cardoso administration, largely because Brazil was simply unable to underwrite the associated costs. While cases such as the prenegotiations for the 1994 Miami Summit of the Americas (discussed in Chapter 2) demonstrate an awareness in both the Andean Community and Mercosul that a continent-wide region might provide benefits for all, the process lacked the political momentum necessary to translate vague commitments into substantive agreements (Chohfi 2002). Integration with Mercosul, which in geographical terms would mean CAN linkages with Brazil, simply lacked the economic underpinning that had been present in the Southern Cone after the revival of bilateral relations during the 1980s. As Tables 4.4 and 4.5 illustrate, the Brazilian market was not an important destination for the general and value-added exports that drove the commercial boom in Mercosul. Indeed, the Chilean and Bolivian decision to join Mercosul as associate members in 1996 and 1997, respectively, had no appreciable effect on the proportion of national exports destined for Brazil, with increases in Chilean exports coinciding with the stabilization of the *real*, and the boom in Bolivian exports, with the opening of a natural gas pipeline to São Paulo. Thus after six years of failed efforts at expanding Mercosul to form the South American Free Trade Area envisioned at the beginning of the Cardoso era a new approach to creating an integrated continental economic space emerged, an approach that sought to precipitate political pressure for integration by developing physical-infrastructure linkages between countries.

Transportation Networks

The suggestion in the discussion of Mercosul is that the political decision to create the bloc was bolstered by policies seeking to encourage the regionalization of economic activity. While the evidence presented in this chapter stops short of indicating the growth of densely integrated production structures across the four main bloc members, the reactions to the 1999 devaluation of the *real* and the 2002 collapse of the Argentine economy point to a reconceptualization of the target market, with firms shifting from a national to a regional focus. Here a seemingly mundane element becomes of crucial importance. The size and industrial capacity of the Argentine and Brazilian economies suggested that expanded bilateral trade held advantages for both countries. Lost in the equation was the logistical problem of physically getting goods to market—how this trade would take place.

Throughout the long years of mutual Argentine-Brazilian distrust Buenos Aires had followed a policy of maintaining the Northwest of Argentina as an "empty quarter," neglecting the elaboration of road and rail networks in order to deprive an invading army of quick access to the political heart of the country (Selcher 1985). The legacy of this policy was one of fragile transportation linkages (*WRH* 8 Jan. 1998) and a serious barrier to the full integration of bloc economies. Indeed, studies of perceived business and export barriers within Mercosul highlight the commercially depressive effects of unreliable transportation networks within the bloc (Silva and Rocha 2001, 598; UNCTAD 2000, 128; CEPAL 2002). This point was not lost on Brazilian policymakers, who recognized the importance that strong infrastructure connections held for regional projects and invested over U.S.$5 billion in Mercosul border crossing points (IPS 19 June 1997; Ouriques 2000).

As the director of the Empresa Brasileira de Planejamento de Transportes (GEIPOT—Grupo Executivo de Integração da Política de Transportes), a Ministry of Transport planning division, noted, when Mercosul was initially created attention was first turned to the expansion and integration of transportation infrastructure. Ten years after the bloc's inception signs of progress were becoming apparent, allowing a shift in attention from large projects such as the "Mercosul Highway" to localized transborder connections that could link national and state road networks with a short bridge and less than 100 kilometers of paved road (Gomes 2001). This gradual consolidation of the regional transportation network's physical aspects allowed the introduction of a new policy element seeking to harmonize and simplify customs and excise procedures surrounding intrabloc goods shipments (GEIPOT 2001). Significantly for the discussion in this chapter, improvements in the condition of regional infrastructure and efforts to smooth bureaucratic procedures paralleled the rise in intra-Mercosul trade, providing the expanded commercial arteries necessary for the shifts in business attitudes alluded to in the previous section.

The linkage between the development of regional infrastructure networks and heightened economic integration becomes particularly apparent if attention is turned to Brazil's Andean neighbors; it is even more apparent if we look at the concentration of intra-Mercosul trade in the southern Brazilian states. The barrier to expanded Brazil-CAN trade was not a lack of interest on the part of Brazilian firms. Indeed, Itamaraty's Mercosul unit found that firms in Brazil wanted access to the CAN market. Rather, the problem was getting goods to market. One Brazilian official remarked on the strange situation surrounding potential high-tech and consumer durable exports from the Amazonian city of Manaus to Peru or Ecuador. Instead of traveling upriver and transferring to road or rail at a port such as Iquitos or Arica, the goods would instead travel down the Amazon, pass through the Panama Canal, and be unloaded on the Pacific coast. Expanding imports from these countries to Brazil faced similar problems, with potential exports being rendered uncompetitive by the high transshipment costs.

The varying quality of transportation linkages with neighboring countries also had a direct impact on Brazil's internal development plans. As GEIPOT's director explained, in the southern states of São Paulo, Rio Grande do Sul, Santa Catarina, and Paraná, the transportation network was dense, with state governments exerting pressure to upgrade and expand the existing federal highway system. The situation in the West and Northeast was completely different, with significantly lower levels of economic activity being reinforced by the paucity of adequate transportation corridors (Gomes 2001). Indeed, part of the problem was the vast distance between many sparsely populated states and the central axis of the Brazilian economy running between São Paulo and Rio de Janeiro. Here we return to the discussion in Chapter 3, which focuses on the decision to internationalize the Brazilian economy as a new route to pursuing domestic and regional development. As José Paulo Silveira (2001), the Planning Ministry's secretary for planning and strategic investment, explained in an interview: "Our approach is to open Brazil up and then this country wants to integrate with its neighbors in order to explore commercial possibilities. . . . But commercial integration is volatile whereas infrastructure integration leads to regional distribution of the production chain, which is more sustainable— the roads are deeper. This means that, looking to the future, if we follow a path for integration based on development, not based only on commercial considerations, this is much more interesting, more sustainable, more fair." The idea underpinning the outward orientation of these areas was to encourage entrepreneurs to engage in new commercial activities, particularly in the Amazonian states, where major cities in neighboring Andean countries are often closer than Brazilian economic centers (Spíndola 2002). Silveira continued by citing a regional infrastructure meeting involving the state of Acre to which the governor brought fifty businessmen to investigate the new opportunities in Peru and Bolivia that might be created by the planned upgrade of roads linking the three countries.

Firmer evidence of the transformative potential of upgraded infrastructure connections comes from Brazilian highway BR-174, the main land route linking the states of Roraima and Amazonas to Venezuela. Prior to 1998, the road was only partially paved. In 1996 the route carried less than half a million dollars in Brazilian exports to Venezuela. As the paving of BR-174 progressed and reached completion in 1998, bilateral trade along the road exploded (Tables 4.7 and 4.8). By the time the last bridge across the Rio Branco was finished in 2000, the newly paved road had induced a forty-nine-fold increase in land-based trade, from U.S.$951,538 in 1996 to U.S.$46.6 million by 2000.

Table 4.7. Exports to Venezuela by Road from Amazonas and Roraima (in U.S.$ FOB)

	From Amazonas	From Roraima	Total Exports to Venezuela
1996	29,013	369,628	454,418,745
1997	9,544,372	700,243	768,145,996
1998	33,034,379	1,119,023	706,298,162
1999	25,426,885	1,546,258	536,669,472
2000	39,109,433	2,099,689	751,065,508
2001	42,351,004	3,384,589	1,092,174,912
2002	43,029,289	4,303,617	796,568,102

Source: Aliceweb, MDIC.

Table 4.8. Imports by Road from Venezuela to Amazonas and Roraima (in U.S. Dollars FOB)

	To Amazonas	To Roraima	Total Imports from Venezuela
1996	834,79	469,418	969,288,000
1997	2,121,551	5,035,821	1,047,559,000
1998	658,286	6,625,226	755,506,000
1999	1,001,039	1,424,839	974,352,000
2000	2,132,569	3,276,137	1,328,009,000
2001	2,877,500	1,645,193	746,983,000
2002	245,627	1,401,803	626,743,000

Source: IADB/INTAL (Institute for the Integration of Latin America and the Caribbean) DataIntal v.4.1. www.iadb.org/intal.

Energy Matrices

Although the increase in Brazil-Venezuela trade prompted by the paving of BR-174 was important, the changes that the road allowed in the overarching bilateral economic relationship were more significant for the evolution of Brazilian foreign policy. The BR-174 upgrade was not pursued with the simple goal of boosting exports from Manaus to Venezuela and the Caribbean through the port of Caracas. A wider view of the project was taken, conceptualizing the highway as the core of an infrastructure corridor that would open access to the hydroelectricity of Venezuela's Guri Dam for the twenty million people of northern Brazil and mirror the changes wrought in the Ruhr Valley by the European Coal and Steel Community (Cardoso and Lafer 2007).

Indeed, the decision to use Venezuelan electricity emerges as part of a larger Brazilian strategy of using energy purchases to shift the balance-of-payments situation with neighboring countries in order to solidify regional linkages. During the late 1980s and early 1990s a conscious decision was made to change crude oil suppliers not only to reduce dependence on the unstable Middle East, but also to address the mounting trade surpluses that threatened to destabilize bilateral relations with Argentina and Venezuela (Lampreia 2002). By the 1990s this policy had accelerated. Where 83 percent of Brazilian oil imports came from the Middle East in 1980, by 1997 this number had fallen to 36 percent (BNDES 1998a, 47). Oil imports from Argentina and Venezuela experienced a corresponding leap: in 1990 Venezuela supplied 4 percent and Argentina 0 percent of oil imports, figures which had jumped to 16 percent and 24 percent by 1995 (BNDES 1998b, 30). Although the situation had changed somewhat by 2002, when Brazil attained a measure of self-sufficiency in oil production (*OESP* 20 Sept. 2002), the clear trend was toward a regionalization of energy supplies that explicitly recognized the potential for continental self-sufficiency (Barbosa 2001, 151; Cardoso and Lafer 2007).

Given the absence of serious armed conflict in South America during the twentieth century, which reduced the possibility that war would limit supplies, the decision to purchase oil from neighboring countries made strategic sense for Brazil (Holanda 2001, 31–33). But the adoption of a regional approach to energy supplies also played an important role in the larger consensual hegemonic project of constructing an active continental space by allowing Brazil to provide a measure of economic stability to several neighboring countries. Tellingly, after retiring, Lampreia observed in late 2002 that a useful way to restart economic relations with Argentina might be to divert aspects of Brazilian trade in order to purchase bulk commodities and energy from its economically troubled neighbor. The efficacy of such actions for the construction of a South American economic space becomes particularly evident in the cases of Paraguayan electricity and Bolivian natural gas.

As one diplomat mused in an interview, there is a segment of the federal government that views the construction of the giant Itaipú hydroelectricity-generating dam on the border with Paraguay to be a mistake; this group believes that the project should have been completed upstream where it would have been entirely within Brazilian territory. Yet Itaipú has had a profound impact on the Paraguayan economy, transforming the country into one of the world's largest energy exporters and the source for 25 percent of the electricity used in Brazil (United States Department of Energy 2002). Under the terms of the Itaipú treaty each country receives half of the production from the dam. But because Paraguay is able to consume only 10 percent of its allotment, an agreement guarantees the sale of the surplus from Itaipú to Brazil for a fixed price, denominated in U.S. dollars. For some officials in Brazil this arrangement is patently absurd, prompting calls to purchase continental energy imports in *reais*, especially in the Paraguayan and Bolivian cases where there is no alternate market for the electricity and gas.

Concern over the drain on the national accounts caused by oil, gas, and electricity imports from neighboring countries surfaced in a 2000 proposition from Brazilian national energy secretary Benedito Carraro that some sort of Mercosul energy currency be created to limit the macroeconomic damage of Brazil's energy dependency (FBIS-LAT 2000–0717). While potentially politically fruitful on the domestic level after the *real* devaluation crisis, Carraro's proposition overlooked the strategic regional effect of the changes wrought by Brazil's energy policy. The enduring reality was that Brazil remained an energy importer. Embedded within the continentally oriented energy-import policy implemented when oil purchases were shifted from the Middle East to Argentina and Venezuela was a conscious decision to use the balance-of-payments aspects of energy dependency to strengthen PICE and the then-nascent South American project. This strategy found further application during the Cardoso era in the decision to purchase Venezuelan hydroelectricity and construct a pipeline to unexploited Bolivian natural gas fields.

Indeed, implementation of the Bolivian project overrode late-1980s internal Itamaraty concerns that the necessary contractual obligations might not favor Brazil in the medium or long term (Carriço 1989; Holanda 2001). *Real* plan–induced currency stability eased many of the fiscal concerns about the Bolivian deal, contributing to the 1996 completion of negotiations and the

1999 opening of the pipeline (BBC AL/W0448/WL). By 2001 natural gas exports valued at U.S.$175 million accounted for 68.2 percent of Bolivian exports to Brazil, figures that jumped to U.S.$332 million and 83.8 percent in 2002 (MDIC-Aliceweb 2002). These figures stand in stark contrast to the 2001 total Bolivian exports of U.S.$1.521 billion (CEPAL 2002). Significantly, payment for Bolivian natural gas was in U.S. dollars, a policy Lampreia (2002) justified in my interview with him with the explanation that gas was an internationally traded commodity. When pressed with the observation that Brazil was the only market for Bolivian gas, his tone changed slightly, noting that, although this was a question that might need to be addressed in the future, it was highly unlikely that Bolivia would willingly accept a change.

The significance of the continental spread of Brazilian energy matrices is that it provided another framework for greater approximation with neighboring countries and offered an avenue for providing some of the rents associated with leadership. As discussed in Chapter 2, construction of the Itaipú Dam with Paraguay contributed to a sense of economic commonality (Cardoso and Lafer 2007) and laid a foundation for the future construction of Mercosul. Completion of electricity-transmission lines from Venezuela in 1998 provided similar economic depth to relations with pre-oil wealth Hugo Chávez' subsequent efforts to draw his country closer to Brazil and possibly seek membership in Mercosul (*APF* 22 May 2001). The 1996 decision to construct a natural gas pipeline to Bolivia predated that country's 1997 accession to Mercosul as an associate member.

Paralleling these concrete achievements in infrastructure-induced economic integration was the repeated failure to make progress on a Mercosul-CAN accord (discussed in Chapter 2), providing the very clear suggestion by the end of the 1990s that the standing Itamaraty approach of using free-trade agreements to construct the South American project had not been successful. Here a disjuncture emerges between the unsuccessful efforts to politically construct South America and the de facto integration that was occurring on an infrastructural level.

By the end of the 1990s, frustration with the failure to politically induce continental integration prompted a major foreign-policy shift in Brazil, with Cardoso instructing Itamaraty to assemble a proposal that would extrapolate the infrastructure axes of the Avança Brasil program to the continental level. The result was the 2000 Summit of South American Presidents in Brasília, leading to the creation of IIRSA (Lafer 2007).

Physically Building South America

The IIRSA project launched at the 2000 Brasília Summit sought to draw on the important role that physical connections played in the growth of intra-Mercosul trade by using firm-level interaction to provide an impetus for bloc-to-bloc negotiations. Particularly effective in this respect were the bioceanic corridors that would cross Ecuador, Peru, Bolivia, and Chile. For the Andean countries the attraction was not so much access to the distant economic core of Brazil as the possibility for sustained growth through the development of transshipment industries. In order to reach markets in the Far East the vast quantities of soybeans grown in Acre, Rondônia, and Matto Grosso had to be shipped first to Brazil's Atlantic coast and then transferred to an oceangoing vessel for a slow voyage via the Panama Canal. Suggestions that this journey might be shortened with a land bridge were already percolating within Itamaraty and were assuming an increasingly important position in Alberto Fujimori's national plan for Peru in the years before the Brasília meeting (Andrade 1989; Nahú 1992). Chilean entrepreneurs had also cast an eye toward the commercial possibilities of a bioceanic corridor and begun purchasing Bolivian railroads in order to form a path from Brazil to ports such as Iquique and Antofagasta (IPS 3 Dec. 1999). Reinforcing business investment and adding substance to the latest presidential-level proclamations for greater approximation was the local-level reaction, which saw the prospect of a bioceanic corridor being greeted enthusiastically by Andean border towns with visions of developing into important transshipment points for Brazilian exports (Gomes 2001).

The official stance emanating from Itamaraty did little to stem this excitement, suggesting that the construction of multiple bioceanic corridors was an important goal for Brazil. Foreign-trade officials supported this assessment, noting that, while transcontinental linkages were not crucial at the end of Cardoso's presidency, in five to six years such connections might play an increasingly important role in Brazilian foreign trade (Spíndola 2002). The axes sketched on the IIRSA integration map revealed an outline similar to a spider's web, drawing on the geographical reality of South America to create a framework encouraging intracontinental trade with a particular focus on Brazil. The political effects here were crucial, drawing as they did on the potential for greater physical integration to facilitate the formal approximation needed to pursue the South American project and form a unified position for FTAA and WTO negotiations.

Although Chohfi (2002) noted in our interview that transportation routes such as a bioceanic corridor offered the prospect of better prices for Brazil's inland producers and an increase in international trade generated by the central-western and northern areas of the country, these observations were paired with the comment that "it [the bioceanic corridor] is also important in terms of the wider scope of our relations with these countries." After leaving office Lampreia was considerably more direct about the commercial aspect (2002): "I think this [the bioceanic corridor] is mostly an exercise of armchair strategists rather than a practical appraisal. With the capability of large ships today it makes a lot more sense to send containers or larger volumes of merchandise from an efficient port like Sepetiba."

Officials in the transport departments offered more measured language, noting that many bioceanic routes were technically possible, but perhaps not immediately economically feasible. While meaningful assistance was provided, including the construction of new crossings to Bolivia and Peru, it was clearly suggested that rapid expansion of such corridors was not a pressing national economic priority (Gomes 2001). With development of the various bioceanic corridors being largely restricted to the upgrade of existing infrastructure rather than the construction of entirely new routes (*Brazil Now* November–December 1998), the chief impact of the proposals, namely, the injection of some impetus into the South American concept, emerges as being political.

One of the significant challenges to the South American project that IIRSA was intended to ease was Andean fear of uncompetitiveness against Brazil's developed industrial capacity, an issue partially addressed by hopes that approximation would bring increased levels of Mercosul investment (Spíndola 2002). Significantly, firm-level competitive concerns were paired with government-level perceptions that Brazil was an approachable source for development aid. Here the shift toward South American infrastructure integration began to have a palpable impact on the construction of a political and economic rationale for South America as a region. A significant goal for CAN members was the use of IIRSA to attract Brazilian funds for the upgrading of the national infrastructure networks that would comprise the twelve axes of integration. This expectation was not altogether unreasonable given BNDES' record of supporting civil engineering projects in other countries through a 1996 alteration to the terms of the EXIM program; that change permitted export financing for all sectors of the Brazilian economy, including engineering and construction companies. The impact of the modification was almost immediate, providing export financing to Brazilian engineering firms engaged in such high-budget projects as a U.S.$1.5 billion infrastructure construction contract with the Venezuelan state oil company Petróleos de Venezuela, SA (PDVSA), a U.S.$140 million contract to bore water tunnels in Ecuador, and a U.S.$77 million upgrade of 180 kilometers of highway in Paraguay (*World Tunnelling* December 2000; *Business News Americas* 28 Feb. 2000; *Project Finance* 1 Feb. 2002).

Clearly, BNDES' export-financing program offered significant benefits to the Brazilian economy, particularly with respect to developing internationally competitive firms. But BNDES financing, operating as an independent factor reinforcing aspects of Brazil's continental foreign policy, also created important political ramifications for the South American project. As the head of Itamaraty's Americas Division noted, neither the Foreign Ministry nor the president of the republic could command BNDES to lend money to a particular enterprise. But this did not preclude formal and informal consultations as well as suggestions from foreign-policy makers (Gonçalves 2002). In some instances the ability to facilitate BNDES financing was presented as being instrumental to the continued involvement of national engineering and construction firms in other South American countries.

One example is the decision by Brazil's Central Bank to suspend the Convênio de Pagamentos e Créditos Recíprocos (CCR—Reciprocal Credit and Payment Convention) in 2000. The CCR was an ALADI mechanism designed to minimize the need for firms to engage in currency exchanges during regional trade by creating special accounts within each country's Central Bank, with balances being settled on the national level at prearranged intervals. For policymakers such as Cardoso and Lafer (2007), who were seeking to push the South American concept, the suspension was a mistake brought about by an excessive nervousness within the Central Bank about the heterodoxy of the instrument. The downstream effect contributed to the exclusion of Brazilian firms from a range of infrastructure projects in Ecuador, including the costly San Francisco hydroelectric dam, by raising the cost of project financing. While it was quickly acknowledged that the suspension of the CCR was well within the rights and responsibilities of the Central Bank, particularly since the structure of the CCR was presenting an increasingly unacceptable credit risk to Brazil's foreign-exchange reserves (*International Trade Finance* 7 June 1996; *ComexNet* 2001; *OESP* 10 Sept. 2002), the possibility that a revised version of the instrument would be restored was greeted with some gratification. Indeed, it is significant that the late-2002 restoration of the CCR accompanied the entrenchment of IIRSA after the second South American Presidential Summit in Guayaquil, reopening a technical device needed to finance the transnational commercial exchanges necessary to pursue regional infrastructure projects.

If we return to the historical antecedents of Mercosul the mix of IIRSA, BNDES financing, and restoration of the CCR become particularly important for the South American project. Although Mercosul emerged from a political agreement between Argentine president Carlos Menem and Brazilian president Fernando Collor, successful creation of the bloc stemmed from the lengthy period of approximation discussed in Chapter 1. In short, considerable sustained effort had been devoted to creating conditions propitious for economic integration in the Southern Cone.

Viewed in this context, the 2000 launch of IIRSA and the expansion of BNDES-EXIM financing for infrastructure projects in other countries emerge as a concerted effort to relaunch stalled regionalist political projects and the South American concept with the concrete connections necessary to sustain integration (Cardoso and Lafer 2007). While traditional diplomatic instruments such as treaty negotiations and economic-accord discussions were not completely sidelined, the integrating impetus shifted from political intent and presidential pressure to the technocratic details of regionally coordinated transportation and Planning Ministry policymaking.

Although this change in tactics was originally resisted by Itamaraty and pursued only at the express order of Cardoso, by 2002 sentiment within the Foreign Ministry was becoming increasingly warm to the approach, especially after it helped accelerate moribund discussions with CAN and provided a physically tangible rationale for expanded continental cooperation in FTAA negotiations.

The subtle aspect of the new approach to South American integration unveiled at the 2000 Brasília Summit was that it used the apoliticism of infrastructure networks alluded to earlier by Silveira to pursue a political project. By constructing linkages to facilitate transnational economic flows within South America the infrastructure-integration project set the stage for the emergence of what Hirschman (1945) would perhaps term regionally oriented commercial fifth columns, each pushing its respective government to pursue heightened continental integration.

Conclusion

By the end of the Cardoso era the economic aspect of the South American project remained incomplete, with trade integration between Mercosul and

CAN being limited to restatement of a strong commitment to further approximation between the two blocs (Mercosul 2002). On this basis the suggestion is that Brazilian leadership in the economic dimension was limited and did not provide the rents necessary to incite a sustained and concerted demand push for a South American region.

Yet such a conclusion would overlook the propositions advanced by this chapter. Although grounded in the political dynamics of the "new" regionalism—a state-based enterprise—my argument is that self-sustaining, cohesive regionalism that extends beyond political platitudes requires an effective transfer of ownership of the regional project from the level of presidential politics to the realm of the firm and the individual, the actors that will breathe life into the structures erected by governments.

Brazilian foreign policy in the economic dimension thus emerges as a subtler approach to the political project of regional integration and draws on thinking similar to Hirschman's concept of a commercial fifth column to seek societal and business pressure for an expansion of intracontinental economic linkages. The pertinent lessons drawn from the relatively successful example of Mercosul highlight the gradual nature of integration as well as the importance of creating the physical linkages that facilitate the logistical realities of commerce, namely, the shipment of goods from producer to market. The Brazilian approach to an extension of Mercosul to include the rest of the continent was consequently modified, shifting from a continuing series of political meetings to the technocratic realm of physical infrastructure network planning. In short, the emphasis was in effect placed on developing Hirschman's fifth column, almost seeking to emulate the pressures of globalization on the regional level by establishing the framework for an expansion of intracontinental trade and relying on business to exploit the new opportunities by creating the intermingling of economic interests that might renew and fortify the political will necessary to fashion a viable South American regional space.

5

The Security Dimension

In his discussion of the rise of a nascent Mercosul security community Andrew Hurrell (1998a, 252) notes that questions of politics, economics, and security are intertwined, with advances in one sustaining and furthering progress in the others. Within this mix regionalism takes on a stabilizing role, working to build the shared ideas and interests that help establish the mutual confidence needed to encourage cooperation and remove armed conflict from the language of diplomacy.

To a certain extent this argument mirrors the pyramidal model of hegemony I employ, suggesting that for one of the aspects to retain strength and resiliency it must be supported by the others. The subject of this chapter is thus how Itamaraty has sought to encourage and lead the growth of internally sustainable security structures in South America in order to create the conditions necessary for the cohesive regional integration that it desires for Brazil's wider international strategy.

Significantly, Itamaraty's ability to lead the continent in its regional projects is to a certain extent conditioned by Brazil's capacity to ensure a reasonable level of security for its partner states. Here an immediate problem arises, namely, an inability to seriously project force to defend the continent from external incursion. The solution to this conundrum can be found in a loose application of the concentric circles of Golbery do Couto e Silva's (1967) geopolitical strategy. In the largest circles, encompassing the global level and the Western Hemisphere, Rio Branco's policy of friendship with the United States is deployed to prevent external threats (Cervo 2002, 15). However, the situation shifts when we move to the South America circle. While the policy is certainly not one of antagonism toward the United States, a clear emphasis is placed on excluding extra–South American actors from internal South American affairs. The analysis presented in this chapter is thus one of how Brazilian foreign policy has sought to foster a continental security environment that remains friendly with, but independent from, the United States.

Only the most optimistic of observers would classify the Brazilian leadership strategy in the security dimension an unqualified success. In traditional security areas such as the prevention of war and the preservation of national sovereignty Brazilian security policy during the Cardoso era proved reasonably successful, particularly as a brake on external intervention in South American democratic practices. Yet it would be pushing the point to credit success solely to the influence and prestige of Brazil; in many instances U.S. opinion and action were an important factor. Nowhere is this more evident than in the new transnational security issues of narco-trafficking, terrorism, and insurgency. As will be argued in this chapter, Brazilian success in the security dimension has been constrained by a lack of national and regional capacities as well as the policy restrictions created by the country's sustained and strict respect for national sovereignty. Indeed, if we set the problem in terms of Golbery's geopolitical circles, the argument is that failure in the security dimension was caused by an unwillingness to meld individual country-bubbles into the South American circle.

The chapter is divided into four sections. The first explains the importance of democracy and development in Brazil's national defense policy and sets up the conceptual framework for three empirical cases. The protection of democracy forms the first case set out in the second section, with an examination of disruptions in Paraguay, Ecuador, Peru, and Venezuela being used to illustrate how Itamaraty deployed regional instruments such as Mercosul and the Rio Group to combat authoritarian retrogressions and build an ethic of security cooperation within the continent. More direct reference to suggestions of interdependence and regionalism forms the basis of the third section, where the use of physical integration as a technique for peace building is explored in the ending of the Ecuador-Peru border conflict and the elaboration of IIRSA. Finally, attention is turned to the weakest aspect of Itamaraty's security strategy, the new security issues of narco-trafficking, terrorism, and insurgency. Here the shortcoming that emerges lies not in the willingness to cooperate, but in differing national capacities and the limitations that a strict respect for sovereignty places on policies designed to address nontraditional threats.

National Defense and Democracy

As a Mercosul-based security community evolved in the mid-1990s (Hurrell 1998a), the Cardoso administration embarked on a reevaluation of the doctrine governing military planning. The resulting 1996 Política de Defesa Nacional

(PDN—National Defense Policy), although criticized by the armed forces for its operational vagueness (FBIS-LAT 1999–0318), provided a clear indication of how foreign-policy makers conceptualized Brazil's security role in South America. The central security problem typically confronting a state—war—is quickly addressed in paragraph 2.6 with the observation that South America is a highly demilitarized region free of unmanageable conflict, a situation partly attributable to redemocratization in the 1980s. Democracy and the preservation of democracy thus acquired formal importance in Brazilian foreign policy (Cardoso 2001, 6).

Here the temptation is to adopt an undiluted reading of democratic theories of peace, a risky tactic because it overlooks the tendency for some countries in the region to use armed conflict as a diplomatic ploy to initiate or gain position in international law-based negotiations (Hurrell 1998b, 532). A more nuanced application of this theoretical school is required, drawing on the explicit link that the PDN (paragraph 1.6) makes between national development, socioeconomic equality, and political inclusion.

Both the PDN and ministerial statements at the time of the policy's release were clear that national development, particularly with respect to economic growth and social inclusion, was seen as the keystone to sustainable national security. In keeping with the ideas aspect (set out in Chapter 3), the PDN also recognized that national development does not take place in a vacuum, but is affected by relations with neighboring countries. Conceptions of national security thus acquired a transnationalized aspect that equated the deepening of citizenship within Brazil and the wider region as integral to the development of the capacities and confidence needed to address globalized, post–Cold War uncertainties (Lampreia 1996b).

José Luiz Machado e Costa (1999, 68), a diplomat involved in drafting the PDN in 1996, strongly suggests that the goal was to expand the emerging Mercosul security community into a continental entity. After reviewing comparative military capabilities and the peaceable nature of intra–South American relations, Machado e Costa (1999, 77–84) outlines a variety of possible future conflict scenarios, all of which are based on the need to strengthen national development frameworks. In a point recalling the *política externa independente* decision to separate Brazilian military capacity from U.S. supply sources, he presents the PDN as seeking autonomy from U.S. approbation and assistance in the security realm. This argument is consonant with the wider goal Brazilian diplomats constantly cite of protecting Brazil's sovereign freedom of action (Lampreia 1998a, 11).

Specific reference is made by Machado e Costa (1999, 86) to the impact of U.S. counternarcotics policies in the region, leading to the suggestion that a coordinated South American approach should be taken to shared continental security threats. It is also in the nature of the U.S. response to the narcotics threat that the deepest challenge to the establishment of a South American security community becomes evident, namely, a faltering ability to address new security issues internally without becoming reliant on extracontinental assistance. Here it is useful to turn our attention to a consideration of Cervo's (2002, 14–15) categorization of the PDN as an idealist document drawing heavily on Kantian principles of democratic peace to emphasize pacifism, disarmament, and cooperation, but not necessarily NATO-style combined operations.

In a 1997 speech Lampreia (1997) drew on the Kantian principle of democratic peace by arguing that the preservation of democracy and the continuation of peaceful relations in the continent would free resources needed for widespread socioeconomic development. Itamaraty secretary-general Sebastião do Rego Barros (1997, 147) reinforced the importance of this principle, noting that economic integration and regionwide democratization fostered confidence between states, creating an atmosphere that automatically guaranteed each country's national security by removing the strategic tensions that led to war. However, such strong allusions to the democratic theory of peace need tempering with the warning that armed conflict has been used as a diplomatic gambit in South America (Hurrell 1998b). The required theoretical nuances may be found in the observation that there is a tendency to take a simplistic view of Kant's initial proposition and overlook the undergirding argument that republican forms of governance lead to a shared set of values and the creation of mutual respect and understanding among nations (Sørensen 1992).

This intellectual and emotional connection initiates a virtuous circle of increasing cooperation, a process which feeds into the logic underpinning Kantian approaches: increases in international trade and the consequent interdependence greatly elevate the cost of war (Sørensen 1992, 399). Given the transnationalized economic agenda outlined in Chapter 4 and the ideational basis of Brazilian foreign policy set out in Chapter 3, Itamaraty's emphasis on the maintenance of a regime type that fostered international stability and increased the credibility of the continent as a reliable business partner is hardly surprising (Cardoso 2001; Lampreia 1998a).

The application of a Kantian ethic to intracontinental relations also has implications for South America's place in larger international security questions as it categorizes the geopolitical space as an area capable of autonomously managing and resolving internal disputes and tensions without the need for international intervention or monitoring. Again, this has important implications for Itamaraty's continental project because the Kantian ethic endows the region with a reputation for stability and self-governance, which is necessary for acceptance as a credible international actor and facilitates some regionalization of the security-provision costs inherent in leadership.

The protection of democracy implied in the PDN becomes clearer if we turn to a critical examination of the theory of democratic peace. The literature on democratic peace is coming to a consensus that democracies are not inherently less warlike; rather, one democracy is not likely to attack another (Gates et al. 1996, 6). The corollary is that democracies are quite willing to attack authoritarian regimes and vice versa. In the 1980s the implications of this proposition became apparent when a rhetoric of democratizing "undemocratic states" was used by Presidents Reagan and Bush to justify invasions of Grenada (1983) and Panama (1989), respectively.

In this regard the preservation of democracy and its most visible forms in South America emerges as an important factor in preventing U.S. efforts to engage in naked forms of direct intervention such as invasion and occupation. We can thus complicate Machado e Costa's (1999, 78) proposition that a democratic peace is pursued because it allows valuable resources to be redirected to national development projects. Further, the maintenance of democracy helps create a space relatively free of direct U.S. intervention where governments can pursue development-oriented policies not necessarily in complete consonance with immediate U.S. interests. But the pertinent critique is that the absence of war between democracies is not synonymous with a lack of interference or covert intervention (Russet 1993, 122–123). In conjunction with the historical reality of U.S. intervention in the Americas (P. Smith 2000), this caveat suggests that the existence of a neighborhood of democracies does not prevent the more powerful from interfering in the internal affairs of the less powerful; it simply makes it politically more difficult. The political skill required to advance interventionist policies within a democratic society becomes one of identifying a publicly acceptable pretext for intervention in another democratic state and can be found in calls for an international approach to the new transnationalized security issues such as narco-trafficking, terrorism, and the suppression of insurgents.

The insertion of new security issues into our discussion creates immediate problems for Brazil's security strategy. Strict respect for sovereignty and noninterference in the internal affairs of other countries were established as policy precepts by Rio Branco in part to prevent the creation of precedents that might later be used to justify international intervention in Brazil. When combined with the spread of democracy in the 1980s and the pursuit of confidence-building measures in the Southern Cone, Rio Branco's principles and the Kantian element found in Brazil's security policy helped initiate a security community in Mercosul that might embrace the entire continent. The underlying assumption was that there was a clear distinction between the national and the international, a proposition which breaks down with the introduction of nonstate-based transnationalized issues such as narco-trafficking, terrorism, and insurgency.

As the following three sections of this chapter will demonstrate, there is thus a fundamental disconnect in Brazil's vision of security for South America. Application of a quasi-Kantian approach to regional security emerges at the core of Brazilian leadership in the areas of the protection of democracy and the creation of peace as a reasonably effective instrument for preserving South American autonomy by excluding external interference in both regional and national affairs. However, this approach breaks down when we look at the new threats to security of narco-trafficking, terrorism, and insurgency. Here an unwillingness to violate the sanctity of sovereignty by taking a leadership role that imposes or at least forcefully suggests regional responses to the new threats left a large space for the United States to reinsert itself in the heart of continental affairs, in effect questioning the validity of Brazil's vision for the security of the emerging South American geopolitical space.

Securing Democracy

Given the important place democracy occupies in plans to form something akin to a continental security community, a central concern in Brazilian foreign policy is the protection of democracy in South America. Yet there is a fundamental disjuncture, driven by two main factors, between Itamaraty's rhetoric and its (non)action to protect and deepen continental democracy. The lesser brake on action relates to the cost of political reengineering programs. Policymakers in Brasília view institutional imposition with some skepticism, and during my interviews pointed out not only that it is a financially and politically unaffordable undertaking for their country (Lampreia 2002), but also that democracy is doomed to collapse if it does not grow from transformations in domestic social, economic, and political relations (Cardoso 2000c; Polanyi 1944; Rueschemeyer et al. 1992; O'Donnell and Schmitter 1986; Haggard and Kaufman 1995; Whitehead 1996; Lowenthal 1991). A more substantive brake on an activist approach to advancing continental democracy comes from concern that it could create a precedent for extraregional countries to impose specific regime characteristics on Brazil's imperfect democracy. For Itamaraty the implication is that, far from being altruistic policy initiatives, attempts to impose democracy or offers to assist with democratization represent a more insidious route to exercising a measure of control over regional states and South America as a whole.

A careful line must therefore be drawn, one which requires adherence to the democratic norms crucial for the consolidation of a South American security community, but without allowing the sort of subtle interference that would weaken Brazil's continental leadership or cause the country to be viewed with distrust. As a brief survey of democratic upheavals in Paraguay, Ecuador, Peru, and Venezuela will demonstrate, Itamaraty's efforts at protecting democracy in South America have been limited to ensuring that all states adhere to a minimal definition of democracy—respect for basic constitutional and electoral norms—and preventing other countries such as the United States and Canada from imposing specific measures that might lead to subtle control over the continent's unsettled democracies.

Paraguay

Gen. Andrés Rodríguez' decision to initiate a democratic transition in Paraguay after he toppled the thirty-five-year dictatorship of Gen. Alfredo Stroessner is a masked example of democracy by imposition (Whitehead 1991; Nickson 1989; Arditi 1995). With the prestige and economic well-being of the Paraguayan elite dependent on a corrupt economic model grounded in patronage and "triangular trade" with Argentina and Brazil, relatively open access to neighboring markets was of utmost importance (Nickson 1988; Nickson 1996; Roett and Sacks 1991; Lambert 1996). Argentina and Brazil made continued market access and trading relations contingent on the adoption of democratic forms, placing a stark choice before the rulers of post-Stroessner Paraguay: democratize or face complete regional isolation (Sarney 1989; Collor 1991b). Despite some substantive changes to the postauthoritarian Paraguayan political framework (Fournier and Burges 2000, 9–10), Colorado Party control of the principal instruments of power, including the presidency, remained the abiding reality (Lambert 2000; Lambert and Nickson 1997). Thus the struggle for the 1993 Colorado Party presidential nomination was not a surprise; Juan Carlos Wasmosy emerged victorious after his patron, Rodríguez, had Gen. Lino César

Oviedo take the ballot boxes into "protective custody" (FBIS-LAT 97–253). Significantly, events during this democratically formative primary elicited no official condemnation from Brazil, and critical voices were muted after a fraud-free vote put Wasmosy in the presidential palace. The implicit suggestion for ambitious Paraguayans was that raw power, not democratic process and legitimacy, unlocked the doors to the presidential palace.

Drawing on the lessons of the 1993 presidential election and his personal impunity during the primaries, Oviedo attempted to transform Wasmosy into a puppet president (Valenzuela 1997, 46–47). In an effort to defend his waning authority, Wasmosy decided to relieve Oviedo of his command in April 1996, prompting an attempted coup d'état by the disgruntled general.

Oviedo's coup attempt emerges as a critical juncture in Brazilian efforts to preserve democracy in the Southern Cone by widening the Mercosul region. The mistake in Oviedo's strategic calculation was to confuse formal silence over questionable party primaries—an issue Brazil considered to be in the purview of Paraguay's judicial system—with tacit acquiescence to an overturning of the democratic apple cart. In part, this miscalculation can be attributed to an ambiguous regional atmosphere, encapsulated in the Mercosul treaty. Although the creation of the bloc was embedded in collective efforts to protect democracy in the Southern Cone (Hurrell 1998a, 244), the 1991 Treaty of Asunción makes no explicit reference to democracy as a prerequisite for bloc membership (Mercosul 1991). The response to the attempted coup, however, clarified this ambiguity.

During the first hours of the revolt the Mercosul and U.S. ambassadors encouraged Wasmosy to resist, warned Oviedo to back down, and threatened an undemocratic Paraguay with suspension from the regional bloc. The combined action of Paraguay's neighbors was certainly helpful, but came second to the civil society–led street protests calling for the general's surrender. This suggests that threatened isolation had little impact because of the relative weakness of Paraguay's business elite (Valenzuela 1997, 51–52). But, as one Brazilian official notes, Paraguayan political and economic affairs are conducted on a highly informal level. Thus, the military's refusal to back Oviedo—perhaps the critical factor in thwarting the coup—might be attributable to pressure from neighboring armed forces and recognition by illicit elites that exclusion from Mercosul would cripple contraband and smuggling networks.

Oviedo's attempted coup prompted the Treaty of Ushuaia addendum to the Mercosul treaty, which in Article 1 makes democracy an explicit condition for participation in the Southern Cone regional-integration process and provides the precedent for similar measures in the South American presidential declarations of 2000 (paragraph 2) and 2002 (paragraphs 20–28). Specifics about the shape and operation of democracy are avoided, emphasis instead being placed on the basic forms that allow the development of self-sustaining representative politics.

While the vagueness of the treaty certainly leaves Brazil and its Mercosul partners open to criticism that they could have done more to assist democratization in Paraguay, the reality is that the threat of expulsion from Mercosul curbed excesses in the authoritarian tendencies of important segments of the Asunción elite. Indeed, during the 1998 presidential election the specter of isolation within Mercosul not only ensured that the vote would take place, but also acted as an effective constraint on the arbitrariness of both military and political elite efforts to overturn Oviedo's nomination as the Colorado Party candidate. The result was a rather tortuous series of legal procedures, which, while ultimately securing the welfare of the vested interests wielding real power in Paraguay, did subscribe to correct legal and constitutional forms (FBIS-LAT 98–012; FBIS-LAT 98–034; FBIS-LAT 98–035; FBIS-LAT 98–068; *WRH* 19 May 1998).

Significantly, the success that Mercosul pressure demonstrated in embedding constitutionality during the 1998 presidential election persisted through the political crisis of early 1999, when the assassination of Vice-Pres. Luis María Argaña threatened to plunge Paraguay into civil war (Instituto de Relaciones Europeo-Latinoamericanas 1999). Although the subsequent course of Paraguayan politics was far from smooth, one Brazilian diplomat noted that pressure applied through the prodemocracy clause of the Treaty of Ushuaia entrenched the operational norms of democracy by opening a small space for civil society and genuine democratizing elite to push for change. More significantly for Itamaraty's foreign-policy objectives, the Mercosul-induced embedding of basic democratic forms in the Paraguayan polity demonstrated that regionalism offered an avenue for South American nations to cooperatively manage their own affairs.

Ecuador

One limitation inherent in the Brazilian approach to protecting democracy in South America, born of historical fears of being branded hegemonic, is the country's unwillingness to engage in projects that might be perceived as violating the sovereignty of other countries (Cooper and Legler 2001, 118). Indeed, early 2000 discussions with Argentina about whether the two largest Mercosul states might help alleviate political instability in Colombia and Ecuador were footnoted with the qualifier that such action would have to be not only specifically requested, but also explicitly respectful of national sovereignty (*EFE News* 17 Jan. 2000). Less than a week after a meeting between Lampreia and his Argentine counterpart, Adalberto Rodríguez Giavarini, the Jamil Mahuad presidency in Ecuador collapsed under pressure from the Confederación de Nacionalidades Indígenas del Ecuador (CONAIE—Confederation of Indigenous Nationalities of Ecuador, Ecuador's national indigenous movement) and disaffected segments of the military (*WRH* 11 March 2000; McConnell 2001). Despite active discussions with Argentina to develop a coordinated response to the collapse of democracy in Ecuador, words of condemnation from Itamaraty was chiefly noticeable for its absence and reduced to a prompt Rio Group statement calling for the maintenance of constitutionality and institutionality (interview with Brazilian diplomat). This added to efforts by the U.S. military attaché in Quito to persuade defense minister Gen. Carlos Mendoza to surrender power to the vice-president, Gustavo Noboa (*LAWR* 25 Jan. 2000; Foley 2000; Workers World 3 Feb. 2000). As one Brazilian official notes, the transfer in power from the provisional *junta de gobierno* to Mendoza and then to Noboa happened so quickly that there was no time for Itamaraty to prepare a formal response. Moreover, in the eyes of the Brazilian Foreign Ministry there was no need to take action beyond subscribing to the Rio Group's joint statement because after a very short period of uncertainty international pressure persuaded the military to follow the Constitution and support Noboa's installation as president.

The Ecuadorian example is useful because it frames Itamaraty's approach to the protection of democracy as revolving around the preservation of constitutionality—as seen in the Paraguayan case—and noninterference in the evolution of domestic political institutions. Moreover, Brazilian responses to the Paraguayan and Ecuadorian cases employed two regional groupings, Mercosul and the Rio Group. The combination of collective response and the eschewal of forceful external intervention set a precedent for Itamaraty's reaction to Peru's 2000 presidential election, a vote that was widely criticized by international observers (Cooper 2001).

One Brazilian official justified Itamaraty's restrained response to the January 2000 coup in Ecuador by emphasizing the difference between the end of Abdala Bucaram's presidency in 1997, where the entire executive branch was replaced without reference to the Constitution, and the forced resignation of Mahuad, which resulted in little variation in government programs and an eventual maintenance of constitutionality. What is striking in this official's statements is that he ignores the Ecuadorian military's conduct during the indigenous population's march on Quito in January 2000. With the presidential palace surrounded by protesting crowds, the high command of the Ecuadorian armed forces in effect mutinied, announcing that it would not protect the president should the uprising turn violent (*Financial Times* 22 Jan. 2000; *El País* 22 Jan. 2000). Furthermore, the marching indigenous were able to reach the capital only after the military allowed passage through a series of checkpoints intended to stop them. Underpinning these (non)actions was the persistence of an attitude within the armed forces that cast the institution as the protector of democracy, duty-bound to prevent an "illegitimate" government from holding office (Borja 1998).

From the point of view of Brazil's Foreign Ministry, however, these were simply unfortunate circumstances forming a backdrop to the more critical maintenance of constitutionality. As in the Paraguayan case, it emphasized the forms of constitutional governance, leaving the resolution of the political upheaval as an internal matter to be addressed through the appropriate legal mechanisms. This stance was also to mark the Brazilian response to democratic upheavals in Peru (2000) and Venezuela (2002).

Peru

The account of the 2000 Peruvian presidential election presented by Lewis Taylor (2001) is clear that the vote was surrounded by procedural irregularities and attempts at institutional manipulation. Indeed, the first-round ballot proved disastrous for the credibility of the election, with the official vote totals for Alberto Fujimori and the leading opposition candidate, Alejandro Toledo, being an almost exact inverse of exit poll results conducted by several respected nongovernmental organizations (NGOs). When combined with the decision of state-owned television networks to abandon election night coverage in favor of "B" movies, the immediate suggestion for many observers was that then-sitting president Alberto Fujimori was involved in a program of deceit to guarantee his own reelection (Taylor 2001, 11–14; *El País* 12 March 2000). With the Oficina Nacional de Procesos Electorales (ONPE—National Office of Electoral Procedures) ignoring OAS mission calls to delay the second round of voting (a suggestion Cardoso also made to Fujimori in a telephone call) in order to correct a number of technical shortcomings, including an unreliable computer system, Toledo announced that he would boycott the 28 May runoff (BBC 10 June 2000).

Hemispheric reaction to Fujimori's reelection was swift and divisive. While there was near unanimity that it would have been best if the second-round vote had been delayed in order to address the concerns raised by the OAS observers (OAS 2000), a North-South divide emerged around the legitimacy of the election. The United States was quick to question the probity of Fujimori's victory, convening a 31 May meeting of the OAS to consider applying Resolution 1080, which automatically excludes nondemocratic states from the organization.

Even though Fujimori admitted that some aspects of the second-round ballot were questionable (*AFP* 2 June 2000), the Latin American response to implementation of Resolution 1080 was not favorable. Commenting on the vote, Cardoso noted that, far from having experienced a coup, the people of Peru had taken part in an election and returned Fujimori to the presidential palace (*EFE News* 4 June 2000). Lampreia offered a blunter assessment that captured regional concerns:"The feeling is, that in a little while, no country in Latin America will be able to conduct its own elections" (*Washington Post* 3 June 2000).

The strong suggestion in the Cardoso and Lampreia statements is that intervention in the Peruvian case might erode respect for sovereignty throughout the region and herald the sort of subtle interference I alluded to earlier in this chapter. A subsequent director-general of Itamaraty's Americas Department amplified this position, explaining that, while his ministry certainly had no problem with the OAS or NGOs acting as reference sources, there was a sense that these bodies were becoming the main actors to the detriment of Peru's democratic development (A. Gonçalves 2002).

The middle ground between condemnation and an absence of comment on the vote was sought by Brazilian diplomats and articulated by Cardoso's suggestion at a June 2000 Rio Group Summit that a viable solution must respect state sovereignty without allowing "sovereignty" to become a shield for human rights violations and antidemocratic practices (*EFE News* 16 June 2000). For Itamaraty a central concern was that the Peruvian case might create a precedent allowing vocal NGOs and dissatisfied states to cancel elections viewed as unfavorable to their interests. Moreover, there was concern that the admittedly flawed reelection of Fujimori might open a new avenue for mandating the particulars of democracy, thereby opening the door for an embedding of the external influence that Itamaraty's democracy-protection policies were trying to avoid. Acquiescence was thus given to the Canadian proposal that an OAS mission be sent to Peru, provided it was limited to offering recommendations for reform and avoided activities that might be seen as passing judgment on the validity of the 2000 election.

The compromise reached in the OAS represented a signal failure to use the hemispheric body as an instrument to combat fraudulent elections in the region. Accusations of fraud were overlooked in part because many regional leaders wished to maintain their positive working relationship with Fujimori (McClintock 2001, 138).

While it certainly appears evident that Itamaraty wished to ensure Peruvian participation in the upcoming Brasília Presidential Summit, as Brazilian diplomats evaded questions about the questioned vote (Lampreia 2000a), this argument overlooks the reality of the report on the vote Stein drafted for the OAS, which criticizes prevoting procedures and preparations without actually branding the ballot an exercise in fraud and deceit (OAS 2000). Indeed, the implicit assumption of fraud is open to question: exit polls from independent monitors such as *Transparencia* mirrored the official ONPE results (Taylor 2001, 12). In this respect the Peruvian case appears to parallel the Paraguayan, where prevoting irregularities played an important role in the outcome of the election without actually derailing the marking and counting of ballots.

Thus, the same approach found in Paraguay emerged as the cornerstone of the position that Brazil, with strong support from Mexico and Venezuela, advocated for Peru through the Rio Group: democratic forms and practices must be the result of internal negotiation and agreement, not external imposition (BBC AL/W0644/S1; *AFP* 17 June 2000). During the extended public debate on the crisis Lampreia noted that the temptation to impose institutions or to propose specific measures and formulas to further democratization in Peru should be avoided (BBC AL/D3859). Indeed, the strong legacy of U.S. intervention in the region (P. Smith 2000), particularly in the creation and manipulation of democratic systems (Robinson 1996a; Herman and Chomsky 1994), mitigated against a welcoming response to North American proclamations that an election should be nullified.

The outcome in the Peruvian case was a restating of the principle of exclusion found in the Paraguayan and Ecuadorian cases. Again Itamaraty deployed regional groupings not only to prevent the creation of an interventionist precedent, but also to limit the role of extracontinental actors in state and continental affairs in South America, a consideration that was to prove crucial when Venezuelan president Hugo Chávez was briefly deposed in 2002.

Venezuela

Lampreia's suggestion that regional governments did not altogether trust U.S. attitudes toward democratic governance was seemingly supported by a patina of evidence as Venezuela's political crisis deepened in February 2002. Long before events in Caracas came to the near-insubordination of ranking military officers resigning as a public protest (*El País* 9 Feb. 2002; *El País* 19 Feb. 2002), there were suggestions in 2001 that the United States might look favorably on a carefully executed coup (Anderson 2001; Arvelaiz and Ponceleon 2002; Main et al. 2002). In the immediate aftermath of the 11 April 2002 rebellion that temporarily toppled Pres. Hugo Chávez, U.S. administration officials forcefully disavowed charges that they had either fomented or tacitly supported the action (Gutiérrez 2002). However, the credibility of this message was significantly diluted by the State Department's failure to speedily welcome the return of constitutionality after the coup collapsed. Instead, a senior U.S. government official working on Latin America refused to recognize the events in Caracas as a coup, noting that "legitimacy is something that is conferred not just by a majority of votes" (*Washington Times* 16 April 2002).

The Cardoso reaction to the toppling of the Chávez regime was significantly different from that of the Bush White House. Within hours of having heard that a coup had taken place in Caracas, officials in the Planalto Palace telephoned foreign minister Celso Lafer at the Rio Group Summit in Costa Rica and instructed him to organize a declaration condemning Venezuela's break with constitutionality. The Brazilian position was explained in the simplest possible terms by Lafer shortly after Chávez was returned to power: "There is no such thing as a good coup or a bad coup. A coup is a coup" (*DPA* 16 April 2002). Where reports indicated that U.S. officials were rumored to be advising the head of the provisional government in Caracas, paragraphs three and four of the 12 April Rio Group statement unequivocally condemned the coup and called for a restoration of constitutional rule (Grupo do Rio 2002). The differences between the Rio Group's and U.S. positions derailed any possible White House effort to remove Chávez from office (Hakim 2002).

Although the White House had fallen in line with the Rio Group's statement by 13 April, a great deal of damage had been done to the prodemocracy credentials of the key Latin American advisors on the Bush foreign-policy team. Indeed, a fundamental wariness about U.S. intentions in Venezuela appeared to underpin strong efforts by Cardoso to call off a U.S.-sponsored OAS meeting to discuss application of Resolution 1080. Addressing concerns that the session would be used to push a resolution condemning Chávez (Powell 2002), Brazil's ambassador to the OAS, Valter Pecly, bluntly noted that "if the assembly does not adopt a constructive position it will not pass a thing" (*DPA* 16 April 2002). In the end the assembly behaved much as Pecly had predicted, passing a resolution which applauded the return to constitutionality in Venezuela and recommended that OAS secretary-general, César Gaviria, offer his good offices to help resolve tensions in Caracas (OAS 2002). Indeed, the measures in the OAS resolution paralleled advice Cardoso offered to Chávez in a telephone call shortly after the coup, namely, that Chávez publicly forgive his opponents and seek reconciliation (Gutiérrez 2002).

Defending the U.S. government's reaction to the coup in Venezuela, U.S. principal deputy assistant secretary of state for Western Hemisphere affairs, Lino Gutiérrez, suggested that his critics reexamine the Rio Group's statement and noted in particular that rather than calling for Chávez' return to office it focused on the holding of free elections (Gutiérrez 2002). Indeed, Gutiérrez might have gone further and pointed out that keeping Chávez in the presidency might prove central to Cardoso administration plans to use Venezuelan hydroelectric power in Brazil's Northeast. In either case the critique missed the point of the stance Brazil urged through the Rio Group, namely, that any solution to the political crisis in Venezuela must follow that country's constitutional norms.

Arguably, the call for fresh elections and respect for the Constitution would have ensured Brazilian interests in Venezuela by seeing a Chávez ally elevated to the presidency. But by rejecting the legitimacy of the Pedro Carmona regime and calling for implementation of the constitutionally mandated mechanisms of succession, the Cardoso administration was able to distance itself from suggestions that it was trying to influence the course of Venezuelan politics. Indeed, the sharp contrast between the soft sounds of regret uttered by U.S. policymakers and the rapid condemnation coordinated by Itamaraty created the impression that the Bush White House was returning to the arbitrariness that marked the Monroe Doctrine. Success in recruiting regional support to block U.S. intervention in Peru and Venezuela as well as preventing democratic collapse in Paraguay and Ecuador allowed Itamaraty to develop an ambience of regional democratic solidity.

In Kantian terms a sense of democratic permanence has obvious implications for the prevention of future conflicts. But perhaps of greater importance in this case was the impact that Itamaraty's style of protecting democracy had on creating the underlying conditions for a long-term sustainable peace. Repeated public expressions of faith in the electorate in neighboring countries helped lay foundation stones for the ideational aspect outlined in Chapter 3 and positioned democracy as a unifying idea for a potential future South American security community.

Integrating Peace

The clear preference within Itamaraty for leading a collectivized approach to intraregional security threats is readily apparent in such initiatives as the 1986 declaration of the South Atlantic as a Zone of Peace and Cooperation and the 2002 Guayaquil declaration of South America as a Zone of Peace. But before the long-term ambitions for a continental security community could be realized existing and potential intracontinental conflicts first needed addressing (Mansfield et al. 1999–2000). Although this task was significantly eased for Brazilian diplomats by the rarity of interstate armed conflict in twentieth-century South America, persistent tensions remained. One such dispute, the long-simmering border war between Ecuador and Peru, erupted into limited combat operations in the Cenapa Valley within weeks of Cardoso's assuming office in 1995 (Palmer 1997). In retrospect, Lampreia (2002 and 1999a) classified Itamaraty's role in brokering an end to the forty-four-year-old conflict as one of the most important moments in Cardoso's foreign-policy agenda. On an immediate level it established Brazil as a credible interlocutor in regional conflicts, one able to bring about peace through discussion rather than military-led imposition. It also offered Itamaraty an opportunity to formulate a subtler approach to a simmering continental border dispute by deploying the mechanisms of regionalism found in Mercosul; this approach would emerge as a tangential aspect of the IIRSA process. Both of the cases presented in this section are important to the development of the security aspect of Itamaraty's larger South American project because they demonstrate that oblique collective diplomacy rather than military imposition can be crucial for the provision of security on a continental level.

Building Peace—Ecuador versus Peru

The decision not to employ regional groupings such as the OAS or the Rio Group as a strategy for resolving the Ecuador-Peru conflict afforded Brazilian diplomats an opportunity to firmly establish a reputation for advancing the cause of security and stability in the continent (E. Oliveira 1999). However, suggestions that Brazilian-led efforts to end the dispute demonstrate an ability to manage South American affairs must account for the presence of the United States along with Argentina, Brazil, and Chile in the group-of-four guarantor countries seeking to apply the 1942 Protocolo de Rio de Janeiro. Although the final stages of the negotiations in 1998 were dominated by announcements made in Brasília, the Ecuadorian president, Jamil Mahuad, and the Peruvian president, Alberto Fujimori, still visited the White House in search of what seemed to be the benediction of President Clinton. Nevertheless, the abiding reality of the peace negotiations was their diplomatic and military direction from Brasília, with the United States effectively minimizing its role when a rapid resolution to the conflict appeared unlikely. More to the point, the final peace strategy pursued by the guarantor nations—a 10 October 1998 letter received by each of the belligerents offering a process of binding arbitration— was covered by the Ecuadorian press in a manner which explicitly recognized Brazilian leadership in the process (*El Comercio* 11 Oct. 1998).

Significantly, the peace deal signed by Ecuador and Peru in Brasília on 26 October 1998 was the result of a process of binding arbitration. The offer of arbitration that came after three and half years of mediation was contingent on each country's agreeing to the text sight unseen. While Ecuadorian commentators greeted this option with open arms, the Peruvian reaction was more subdued, indicative of a sentiment that the country would be surrendering a position of strength (*El Comercio* 12 Oct. 1998).

For Brazilian diplomats acceptance of the arbitration offer was support for Itamaraty's larger goal of forming a continental security community because it clearly indicated that neither country feared an imposed settlement as a pretext for Brazilian (neo)imperialistic intervention. More significant was the leading role Itamaraty played in conceptualizing and drafting the final text formalizing the details of the agreement, a factor which perhaps mitigated Ecuadorian and Peruvian concerns that the United States might be trying to manipulate the process. On a larger level, the handling of the arbitration document highlighted Brazil's capacity to engage in the diplomatic tasks of leadership in the security realm in the inclusive manner necessary for the elaboration of a continent-wide security community.

As one Brazilian official close to the peace process noted, Itamaraty's involvement in ending the war was dominated by two priorities. The first and perhaps most significant goal for long-term formulation of common South American approaches to hemispheric and global challenges was to establish a substantial peace. A simple signing of yet another treaty was not considered adequate. Instead, the aim was to radically reconfigure all levels of relations between Ecuador and Peru to make peace a reality sustained by a dense network of transnational linkages. At the early 1998 ceremony announcing a timetable to complete the peace process Lampreia dwelt extensively on the importance of the basic elements of integration in the Ecuador-Peru case that would eventually form the core of IIRSA. Peace and the mobilization of popular support for peace was predicated on a strengthening of communication and transportation linkages between Ecuador and Peru, with particular emphasis being given to the restoration of free navigation on the Amazon and its tributaries. The goal was to establish a sense of solidarity and fraternity between people on both sides of the border (Lampreia 1998b). As Brazilian officials noted, elaboration of the infrastructure linkages necessary to create this sense of shared community and interest was critical for overcoming the unrealistic expectations which some parties brought to the negotiating table (Lampreia 1999a, 217); this allowed a final settlement to emerge that was palatable to both sides of the conflict.

The second goal identified by Itamaraty was to use Brazilian leadership to develop new forms of relations with other countries on the continent as well as with the United States. In this respect the emphasis was on demonstrating that Brazil possessed the diplomatic and military capacity to disentangle the entrenched antagonisms perpetuating some of the region's simmering border disputes.

On the military front a new chapter in international cooperation was opened when the Pentagon acquiesced, and the Chilean as well as the Argentine armed forces agreed to Brazilian leadership of the Missão de Observadores Militares Equador/Peru (MOMEP—Military Observer Mission Ecuador/ Peru). Although the command structure of MOMEP formally indicated that the operation would be run by four coequal colonels, the role of coordinating activities was given to a Brazilian, with the U.S. military providing logistical and airlift support. As U.S. colonel Glenn R. Weidner (1999, 48) notes, the Pentagon's decision to retain veto power over the deployment of U.S. helicopters implicitly challenged the authority of the Brazilian commander in the initial stages of the operation, but nevertheless entailed formal acceptance of Brazilian command over the combined force.

Different appraisals about how long it should take to settle the conflict led to the United States' withdrawing the transportation and communications infrastructure being used by MOMEP just twelve months after the mission started. This presented an opportunity for Itamaraty and the Brazilian military to demonstrate a capacity to deal concretely with regional issues without logistical or operational support from the United States. The decision was made in Brasília to expand the country's leadership role in MOMEP not only by purchasing four Blackhawk helicopters and dedicating two fixed-wing aircraft to the mission, but also by absorbing the costs of establishing and maintaining a communications network for the observer mission along the contested Amazonian border (Cannabrava 1997). The observation Eliézer Rizzo de Oliveira (1999, 148) offers about Brazil's expanded role in MOMEP is that it provided concrete proof that the country was able to undertake and coordinate the military aspect of a response to a regional crisis. This capacity could prove crucial in the elaboration of a cooperative, continent-wide security policy that was not dependent on external assistance.

Perhaps more important than the capacity to interpose a monitoring force between the two combatants was the ability to keep the Ecuadorian and Peruvian governments engaged in a meaningful dialogue. Itamaraty's success at this task was due to a sensitive understanding of the dynamics of the conflict as well as recognition that the ostensibly trivial could carry tremendous symbolic importance. Patience and understanding, Lampreia (2002) explained in our interview, were the keys to managing the contending sensitivities of the belligerents (see also Oliveira 1999, 154).

Recognizing that dealing with the entire conflict in one session would prove unmanageable, Brazilian diplomats proposed breaking the negotiations into parallel sessions, with a single-undertaking approach being adopted to assuage Ecuadorian concerns that they would be tied to an unfavorable partially completed agreement (Herz and Nogueira 2002; Palmer 1997). Four negotiating panels were established—land border demarcation; navigation and commerce; border economic integration; and security-building measures—with the most contentious issues being set aside for future consideration through a process called "subsistent impasses." Although both sides were subjected to tremendous international pressure to settle the dispute, there was a realization within Itamaraty that the preexisting state of bilateral Ecuador-Peru relations made lasting peace a questionable prospect. It is on this point that the choice of the four negotiating panels, three of which had little to do with the direct cause of the conflict, emerge as part of a concerted strategy to construct a "new reality" between the two countries.

Rather than beginning with the specifics of the conflict—the main subsistent impasse, which dealt with disagreement over the line that the border should follow through the Cenapa Valley—Brazilian diplomats focused their attention on breaking the cycle of antagonism that had kept the dispute simmering for over forty years. The idea was to shift the problem from one of competition, implying a win-lose dynamic, to one of problem solving, which carried strong possibilities for mutual benefit. The mediation process, particularly through the use of the last three negotiating panels, concentrated on actively involving the belligerents in a search for ways to exploit the opportunities that would come with normalized relations (Herz and Nogueira 2002, 86–87).

In addition to the expansion of infrastructure linkages that would allow grass-roots ownership of the peace, attention was given to obtaining funding from international development agencies to stimulate border-zone integration. Although the goal of U.S.$1 billion spread over ten years was not reached, the Inter-American Development Bank (IADB) committed U.S.$500 million for projects along the Ecuador-Peru border.

In a strategy that recalls our earlier discussion of the democratic theory of peace, development financing was used to encourage businesses on either side of the border to explore joint-venture possibilities in the hope that a rise in interdependence might obviate a renewal of hostilities by making war excessively costly (*El Universo* 26 Oct. 1998). The guarantor nations also engaged in a pro–peace marketing campaign, holding seminars and conferences to encourage the understanding and interpersonal linkages necessary to break the cycle of hostility.

While the prospect of large volumes of development funding from the IADB certainly helped build support for the October 1998 agreement, the impact was not quite as great as might be expected. Polling numbers collected by the Brazilian embassy in Quito suggested that, before details of the agreement were released, which included the announcements of multilateral financing, support for peace stood at about 60 percent, a figure which rose into the 70 percent range on publication of the treaty's text. Rather than focusing on increased aid flows, public figures and the media emphasized the returns that could be gained from expanded bilateral trade. Indeed, a sort of peace-induced euphoria after the signing of the treaty in Brasília prompted optimistic talk of complete market integration between the two countries (*El Universo* 6 Nov. 1998). More sedate reaction focused on the expansion of business opportunities that would come with normalized bilateral relations (*El Comercio* 1 Nov. 1998).

Smoothing Away Tensions—IIRSA

Addressing the importance of the final settlement in the Ecuador-Peru war, Lampreia (2002) noted in our interview that the persistence of animosities along the frontier "would have disqualified the concept of South America," creating a significant block to a continent-wide security community, let alone the project of consensual hegemony. While the conflict settled in 1998 was certainly the most extreme manifestation of cross-border tensions in the continent, it was not the only one. For the South American project first articulated during Cardoso's tenure as foreign minister to progress a critical question Itamaraty needed to address was the persistence of border tensions throughout the region. In the Ecuador-Peru conflict the emphasis Itamaraty placed on fomenting positive bilateral relations through the elaboration of expanded infrastructure and societal linkages found symbolic expression after the peace agreement in assistance with the construction of a bridge across the border.

The principle underlying this act, that ease of transnational interaction is the best method of reducing the tensions which lead to a shooting war, was to become imbedded in the IIRSA process launched at the 2000 Brasília Presidential Summit. Indeed, an examination of the twelve infrastructure axes proposed by Brazil and adopted by the continent's presidents in the IIRSA plan reveals that the corridors of development have been formulated without reference to existing tensions in a range of bilateral relationships. Guyana thus finds itself in the middle of an axis linking it to Brazil as well as Venezuela and Suriname, two countries with which it has standing territorial disputes (Jagdeo 2000; Guyana 2000a and 2000b). The Bolivian role in three proposed routes for a bioceanic corridor requires close cooperation with Chile, which could necessitate formal recantation of standing claims for a wedge of national territory providing access to the Pacific Ocean. Ecuador and Peru, building on the understanding that came from the end of their war, are crisscrossed by coastal, bioceanic, and trans-Andean infrastructure networks. Returning again to our initial discussion of peace and democracy in Brazil's security policy, the suggestion that emerges here is that Itamaraty consciously sought to deploy interdependence as a device to advance the sense of security and stability needed to make the South American regional project a sustainable reality.

Indications of Itamaraty's intention to deploy the infrastructure axes as subtle tools for reducing persistent tensions in the region can be found in unofficial reactions to the 2002 Guayaquil Presidential Summit's announcement that Venezuela and Guyana wished to construct a road across their disputed frontier. As one ranking diplomat explains, the unveiling of this new project came as a pleasant surprise. At an IIRSA ministerial meeting six months before the Guayaquil Summit the Venezuelan representative had proposed reformulating the Venezuela-Brazil-Guyana-Suriname axis into two axes in an attempt to avoid discussing the disputed Essequibo area in Guyana. The proposal was rejected by ministers from the other countries specifically because there was a consensus that political factors should not influence the design of axes which were intended to function as long-term, sustainable development instruments (A. Gonçalves 2002).

In terms of fostering a continental environment that reduces the possibility of armed interstate conflict, the willingness of Venezuelan authorities to accept the IIRSA consensus provides some evidence that the same logic implemented in the Ecuador-Peru conflict—defusing persistent sources of conflict through integration—may prove effective in a wider South American context. This suggestion becomes stronger when consideration is given to the tumultuous state of politics in both Guyana and Venezuela, a reality that might otherwise prompt a rise in nationalist rhetoric as a diversionary tactic.

An examination of the list of projects being pursued under the IIRSA framework in 2002 reveals a concerted effort to create a perimeter reaching from the northern shores of the continent, around the Colombian tip of the Andes, and down the western side of South America. The change in position by the Venezuelan and Guyanese governments had larger implications for the security aspect of the South American project, suggesting that intracontinental disputes could be effectively addressed through the mechanisms developed during the resolution of the Ecuador- Peru conflict. Indeed, diplomats within Itamaraty appeared to view the bilateral approximation of Brazil's northern neighbors as evidence that the potential economic gains of participation in the IIRSA process were of sufficient magnitude to resolve lingering bilateral disagreements throughout the continent (A. Gonçalves 2002; Sistema Económico Latinoamericano y del Caribe [hereafter SELA] 2002). This was particularly important along the northern coast of South America, where tensions simmered between Colombia and Venezuela and Guyanese relations with Suriname had threatened to erupt into broader conflict (Guyana 2000a). In this instance heavy emphasis was placed on the futility of a border war, prompting interest in the possibilities inherent in improved bilateral relations.

Such logic found a parallel in the evolution of Bolivia-Chile relations after the development of Bolivia's large natural gas reserves. As was discussed in the previous chapter, Chilean firms proved particularly interested in the expanded business and transshipment opportunities opened by Bolivia's approximation to Brazil. The subsequent increased importance attributed to this bilateral relationship found a somewhat perverse expression during the 2002 Guayaquil

Summit when Chilean president Lagos announced that he would not be attending the inauguration of Bolivian president-elect Gonzalo Sánchez de Lozada. Extensive discussions with Sánchez' predecessor about the construction of a pipeline to a Chilean port to ship liquefied natural gas to the United States met with success, suggesting that there was sufficient governmental will to set aside over a century of antagonism in favor of cooperative economic development. But the viability of the project was cast into doubt by the rancorous tone of Bolivia's presidential election and the proclivity of some candidates to draw on a nationalist sentiment by reviving memories of the 1879–1883 War of the Pacific and its relation to the proposed pipeline route. While the reference to historical grievances with Chile was certainly not a new phenomenon in Bolivian politics, Lagos' reaction points to a deeper transformation percolating in the political economy of South America.

Where strategic thinking in both economic and security terms used to be heavily directed toward the United States and Europe, a slow reorientation toward South American opportunities and solutions was emerging. This bolstered the Brazilian strategy of lessening the influence of extracontinental actors in South America and solidifying the continent as a viable geopolitical entity. Here the patient construction of a consensual hegemony—the weaving of a tapestry of interlocking ideas and economic aspirations—was important, leading to the shared conceptualization of national and regional interests necessary to foster an internally sustainable security framework. Moreover, the emerging security framework was one that explicitly excluded armed conflict between South American states as a viable diplomatic strategy. The challenge facing policymakers, however, was that the state was not the only armed actor in the continent, raising the question of how the consensual hegemonic project might deal with new, nonstate-based security threats.

New Security Threats

Itamaraty's approach to protecting democracy and preventing the outbreak of war in South America was marked by the use of indirect influence to bring about subtle changes in thought and redirection of attention through regional instruments such as Mercosul, the Rio Group, and IIRSA. In what could well be a simultaneous statement of praise and warning about the security policy followed during the Cardoso era, Hurrell's discussion of the new Latin American security reality gives credit to regionalism as a force for peace and stability in traditional security areas such as the prevention of war and the preservation of national sovereignty, but with a crucial caveat. While the increased interdependence that comes with regionalism fosters the reduction in tensions and growth in trust needed for the construction of a security community, the rise in interconnectedness also makes each state more vulnerable to new transnationalized security issues such as narco-trafficking, insurgency, and terrorism (Hurrell 1998b, 539–540). This presented a challenge to Itamaraty's strategic goal of excluding external interference in domestic Brazilian affairs and seeking a measure of internal self-sufficiency for South American security. The implication of Hurrell's observation is that effective policy dealing with the new security issues must be transnationalized, requiring international cooperation and a willingness to become involved in the internal affairs of other countries.

Awareness of the danger highlighted by Hurrell is suggested both in a 2000 speech Cardoso (2000g) gave to the Fourth Conference of Defense Ministers of the Americas, and in paragraph 2.12 of the 1996 PDN, which notes that threats to Brazilian security can emanate from insurgency and criminal activities in neighboring countries, particularly in the Amazon region. Yet despite the awareness that some of the deepest threats to Brazilian security were now transnational and nonstate-based in nature (*LAWR* 22 Nov. 1996), foreign policy in these areas remained remarkably defensive during the Cardoso era, seeking to exclude the problem from the national territory rather than engaging in a proactive policy of regional engagement. The Itamaraty response to the new security agenda thus emerges as a mix of attempts at cooperation and exclusion. In each instance the pattern of opting for diplomatic measures and strong rhetoric in place of concrete action in the areas of protecting democracy and preventing armed conflict remained prevalent.

Narco-trafficking

By the late 1980s the U.S. focus on closing existing drug-smuggling routes from Colombia had resulted in a redirection of narcotics trafficking through Brazil and increased use of an Amazonian coca variant known as *epadu* (Mora 1996). The shift in transshipment routes also brought a corresponding rise in the availability and use of narcotics in Brazil. In addition to the socioeconomic problems caused by an increase in the proportion of the population addicted to illegal drugs, the Brazilian state's control over the national territory loosened as three main integrated smuggling rings developed and entered into cooperative agreements with suppliers and distributors in other countries (Procópio and Vaz 1997). In part the problem was that the Brazilian armed forces and police had no way of tracking activities in the vast Amazonian jungle, let alone patrolling urban *favelas*.

One initiative that was intended to help with issues such as drug smuggling was Calha Norte. President Sarney initiated the Programa Calha Norte (Northern Gutter Program), creating a series of new communities and military installations in the border areas north of the Solimões and Amazon rivers. Using these new settlements as bases, the armed forces implemented a schedule of regular patrols meant to deter border incursions. Embedded within the national security prerogatives of Calha Norte was a state-building exercise, which called on the military to provide some of the basic social services such as health care and education that were intended to generate a sense of belonging within the Brazilian nation. Indeed, the social element, working to advance national security by permanently populating the region with Brazilians, was arguably the initial priority (Ministerio de Defesa).

The problem with respect to narco-trafficking is that Calha Norte created only a porous buffer against land- and river-based smuggling. It was a relatively simple matter for drug runners to use small planes to fly between rough landing strips hacked out of the forest. As a Brazilian Air Force brigadier explained, five radar stations provided patchy cover of the Amazon basin, making it one of the world's largest air traffic control blind spots (*Newsweek* 28 Oct. 2002).

Concern about the resultant lack of state control in the Amazon rose throughout the 1990s, particularly after the United States expanded its antidrug program and began conceptualizing the preliminary elements of Plan Colombia and applying pressure on the Cardoso administration to close the smuggling networks (AP 31 March 1996).

Lingering concerns from the late 1980s and early 1990s that human rights and environmental protection might become a pretext for transforming the Amazon into an international protectorate similar to Antarctica found new incarnation in the drug debate (Cavagnari Filho 2002; *New York Times* 19 Nov. 1991). In addition to the obvious threat presented by drug-induced socioeconomic tensions, a significant concern voiced by the Brazilian military was that the fight against narco-trafficking might be used as a pretext within the context of the U.S. War on Drugs to establish a permanent foreign military presence in the Amazon region, and a possible future attempt at controlling the area's natural resources.

Yet despite the clear recognition that the drug issue presented a threat to traditional and new conceptions of national security, the Brazilian military staunchly resisted efforts to directly involve it in drug-interdiction programs.

Instead the Defense Ministry emphasized expanded police action and international cooperation as the appropriate response to narco-trafficking and organized crime (Quintão 2000), holding military units in reserve to provide combat and logistical support to Brazil's antidrug police units. To a certain extent military planners saw room for an overlap in police and military functions, particularly in the Amazon, with law enforcement's antidrug activities effectively defending the national territory through a blocking action in border areas (BBC AL/D3939/L). While such propositions drew on increases in police patrols seeking narco-traffickers (*AFP* 31 August 2000), the underlying assumption was that smugglers and guerrillas could be excluded from Brazil, which was made problematic by a lack of real-time intelligence. As one observer noted, even with accurate intelligence, efforts to control transnational criminal activity were severely hampered by a lack of substantive regional cooperation and the comparative weakness of neighboring military and police units (Krause 2002).

The inability to track and prevent the movements of narco- traffickers in Amazônia became a major concern for U.S. policymakers in the 1990s, with particular emphasis being placed on the inability to curtail smuggling flights along the eastern side of the Andean cordillera. Under mounting pressure to allow the United States to establish some sort of monitoring capacity in the Amazon, Cardoso responded by creating the Sistema de Vigilância da Amazônia (Sivam—Amazon Vigilance System), an integrated network of radar stations, satellites, aircraft, and motion detectors capable of monitoring forest overflights and movements along the ground and rivers. Although the Sivam project was assembled by U.S. defense contractor Raytheon and benefited from U.S. military advice, ownership and control remained in Brazilian hands.

In political terms Sivam was presented as an inwardly directed project designed to ensure that Brazilians were able to retain control over their own national territory. But the monitoring capabilities of Sivam extended well beyond Brazilian national territory, especially in the extreme northwest of the country along the border with Colombia and Venezuela (an area known as the Dog's Head) where narco-trafficking and guerrilla activity were concentrated.

While Sivam's strategic implications for U.S. antidrug strategies in neighboring countries were obvious, U.S. offers to systematically share data with Brazil did not occur until the final stages of the Cardoso administration (*Bulletin of Atomic Scientists* 2003; *Liberation* 30 July 2002). Indeed, with a U.S. Air Force officer classifying Sivam-operating Brazil as "a linchpin in South America" (Krause 2002), the integrated surveillance system emerged as a powerful bargaining chip in bi- and multilateral negotiations about how security threats such as narco-trafficking should be addressed.

As Cardoso explained to a 1998 Special Session of the UN General Assembly, Brazil's approach to countering narcotics operated around two main pillars, demonstrating a fundamental divergence from the U.S. approach. Rather than expressing the issue as the supply-driven, externally imposed threat suggested by the U.S. War on Drugs, the Brazilian response placed primary emphasis on demand reduction, which in effect identified consuming countries as the cause of drug production (Cardoso 1998b). Narco-trafficking thus became a global issue, one requiring a cooperative approach.

With this principle in mind the Cardoso administration concluded a series of treaties with neighboring countries to restrict the flow of narcotics, precursor chemicals, and drug money. Although the agreements encompassed cooperation on the tracking and apprehension of narco-traffickers, suggestions of Plan Colombia–style direct intervention were assiduously avoided. Indeed, paragraphs 48–51 of the 2000 *Brasília Communiqué* specifically call for adherence to multilateral approaches to combating and evaluating drug trafficking.

Again, the guiding principle of any multilateral initiative was to be cooperation, not the creation of new, transnational paramilitary forces with the authority to operate freely across national frontiers (Oppenheimer 2003). In keeping with this noninterventionist stance serious suggestions from Brazilian policymakers that Sivam coverage might embrace border regions in neighboring countries were not made until the final stages of the Cardoso era, and then on a cost-recovery basis focusing on bilateral linkages that implicitly challenged U.S. efforts to incorporate the radar system into a wider version of Plan Colombia or the Andean Regional Initiative (Beers 2001; Amatangelo 2001).

The launch of Sivam was also accompanied by a financial and human recapitalization of Calha Norte and an expansion of police drug-interdiction programs through Operation Cobra, providing the military and police with the resources needed for a rapid response to new intelligence (BBC AL/W0646/ S1; *Gazeta Mercantil Invest News* 17 Oct. 2000; *AFP* 1 Nov. 200; *OESP* 16 Sept. 2000). Again, the focus was largely inward, relying on corresponding efforts by antidrug forces in neighboring countries to slow the flow of narcotics as a knock-on effect of largely independently formulated and pursued programs.

The pattern that emerged in Amazônia was repeated in the triple frontier border area between Brazil, Argentina, and Paraguay, where pressure to curb contraband and narco-trafficking networks around the Paraguayan border city of Ciudad del Este did not extend to direct Brazilian intervention. In an area where illicit economic activity was rife (Goldberg 2002; Aquino 1997), efforts were instead restricted to stop-and-search patrols on the Brazilian side of the border, the pursuit of a mechanism for coordinating regional police activities (Pion-Berlin 2000, 53–54), and the creation of investment protocols designed to encourage the emergence of a legitimate business sector distinct from the Colorado Party and the military (interviews with Brazilian diplomats).

The approach differed fundamentally from that in Plan Colombia, which included the active involvement of U.S. armed forces personnel in monitoring drug activity and missions to destroy coca plantations and processing facilities. Indeed, this is precisely the sort of policing role Itamaraty tried to avoid, in part because Brazil lacked the necessary financial and military resources, but also because it ran against the tradition of strictly respecting the sovereignty of other states. Again, there was a conscious effort on the part of Itamaraty policymakers to avoid precedents that might be used at a later date to justify unwanted external intervention in Brazilian affairs (U.S. State Department 2002). Instead, there emerged a preference for the sort of ideas set out in paragraph 52 of the 2000 *Brasília Communiqué*. This focused on the development of internal institutions and capabilities in each country, a view which also encompassed the recognition that drug-related security threats were partially driven by the economic, political, and social shortcomings prevalent in the continent. Within this context initiatives such as Sivam and Calha Norte emerged as the central instruments on which a cooperative subregional approach to the drugs issue might be constructed, one which need not depend on or countenance a strong U.S. presence in South America.

The problem with the cooperative approach envisioned by Brazil is that it required an operation similar to Calha Norte from each country, which would have the effect of stifling drug flows by closing border areas to narco-traffickers. But as has been noted, Brazil's neighbors had a limited capability to make the presence of the state felt beyond areas immediately surrounding border crossing points and major transportation arteries (Krause 2002; Mendel 1998). In the Southern Cone the narco-trafficking situation was complicated by Paraguay's political reality. Brazil supplied much of the Paraguayan military's equipment and advanced training (Pion-Berlin 2000, 56–57), suggesting that cooperation to fight narco-trafficking could be easily facilitated, except that it was the police who ran antidrug programs in both countries. More to the point, the reason for the Paraguayan military's reticence is attributed by some observers to

an ambiguous combination of a stated desire to maintain institutional professionalism and suspicions that some high-ranking officers were involved in drug
trafficking (Fournier and Burges 2000, 20–21). Persistent efforts to encourage
the Paraguayan military to help reduce the flow of arms, illegal goods, and
narcotics through the triple frontier area, including the 1996 formation of the
Tripartite Command of the Triple Frontier and the 1999 Mercosul approval
of the Plan for Reciprocal Cooperation and Coordination for Regional Security (A. Cardoso 2002), met with official approval in Asunción, but lackluster
implementation in Ciudad del Este (*Telam News Agency* 27 May 1998; BBC
AL/D3239/L). The implication is that on paper the Itamaraty strategy of creating intracontinental mechanisms to advance South American security was
a success, but that reality offered a more pessimistic picture, one which called
for a more active coordinating role from Brazil that might involve negotiated
transgression of the traditional policy of strictly respecting the sovereignty of
other states.

Insurgency and Terrorism

Suggestions that the Cardoso administration's approach to the construction of
an internally sustainable South American security system faltered because of
an unwillingness to pursue a more engaged policy had direct application to the
Colombian border and the operation of the guerrilla Fuerzas Armadas Revo-
lucionario Colombiano (FARC—Colombian Revolutionary Armed Forces).
Indeed, consideration of FARC significantly complicates the narco-trafficking
question because the guerrilla army turned the provision of protection and
logistical assistance to the drug cartels into a lucrative fund-raising operation.

The official Brazilian position, however, looked past the intertwining of
narco-trafficking and insurgency in Colombia. Policymakers discounted the
potential threat the guerrillas might pose for the Amazon region, preferring to
treat the issue as an internal Colombian matter (*AFP* 5 Sept. 2000). The logic
underpinning this stance recalled the Ecuador-Peru border conflict, where
Brazil drew on its noninterventionist history in South America to fill the role
of an intermediary viewed as honest and trustworthy by both disputants (Corrêa 1999b).

Efforts to similarly position Brazil for a future role as mediator in the Colombian civil war had practical policy implications during the Cardoso era,
leading to some reticence in bilateral relations. One mark of this caution was
the cancellation of an agreement that allowed the Colombian military emer-
gency use of a Brazilian base after it became apparent that the aircraft evacu-

ating wounded soldiers were also delivering reinforcements to engage FARC (*AFP* 6 Nov. 2000).

Despite Itamaraty's unwillingness to give the appearance of being officially involved in Colombia's insurgency problem, the Brazilian military devoted considerable effort to excluding FARC and Peru's Sendero Luminoso (Shining Path) from Brazil. In September 1998 reports emerged that Brazilian special forces had been scrambled to deal with FARC units that were fleeing a Colombian antiguerrilla operation (BBC AL/D3334/L). Similar reports surfaced again in June 1999 after military intelligence services received indications that both FARC and the Sendero Luminoso had established support bases in Brazilian territory (BBC AL/D3582/L).

As in the case of narco-trafficking, attention was turned to improving the military's capacity to exclude neighboring guerrilla armies from Brazilian territory (Mendel 1999). An expansion of the human and physical capacity of Calha Norte was accompanied by an increase in patrol activity as well as a series of large maneuvers and training exercises intended to intimidate guerrilla units (*Valor Econômico* 15–06–2000; BBC AL/W0646/S1). Yet, just as in the case of narco-trafficking, the construction of this security barrier proved only partially effective. Members of FARC and other regional insurgency groups remained a persistent presence, albeit one that exercised considerable discretion in its movements and activities. For example, FARC developed a network of jungle pathways that were used to export narcotics and import arms from countries such as Brazil and Ecuador (*AFP* 26 March 2001). Indeed, the capture in Colombia of Luis Fernando da Costa (better known as Fernandinho Beira-Mar), head of the Rio de Janeiro drug gang Comando Vermelho, came as part of an operation seeking to close down a FARC-run drug and arms network (*AFP* 22 April 2001).

An unwillingness to become embroiled in the domestic political dynamics of Colombia's civil war despite its overflow into Amazônia and, via drug trafficking, the *favelas* of major cities was also apparent in Itamaraty's reaction to post–11 September 2001 suggestions that terrorist cells operated in the "ungoverned space" around the Paraguayan city of Ciudad del Este (Oppenheimer 2003; Goldberg 2002). Where U.S. officials made clear their view that Ciudad del Este was an Islamic terrorist base, Brazilian reaction was somewhat more sanguine (VOA 10 Jan. 2003; *LAWR*-WR-02–42; *New York Times* 15 Dec. 2002). With the notable exception of two early-1990s bombings in Buenos Aires, the alleged activities of supposed Islamic terrorist cells presented little in the way of immediate regional security threats to either Mercosul or Brazilian interests. The lack of a popularly perceived threat in the area was highlighted by the large street protests that greeted crackdowns on the Arab residents of Ciudad del Este and the neighboring Brazilian city of Foz de Iguaçu after the attacks on Washington and New York (*Washington Times* 13 Nov. 2001).

More telling was the outcome of a 2002 "3+1" antiterrorism meeting between Argentine, Brazilian, Paraguayan, and U.S. officials. Far from calling for the establishment of a regional antiterror squad, the declaration released by the participants found no evidence that Islamic terrorists were active in the Southern Cone (Argentina 2002). The focus was instead placed on deepening and continuing earlier subregional plans to expand cooperation to combat crime and terror within Mercosul (Miyamoto 2000). Again, the emphasis was on reducing extracontinental interference as part of a larger strategy to bolster intra–South American security frameworks, a policy that saw signs of progress with a 2001 Uruguayan proposal to create a Mercosul permanent working group to coordinate member-state antiterror programs (*Vale Pariabano* 30 Sept. 2001). However, the emphasis remained on cooperation between existing police forces and military units (A. Cardoso 2002), leaving suggestions ranging from of a transnationalized regional response to possible participation of Uruguayan forces as an observer unit in the triple frontier area (*AFP* 8 June 2001).

Here we return again to the major flaw in the security vision Brazilian policymakers elaborated for South America. The clear suggestion in discussions about the new security threats such as narcotics, terrorism, and insurgency was that the most appropriate plan of action involved an enhancement of coordination and cooperation between the relevant national institutions. To this end Itamaraty and the Brazilian security services concluded a raft of protocols and inserted promises for expanded cooperation in a stream of multilateral agreements, including the declarations of the two South American Presidential Summits. Overlooked in this flurry of diplomatic activity was the disparity in the capability of each country to contribute to the collective provision of regional security. The obvious solution would appear to have been the formation of some sort of continental policing unit along the lines of something like NATO or the MOMEP observer force, particularly one tasked with combating narcotics and insurgency movements. But such an undertaking would have required substantial levels of trust between armed forces that remained wary of each other despite a cascading series of symbolic joint exercises and protocols that culminated in the 2002 declaration of South America as a Zone of Peace (Pion-Berlin 2000, 63). Moreover, it would have required Brazilian confidence in the security services of neighboring countries, something that my interviews with Itamaraty officials suggest was weak, at best. The new security agenda thus points to an underlying dynamic suggesting that even within Mercosul substantive economic and political approximation was not viewed as an irreversible trend capable of banishing suspicions of more traditional military rivalry.

Conclusion

Itamaraty's goal of forming an internally sustainable security structure for South America emerges as a partial success. Certainly Brazil emerged as a credible defender of the national-sovereignty norm in the continent, building on a track record of acting in good faith. Yet traditional threats to national sovereignty were not the major security concern in a continent markedly free of armed interstate conflict; the destabilizing actions of narco-traffickers as well as insurgency and terrorist groups presented the most pressing threats to states in the region. Here Itamaraty's reliance on national sovereignty resulted in a policy stance that sought to exclude these new threats from Brazil, treating the issue as an internal matter that could be addressed in a coordinated, although individualized, manner. Founded on the foreign-policy precepts set out by Rio Branco—strict respect for sovereignty and studied noninterference in the internal affairs of other states—the security policy pursued by Itamaraty proved best when dealing with clearly identifiable, state-level actors. Yet, given the transnationalized, informal nature of the actors driving the new security threats, Itamaraty's explicit, forceful, and continuous adherence to the precepts of sovereignty acted as a brake on the sort of leadership which might cope with these challenges.

The suggestion that emerges in this chapter is that the limitations inherent in the policy pursued by Itamaraty provided what amounts to leaky shelter, indicating that leadership in the security element of the regionalist project was not strong or self-sustaining. As my discussion of the new security threats hints, strengthening this aspect of leadership required a reconceptualization that would extend Brazilian notions of security beyond the country's borders. In a region of differing capacities and political realities the new threats to security cannot be controlled through strengthened border patrols, indicating that the concept and application of sovereignty may need to be rethought, perhaps suggesting the pursuit of a force such as MOMEP, deployed in Ecuador. As the U.S. example with Plan Colombia and the Andean Initiative illustrates, leadership in the security realm requires an ability to absorb the cost of providing security goods outside the national territory, in effect, pulling other states in the region into the innermost of Golbery's concentric circles in order to exclude the new threats to national sovereignty. Thus, my conclusion is that, in the security dimension, the foreign-policy strategy pursued during the Cardoso administration was successful in laying the foundations for Brazilian leadership in South America, but that this aspect of leadership will remain shaky until the application of key conceptual principles in Brazilian foreign policy is reexamined.

Continuity and Change during
the First Lula Presidency

In the Introduction we looked briefly at the slow pace of change and the sense of continuity that has marked Brazil's foreign policy. One of my major arguments is that the presidency of Fernando Henrique Cardoso is an important and worthy subject of sustained study because it precipitated and implemented a substantive shift in the tenor, orientation, and practice of Brazilian foreign policy. While the turn to an increasingly active sense of leadership through the mechanisms of consensual hegemony and regionalism built around South America during the Cardoso era has been firmly established, the extent to which this new pattern became embedded within Brazil's foreign-policy thinking remains unexplicated. The task of this chapter is thus to briefly take up the theme of "continuities" and provide a preliminary indication of how the foreign-policy trajectory established by Cardoso persisted during the first three years of Luiz Inácio Lula da Silva's presidency.

The transition from Cardoso to Lula provides an ideal opportunity to examine the extent to which the foreign-policy strategies outlined in this book represent a shift in Itamaraty's style and intent beyond the passing political fads that might be seen as consonant with an approach predicated on presidential diplomacy (Danese 1999). Although the Cardoso era was prefaced by the impeachment of Fernando Collor de Mello and witnessed a presidential succession when Cardoso replaced Itamar Franco in 1995, the reins of power remained very much in the hands of the country's social, political, and economic elite. The shift from the center-right of Cardoso's *Partido da Social Democracia Brasileira* (PSDB—Social Democratic Party of Brazil) to Lula's *Partido dos Trabalhadores* (PT—Workers' Party) represented more than a slide along the political spectrum reflective of a general continent-wide rebellion against a decade of neoliberal economic reforms. It also brought a radical change in the sort of people running the Brazilian state and the priorities actively placed at the heart of their administration (Almeida 2003; Daudelin 2008).

Besides being a staunch opponent of the military dictatorship, Cardoso in many ways epitomizes the self-conception of the Brazilian elite—the cosmopolitan son of a general, fluent in four languages, a scholar of international rank, and sophisticated political operator who guided the constituent assembly that drafted the national Constitution in 1988 (Cardoso 2006; Goertzl 1999). In marked contrast, Lula is a monolingual former São Paulo metalworker and union leader who not only did not have an opportunity to complete formal schooling, but also was forced to move from his native Northeast as a child when his family joined the mass of internal migrants seeking employment in the south (Branford 2003b).

The policy priorities of the PSDB and PT governments appear to differ markedly as well. Where Cardoso's agenda focused on the more theoretical deep structural reform of Brazil's political economy and society (Font 2003; Font and Spanakos 2004), Lula's concentration has been on the more practical, immediate, and prosaic goal of ensuring that everyone in his country has two decent meals a day. Indeed, the emphasis that Lula has placed on enhancing opportunities for Brazilians and the PT's constant call for an expansion and sophistication of the national economy suggest that there might be a renewed inward turn in Brazilian policies; this possibility is given credence by Lula's appointment of the highly nationalistic Samuel Pinheiro Guimarães as secretary-general of Itamaraty. Indeed, before Lula was inaugurated the writings of some key figures on Lula's foreign and economic policy teams (Guimarães 1999; M. Garcia 2003; D. Costa 2003) suggested that there might be a return to some form of import-substitution industrialization and an abandonment of the externally oriented international-insertion approach to development established during the Cardoso era.

At first Lula's victory might seem surprising because it brought almost no change in Brazil's economic policies during the first three years (Mollo and Saad-Filho 2006). During our interview Cardoso went as far as to ask: "What is the difference between my government and the Lula government? We have differences, but not in terms of liberalism" (Cardoso and Lafer 2007). In part he made this claim because in the immediate aftermath of his electoral victory Lula was under tremendous pressure from the international markets to prove that he would govern in a fiscally responsible manner. True to his pragmatic nature, Lula realized that the only way of ensuring the national economic health necessary to achieve his public-policy goals was to prevent an economic collapse by keeping the markets happy. In the context of the leftist ideology prevalent in some sectors of the PT this was viewed as kowtowing to international capitalism.

Reality, though, has been somewhat different, with massive changes in orientation taking place in key interest groups such as the Federação das Indústrias do Estado de São Paulo (FIESP—São Paulo Federation of Industry) in response to the emergence of Brazil as a global agroindustry superpower. The external orientation that Cardoso sought to inculcate in Brazilian business was taking hold, with firms actively seeking extracontinental markets. This in turn pushed a far more activist stance from the Foreign Ministry in international fora such as the WTO.

While the economic situation in Brazil continued to improve during Lula's first three years, with a coalition of business and industry groups such as FIESP and the agricultural trade think tank Instituto de Estudos do Comércio e Negociações Internacionais (ICONE—Institute for International Trade Negotiations) working very closely with the government to deepen and entrench Brazil's global trading links, Lula remained subject to strong political pressures from within his own party to keep to a leftist path.

Beyond the obvious economic precariousness at the end of 2002 and beginning of 2003, Lula was left with a substantial challenge from the earliest days of his presidency. Electoral victory had only been achieved because he was able to assuage the fears of the Brazilian middle class and business elite that he would responsibly manage the economy. Yet his party faithful and core political constituency demanded the sort of radical nationalist policies that had come to mark the rhetoric of the Chávez presidency in Venezuela. The solution Lula pursued was an effective bifurcation of his government, which many observers and bureaucrats I interviewed characterized as resulting in the economically important ministries such as the Central Bank, Finance, Agriculture, and the MDIC being left in the hands of centrist and center-right figures, while the symbolic, but ultimately less domestically important, ministries such as the Foreign Ministry were given to the leftists. Rather than reflecting a judgment about the quality of the staff at Itamaraty, this decision simply mirrored a political reality in Brazil that placed almost no importance on foreign affairs because it lacked traction in the public imagination and offered little opportunity to deliver the political rents that are the bread and butter of Brazilian politics.

Lula's appointments at Itamaraty made a powerful political statement about foreign policy at the very beginning of his presidency. In a break with tradition, Samuel Pinheiro Guimarães, a diplomat whom Celso Lafer had suspended for continuously attacking the very notion of potentially closer economic relations with the United States, was appointed as secretary-general of Itamaraty despite never having served abroad as an ambassador. An initial temptation to further break with tradition by appointing nondiplomat Marco Aurélio Garcia as foreign minister was resisted, with Celso Amorim being returned to that post and Garcia ensconced within the Planalto Palace as the president's main foreign-policy advisor and unofficial foreign minister for South American affairs.

While these appointments did not result in a significant thematic shift in the South America–oriented, consensually hegemonic nature of Brazilian foreign policy, there was an expansion to a wider South-South logic as well as an important change in focus and priorities within this framework. Where the Cardoso era had seen a marked focus on the creation and use of economic foundations to support the ideas and political ambitions of Brazilian foreign policy, Lula during his first three years brought a decided shift to the political end of the equation. Figures such as Guimarães and Garcia have acknowledged the PT's long history of notions of South American solidarity and developing-country solidarity to advance a foreign policy that takes almost idealist notions of southern solidarity as a given and as being of sufficient force to support Brazil's efforts to lead a developmentalist surge in the face of the persistent pressures of globalization and neoliberalism (Almeida 2004; 2005).

The result of the shift in Brazilian foreign policy from the economic imperative of Cardoso to the political of Lula has seen an acceleration in South-South integration efforts that range from the highly economic and pragmatic G-20 group of developing countries, through the issue-specific India–Brazil–South Africa Dialogue Forum, to the politically idealistic transformation of IIRSA into the Community of South American Nations, or CASA (Soares de Lima 2005; Soares de Lima and Hirst 2006; Burges 2007; Alden and Vieira 2005; Vigevani and Cepaluni 2007). While many aspects of the consensual hegemony trajectory established during the Cardoso era have been solidified and entrenched, the style of leadership has shifted to see a shedding of Itamaraty's traditional public reluctance to use the language of leading and leadership.

This ultimately has introduced a problematic contraction in Brazil's foreign policy, with other South American countries not so much rejecting Brazilian leadership as questioning why they should accept it if Brazil is unwilling to provide the public goods and benefits expected of a leader. Indeed, the continuation of the cost-free forms of leadership outlined in Chapter 2 has become problematic as the emphasis has shifted to increasingly political language in Lula's foreign policy that attempts to mask the privileging of Brazil's national interest.

Infrastructure and diversionary trade tactics continued during Lula's first three years to play a critical role in the attempt to establish Brazil as the center of a viable South American region as well as a potential global leader of developing countries, but with an at-times rather less carefully masked mercantilist barb. On the surface the provision of security goods appears to have followed the same pattern seen during the Cardoso era. The disjuncture came when Brazil's emphasis on the right to national autonomy in the determination of political systems and electoral results was contradicted by Lula's public pronouncements in favor of a particular candidate or strategic decisions to look away from democratic transgressions to advance other foreign-policy ambitions (Burges and Daudelin 2007). The prime example here is Brazil's involvement in Haiti, a venture driven more by a desire to secure a permanent seat on the UN Security Council than any sense of hemispheric democratic solidarity.

The keystone to Brazilian foreign policy remained unchanged during the first three years of Lula's presidency; the transformation came as a willingness to publicly unveil the understated and masked aspects of leadership outlined in the rest of this book. The Lula administration's at times overt declaration of intent to lead also offers a critical comparison with the foreign policy attributed to Itamaraty. Where Brazil often seemed pedantic in the operation of its foreign policy during the Cardoso years, expectations from the other countries on the continent were also depressed by Brazil's consistent refusal to clearly acknowledge or accept the mantle of leadership. The unambiguous statement of a desire to lead that has marked Brazilian foreign policy from the outset of the Lula presidency began to establish a set of expectations for the provision of public goods on at least a continental level; these expectations cannot be met simply by the practical, economic, and military restraints inherent in the consensual hegemony strategy.

Leadership

A decidedly uncharacteristic kink in Brazil's foreign policy was added by Lula's ascension to the presidency. Where diplomats had gone to great pains throughout the Cardoso era to publicly disavow the appearance of leadership and leading, central foreign-policy figures in the Lula administration such as Marco Aurélio Garcia (2003) did not shy away from positioning Brazil as a potential leader in South America and the global South, despite later forcefully disavowing such notions (Garcia 2007). Indeed, diplomats during the early Lula years talked far more freely about the idea that Brazil was deliberately leading South America, with one mid-level official going as far as to bluntly state that Brazil could and did tell some of the other countries on the continent what to do.

This dramatic break with Brazil's tradition of understated, oblique leadership certainly made many diplomats privately uneasy and prompted one of the first public statements from Cardoso about his successor's presidency. He criticized the new administration for actively voicing a desire to occupy an international leadership position beside the world's conventional powers (*OESP* 17 Jan. 2003; 30 Jan. 2003; 25 March 2003).

While global leadership aspirations were initially downplayed by Itamaraty, notions of the international acceptability of Brazilian leadership, at least on a continental level, were emphasized, with Amorim at one point going as far as to suggest that the United States would like to see Brazil serving as some sort of a centralized spokesperson for Latin America (*OESP* 10 June 2003). The problem for Itamaraty was that the rest of the continent was not particularly enamored with this idea, especially since little in the way of carrotlike payoffs were being offered to the other South American countries in return for acquiescence.

As one Brazilian diplomat described it, Lula's decision to actively embrace and assert the role of leader was only partly a reaction to the rising notion of *auto-estima* in Brazil that led to the PT's electoral victory. Of far greater importance were notions of ego and the desire for prestige. The diplomat traced this to events at the January 2003 presidential investiture ceremonies of Lucio Gutiérrez in Ecuador, where Gutiérrez called for Brazil under Lula to actively lead South America. The notion appealed to Lula, leading to a marked emphasis in his statements and policy proposals that Brazil should either assert its leadership or take on the provision of public good in South America and the global South (da Silva 2003c; 2004b). This was manifest in attempts to transform IIRSA into a larger South American community of nations as well as Lula's musings that the G-20 might become a southern trade bloc.

For their part, South American leaders were not entirely uncomfortable with the potential reality of Brazilian leadership under Lula. Reflecting on the

pattern of Brazilian relations with the continent, Hugo Fernández Araoz, Bolivia's vice-chancellor under Evo Morales, explicitly drew on the same parallels
to Europe that Helmut Kohl had pushed on Cardoso in the mid-1990s, noting
that "Brazil cannot be a regional leader without accepting the 'costs' of promoting a more just situation for the other countries in South America.... The
big countries [such as Brazil] cannot look upon this price as a cost, but must
see it as an investment" (*OESP* 4 July 2007). But as the former Uruguayan
ambassador to the WTO, Carlos Pérez del Castillo, noted, Brazil was simply
not playing the leader's role: "If a country wants to be leader, it must involve
itself in regional problems" (*OESP* 31 July 2007). While del Castillo certainly
had personal reasons for savaging notions of Brazilian leadership (addressed
below), his comments about serious lacunae in the reality of Brazil's activities
as leader had considerable traction throughout the continent.

Two of the most dramatic examples of discontent with Brazil's leadership
in the continent during the first three years of Lula's presidency came at presidential Summits in 2005. Official events at the Brasília Arab–South American Leaders Summit held in Brasília in May were disrupted by the dramatic
departure of Argentine president Néstor Kirchner, who abruptly returned to
Buenos Aires less than twenty-four hours into the meeting complaining of
Brazilian hegemonism and the problems this was causing for Mercosul. More
understated was the parallel departure of Chilean president Ricardo Lagos,
who saw little point in remaining at an event that would eventually release a
weak and controversial declaration offering few substantive opportunities for
the participants (*Oxford Analytica* 17 May 2005). Later in the year a Summit
of the presidents of the member states in the Community of South American
Nations (CASA)—the continental integrationist scheme launched at a December 2004 Summit in Cuzco—was marked not only by the absence of five
heads of state, but also by forceful demands from Venezuelan president Hugo
Chávez that CASA abandon the neoliberal model embedded in Mercosul and
CAN (*LAWR* 4 Oct. 2005). In political terms the CSN process ostensibly
represented an advance in the continental regionalist project launched at the
2000 Brasília Summit of South American Presidents, but the content of the
sparsely attended October 2005 meeting pointed to the underlying challenge
left unaddressed by Brazil's strategy of consensual hegemony and its active
claim to leadership, namely, the lack of trade flows needed to sustain a continent-wide region (Burges 2005a).

Serious tension was added to the strains on Brazil's leadership by the rapid
increase in global oil prices during Lula's first term. As Cardoso and Lafer

(2007) both readily acknowledge, they had a reasonably easy time constraining the policy proposals of Hugo Chávez because the Venezuelan leader lacked the funds necessary to become an autonomous force in South America. This has changed markedly, with Chávez emerging not just as a competitor for South American leadership, but also as an actor quite willing to expend economic and political capital to achieve his ambitions (Burges 2007).

A number of countries have been quick to pick up on the opportunities inherent in this newly competitive environment. Argentina, enormously dissatisfied with Brazil's failure to provide even the symbolic support of buying a few million dollars' worth of bonds, something Lula could not do lest international markets assume that he would default on Brazil's debt, was quick to sell billions of dollars in bonds to Chávez. Political observers in Paraguay began to take advantage of these opportunities as well, publishing a series of editorial contributions in *ABC Color* suggesting that the Duarte government play Brazil and Venezuela off against each other. Uruguay, for its part, expressed its disenchantment with a Brazil-led Mercosul in almost the most direct manner possible by loudly voicing a desire to negotiate a bilateral deal with the United States.

While these suggestions elicited a temporary loosening of inspections at the Brazil-Paraguay border and sustained discussions about new programs to revitalize Mercosul, the real challenge came from Bolivia. Vice-pres. Álvaro García Linera made a little-publicized trip to Brasília shortly after Evo Morales' inauguration as president to make it clear to Lula, Amorim, and Petrobrás head, José Sérgio Gabrielli, that Bolivia's gas industry had to be nationalized if there was to be any hope of political stability in that country. Despite the early 2006 visit, the nationalization caught Brazil by surprise. The impression in Itamaraty and Petrobrás was that the nationalization was to be negotiated in an orderly fashion, not enacted by decree on May Day 2006 and enforced by the Bolivian military, which occupied Petrobrás facilities in that country. What particularly irked Brazilian diplomats was the heavy involvement of Hugo Chávez in the process, both as a source of moral support and as the provider of technical experts to advise the Bolivian government in the days after the nationalization. The Brazilian response to these events, particularly through Petrobrás, was extremely firm. Suggestions that Brazil was dependent on Bolivian gas were cast as a short term challenge when Petrobrás announced it would accelerate development of vast gas reserves in the Bacia do Santos and Campos. Direct pressure was also put on the Bolivian state when Petrobrás, over questions of unpaid invoices, temporarily suspended the shipment of diesel fuel.

The Lula government called for amicable discussions between Bolivia and Petrobrás to come to terms, but consistently allowed state-owned Petrobrás to privilege commercial priorities over notions of regional political or economic solidarity. The result was a game of economic hardball, with Bolivia sans Venezuela eventually managing to extract only the minor concession that Brazil pay a small premium on the particulate matter contained in the gas.

Itamaraty responded to Venezuela by quietly reshaping its internal structures. A small group of diplomats was made responsible for close and constant observation of Venezuela in order to prevent Chávez from becoming a serious and lasting obstacle to Brazil's plans for the continent. What was absent in this planning, which will become evident in the discussion of economic factors below, was the idea that serious costs should be absorbed from and benefits provided to the other South American countries as part of Lula's increasingly explicit leadership strategy.

Discontent with the failure to implement programs providing the payoffs necessary to sustain Brazil's leadership of a larger regionalist project aside, geographic expansion of the Cardoso-era ideas-based inclusive approach to leading did achieve several important successes for the early Lula presidency. The constant internal bickering and dissatisfaction with Brazilian trade policy that marked the evolution of Mercosul (Malamud 2005) was not repeated on a larger international scale in WTO negotiations. Here the ability to coordinate divergent states and deliver highly polished and technically sophisticated draft documents was evident in the formation of the G-20 coalition of developing countries. As was the case during 1994's Miami Summit of the Americas, the G-20 was formed in response to developments outside of Brazil and the wider global South, in this instance a joint EU-U.S. agricultural proposal for the 2003 Cancún WTO ministerial meeting. Drawing on the increasing level of trilateral cooperation with India and South Africa that had emerged during the summer (Alden and Vieira 2005; *Oxford Analytica* 22 April 2004), Brazil played a leading role in organizing a coalition of twenty-two countries that not only rejected the EU-U.S. offer, but also arrived in Cancún with a carefully formulated counteroffer (Narlikar and Tussie 2004; Narlikar and Wilkinson 2004).

For some, particularly the United States, the events in Cancún represented a failure of the negotiating process and the emergence of an obstructionist southern bloc led by Brazil (*OESP* 18 Sept. 2003). Yet in time it became clear that Brazil was repeating the ideas-led style of leadership. The Brazilian position was clearly spelled out by Amorim in the *Wall Street Journal* of 25

September 2003, shortly after Cancún: "Our platform is about 'leveling the playing field,' through the full integration of agriculture into the multilateral rules-based trading system." Emphasis thus remained on the traditional characteristics of Brazilian foreign policy, namely, the articulation of a multilateral, rules-based international system as well as the creation of consensus.

With this end in mind, Itamaraty accepted detailed and comprehensive technical support from the São Paulo–based think tank ICONE. It used this input to generate detailed negotiating proposals that were put to the rest of the G-20 membership. These proposals were then taken up at a number of joint strategy-planning sessions, modified slightly, and presented to the WTO as the official G-20 position on agriculture negotiations for the Doha negotiating round (*Oxford Analytica* 22 March 2004 and 5 April 2005; G-20 2005). The result was a clear positioning of Brazil as a major representative for developing-country interests within the WTO system and the country's inclusion as one of the Five Interested Parties that has met regularly starting in July 2004 to seek a resolution to the deadlocked agricultural talks (IPS 12 July 2004).

As was the case during the preparations for the 1994 Miami Summit of the Americas, by organizing and working through the G-20 Brazil was able to push its own agenda in a seemingly disinterested manner that created a space between Brazilian desires and attributions of ownership for a particular policy proposal. More to the point, a solid-looking package of opportunities was created without the need to devote concrete, fungible resources to the project. Within the WTO and the hemispheric-trade context attention was firmly focused on the provision of technical support, with a marked preference being given to seeking simple consensus from other developing countries for the draft texts emanating from ICONE. Indeed, Amorim went as far as to bluntly tell the G-90 group of least-developed countries that they should trust Brazil to protect their interests in global trade talks; this initiative was repeated in the G-20's 2005 Bhurban Declaration, which again gave explicit attention to a desire for intra-South cooperation and the shared goals of developing countries (Amorim 2004; G-20 2005).

Where Brazilian leadership during Lula's first three years extended beyond the provision of drafts of negotiation language, it was often in the form of technical assistance or the sharing of established practices. Within South America Itamaraty sought to strengthen the region by helping the Andean countries identify untapped markets in Brazil, although, as will be detailed later, this process was somewhat limited (*Oxford Analytica* 26 Oct. 2005).

The overt actions that Brazil undertook globally at the start of Lula's presidency varied between the symbolic—Lula donated his U.S.$55,000 Prince of Asturias prize to the UN Hunger Fund—and the purely technical—assistance to African countries consisting mostly of offers of development advice, the sharing of best practices, and minor diversion of trade flows (Burges 2005b). Efforts to promote interregionalism in the face of Brazil's Mercosul partners' skepticism resulted in the formation of the India–Brazil–South Africa Dialogue Forum (IBSA), which sought to expand intra-South cooperation, but without committing any of the participants to comprehensive new expenditures (Alden and Vieira 2005; *Oxford Analytica* 22 April 2004). This reluctance to devote substantial resources to the leadership agenda or to accept the costs associated with region formation and coalition leadership (Mattli 1999; Narlikar 2003; Pedersen 2002) carried a substantive price for Itamaraty's wider international institutional ambitions. Efforts to secure the director-generalship of the WTO in 2005 for Luiz Felipe Seixas Corrêa, former Itamaraty secretary-general and ambassador to the international organizations in Geneva, were scuppered by a lack of Mercosul and wider southern support. Indeed, Corrêa was in direct competition with the Uruguayan president's special advisor on international trade, Carlos Pérez del Castillo.

This particular example was not, in the end, terribly problematic for Itamaraty; many observers in Geneva characterized the Corrêa candidacy as a deliberate act of sabotage meant to do in del Castillo's bid in retribution for the Cancún agriculture-related text he presented, a document which some Brazilian negotiators felt was overly dismissive of the country's priorities. A more striking failure came during the 2005 search for a successor to IADB head Enrique Iglesias. In this instance the highly qualified and experienced Brazilian economist João Sayad, who was serving as an IADB vice-president, lost out to Luis Alberto Moreno, then Colombia's ambassador to the United States.

The picture that emerged during Lula's early years was thus one of an active declaration of intent to lead resulting in limited success because Itamaraty was unwilling to commit Brazil to the sort of leadership costs highlighted by Kindleberger (1989). Finally, any hopes of securing a permanent seat on the UN Security Council—a central Brazilian diplomatic ambition since 1945 and almost a personal obsession of Amorim's—collapsed amid indifference from the five permanent members and active opposition from other Latin American countries.

Ideas

The leadership project of the early Lula presidency continued to place the ideas dimension at its core. As was the case during the Cardoso era, Lula's foreign policy sought to deploy ideas and the ability to generate and inclusively disseminate ideas as the currency underwriting the leadership project. Democracy and the need to resolve inequities in the global political economy remained a central part of foreign-policy rhetoric, even if substantive action to clearly support democracy remained somewhat questionable (Burges and Daudelin 2007). The change and added sophistication that Lula has brought to the ideational element of Brazilian foreign policy appeared to have drawn almost directly on the sociology literature underpinning Wendt's constructivist take on international relations (Berger and Luckman 1966; Wendt 1992; Wendt 1999). In a Fanonian vein that points to the heart of the shift to a political emphasis in Lula's foreign policy, specific attention has been given to the idea that southern states can reconstruct and direct their own reality by giving careful thought to the social implications of their conceptions of their capacities, capabilities, and future direction in the global system.

Lula's ideas-based foreign policy followed a rhetorical logic revolving around the concept of *auto-estima*, the sense of national self-confidence that resulted in Brazilians trusting their own judgment in electing Lula despite widespread international concern about the sanity of such a decision (Burges 2005b). In a foreign-policy project sense *auto-estima* was advanced as a device for southern empowerment. In a prepared speech drawing on the writings of the Martinican psychologist Frantz Fanon, Lula bluntly stated to the UN General Assembly in 2004 that the developing world had the power to make its own choices, a power that it only had to claim (da Silva 2004a). This assertion of what he hoped to make a new, albeit potentially uncomfortable, reality for the global South built on previous statements in which he emphasized that Brazil was not a developing country, but an unequal country. Moreover, in an unconscious nod to Cardoso's dependency theory, he stated that he considered the inequality and swathes of underdevelopment in Brazil and much of the rest of the global South to be substantially the result of internal decisions, not of the imperial or colonial designs of the United States or Europe (da Silva 2003a).

The key to the idea of *auto-estima* at the heart of Lula's early approach to the foreign policy of consensual hegemony established by Cardoso was thus a willingness to accept domestic realities. In the sense discussed by Fanon (1967), this attitude involved a belief that influences from the North not only mattered, but also interacted with homegrown ideas and traditions to create new paths and opportunities, not necessarily the constraints often associated with the classic North-South relationship. Hope for a brighter future born of the full realization of domestic potentials and capacities was thus the central message, one that emphasized the ability of the South autonomously to create a beneficial insertion into the global political and economic system. This projection of political will as a way forward was paralleled by a shift in global perceptions of countries such as Brazil, most notably through the Goldman Sachs paper launching the BRIC emerging market concept of Brazil, Russia, India, and China as the powers of tomorrow (Wilson and Purushothaman 2003).

An interesting contradiction lies embedded within the centrality of the *auto-estima* concept to the ideational basis of Lula's foreign policy. If anything, the dependency logic of the Cardoso era was given a harder, more traditional line by several key Lula appointments. Marco Aurélio Garcia came from a staunch leftist academic career and internal PT policymaking to be the presidential palace's advisor on foreign relations. Samuel Pinheiro Guimarães, appointed secretary-general of Itamaraty, wasted little time in making his book *Quinhentos anos de periferia* (Five hundred years on the periphery) required reading for the country's diplomats. BNDES, too, received an intake of nationalist thinking devoted to finding southern solutions to the challenge of global development and the elimination of poverty. In this vein Darc Costa, a BNDES vice president, published a book in 2003 that in effect restated the utopian South American integrationist logic of the 1960s, but with the added dimension of Brazil's acting as an accepted leader of a continentally driven development project. While Costa's account perhaps reaches the extremes of the southern isolationist ideas circulating within the foreign-policy establishment at the outset of Lula's presidency, a softer version comes through clearly in statements made by Lula and Amorim. A Costa-style unlinking from the North was not advanced as a serious option, although relations with the United States were characterized by some, including Lula's ambassador in Washington, Roberto Abdenur, as being allowed to fall into something close to benign neglect (Cabral 2007). Instead, questions were asked about why South-South trade and cooperation flows remained so low, prompting a search for ways of increasing these exchanges and giving greater impetus to processes such as the G-20 and IBSA. In effect, Lula was advocating a new economic geography, one that would redraw global trade routes by exploiting the unrealized opportunities of intra-South trade (da Silva 2003b; 2004b).

Like Cardoso, Lula was not suggesting destruction of the current global political economy; the message that international institutions and the operation of the international system were in need of reform remained a steady theme in the early days. Indeed, Lula's emphasis on creating a new economic geography pushing expanded southern commercial, cultural, educational, and scientific linkages deepened the core Cardoso message that the country had to globalize and open in order to recruit the knowledge and resources necessary to exploit its potential. The result was a neat twist on the current CEPAL argument that autonomous development was no longer possible, that the entire process requires a carefully formulated insertion into the global system (Ocampo and Martin 2003), and that geography does not pose an insurmountable barrier to national or regional development (Gallup et al. 2003). Declarations such as those at the heart of the India-Brazil-South Africa Dialogue (IBSA) emphasize the potential for expanded trade and concentrate on creating the bureaucratic and intergovernmental frameworks necessary for facilitating the scientific and technical cooperation seen as crucial during the Cardoso era and highlighted as essential by CEPAL (IBSA 2004). This internationalizing of the sources of opportunities for Brazilians has been extended by Lula's sustained pressure on national firms to globalize their operations (da Silva 2003c) as well as his repeated suggestions that either the G-20 be turned into a southern economic bloc (a proposal rejected by the other members and treated in a somewhat lackluster manner by Itamaraty [Burges 2005b]), or that IBSA be expanded to include China and Russia. In each instance the goal was to engage in an exchange of technical knowledge or, with regard to China, a trade of Brazil's resource base for China's scientific capacity (*Oxford Analytica* 15 June 2004; 19 Nov. 2004).

Lula's ideational agenda of shifting the implicit boundaries of what Brazilians and citizens of other developing countries might consider possible has added a decided neoliberal kick to the leftist ideological nature of his PT electoral base. Market economics, with a gently guiding rather than a forcefully directing hand from the state, remained at the core of foreign policy after the presidential transition in January 2003. Articulation of the G-20, dissemination of the *auto-estima* concept, and sustained efforts to encourage an expansion of South-South trade all but explicitly imply that the neoliberal principle of a national opening to international forces is a necessary and, ultimately, a good thing. The change that Lula has brought to this ideology is that, rather than relying on reasoned argument to bring about international institutional reform in a Cardoso-style pattern, Brazil can turn to a more traditional approach based on coalition politics; it can use the internal divisions between the rich and the poor as a device to strengthen and test policy proposals being put to potential external partners. Creation of heightened self-confidence in the South has laid the foundations for patterns of interaction that have begun to bypass the North, which in turn has opened opportunities for cooperation in major international economic institutions such as the WTO.

Despite disparaging assertions to the contrary after the 2003 Cancún WTO meeting of ministers, the Brazil-led G-20 was firmly focused on achieving a successful conclusion of the Doha round, but with an agreement that followed a more ideologically pure reading of global trade liberalization. Its rhetoric eschewed the mercantilistic concession-trading dominant through the 2001 Doha ministerial meeting in favor of a more idealistic approach arguing for the elimination of agricultural subsidies and supports because this action would be entirely consonant with the liberal economic theory widely presented as being at the core of the emerging global economic system.

Brazil's rise as one of the world's most competitive agroindustrial producers has been obfuscated by the G-20's developmentalist language. Coordination of the G-20 has nevertheless combined with the newfound BRIC label to give the country substantial heft as a leader in the WTO. The WTO negotiating coalition founded on the ideas-led leadership style implicit in the Cardoso era's consensual hegemonic strategy is more in keeping with traditional coalition formation, although in the Lula manifestation it is a much more fluid and issue-specific form than was seen in intra-South relations of the 1960s and 1970s (Wilkinson 2000; G-20 2005; Narlikar and Tussie 2004). Within this context the goal, as outlined in the previous section, remains the mobilization of other countries around the continued ideational program. As will be explained in the next section, global acceptance of the core precepts of an open trading system and the heightened self-help responsibility implicit in *auto-estima* have created a space for Brazil to attempt to continue building the economic aspects of consensual hegemony begun during the Cardoso era.

Economics

The continued importance of the regional context for Lula's foreign policy was made clear by Amorim (2002) in December 2002 when he noted that it would be difficult to imagine a strong Brazil if Mercosul or the continent were to exist in a fractured state. Indeed, Amorim's investiture speech as foreign minister emphasized the importance of strengthening Brazil's regional context, particularly through the upgrading of infrastructure linkages planned in the IIRSA process (Amorim 2003b).

From the outset the rhetorical emphasis of Lula's foreign policy was on continuing the Cardoso era's continental project. I stress "rhetorical emphasis" because Lula's decision to actively and publicly acknowledge his leadership ambitions created demands for the delivery of substantive payoffs extending beyond those of the carrotless/stickless style of leading. As President Kirchner's eruption at the Arab–South American Summit highlights, the other South American countries were becoming increasingly impatient with regional arrangements that promised much, but appeared to be delivering little in the way of concrete economic gains.

The pattern of economic bickering that characterized Mercosul after the devaluation of the Brazilian *real* in 1999 continued through the first three years of Lula's presidency. Initial discussions with Argentina placed a priority on revitalizing the bloc (*OESP* 15 Jan. 2003; 5 Feb. 2003), but these hopeful signs soon broke down as Brazilian imports to Argentina began a recovery in March 2003, and the recovery of the peso made these products increasingly competitive (*OESP* 11 March 2003; 5 June 2003). Despite the signing of a memorandum committing both countries to resolving their differences and stabilizing bilateral trade (*OESP* 23 August 2003), by 2004 commercial relations between Argentina and Brazil had deteriorated to the point where there were constant trade-related spats over allegedly unfair flooding of markets by Brazil, especially in the sensitive white goods and footwear sectors (*OESP* 12 July 2004; 9 Feb. 2005).

Increasing dissatisfaction with the pattern of trade, which was witnessing the emergence of Brazil as the value-added manufacturing hub for South America envisioned by Cardoso, prompted Argentina's secretary of industry, Alberto Dumont, to complain that the benefits from Mercosul were unfairly distributed and that Brazilian policies were in effect destroying industry in the other bloc countries (*O Globo* 24 Feb. 2005). The figures set out in Table 6.1 illustrate Dumont's complaint. While Brazilian imports across South America did increase steadily throughout Lula's first term, exports increased even more quickly. The surge in exports to Argentina was particularly abrupt, leading to a doubling of Brazil's trade surplus with the country in a single year between 2003 and 2004. Similar trends were seen in trade relations with Paraguay, Uruguay, and the Andean countries. Indeed, only Bolivia managed to sustain a growing surplus with Brazil, and this was due entirely to that country's dependence on Brazil as the market for its natural gas.

Table 6.1. Brazilian Exports and Imports (in U.S.$)

	2002	2003	2004	2005	2006
Argentina					
Exports to	2,346,508,274	4,569,767,654	7,390,967,394	9,930,152,936	11,739,591,939
Imports from	4,743,785,116	4,672,610,523	5,569,811,952	6,241,110,029	8,053,262,647
Balance	-2,397,276,842	-102,842,869	1,821,155,442	3,689,042,907	3,686,329,292
Bolivia					
Exports to	422,205,557	362,425,706	540,439,784	585,252,917	701,601,938
Imports from	395,829,631	520,432,027	713,360,511	989,773,678	1,448,228,137
Balance	26,375,926	-158,006,321	-172,920,727	-404,520,761	-746,626,199
Chile					
Exports to	1,464,798,651	1,886,978,683	2,555,916,452	3,623,663,246	3,913,549,324
Imports from	648,733,881	821,233,607	1,398,651,997	1,746,017,339	2,866,267,360
Balance	816,064,770	1,065,745,076	1,157,264,455	1,877,645,907	1,047,281,964
Colombia					
Exports to	638,528,003	751,635,382	1,043,534,982	1,412,193,504	2,139,882,717
Imports from	108,499,896	98,518,338	143,269,823	137,748,159	247,902,662
Balance	530,028,107	653,117,044	900,265,159	1,274,445,345	1,891,980,055
Ecuador					
Exports to	389,283,340	356,858,207	494,888,862	648,647,252	877,497,508
Imports from	14,906,908	18,892,504	82,781,123	91,706,707	30,392,909
Balance	374,376,432	337,965,703	412,107,739	556,940,545	847,104,599

Guyana

Exports to	8,754,947	9,695,198	13,633,697	16,604,009	20,204,149
Imports from	25,641	35	10,379	11,559	0
Balance	8,729,306	9,695,163	13,623,318	16,592,450	20,204,149

Paraguay

Exports to	559,625,414	708,750,484	873,352,694	962,720,724	1,233,638,638
Imports from	383,087,752	474,750,083	297,825,436	318,935,985	295,935,121
Balance	176,537,662	234,000,401	575,527,258	643,784,739	937,703,517

Peru

Exports to	438,663,064	491,596,340	636,164,378	938,664,676	1,509,564,004
Imports from	217,782,733	235,237,054	349,383,743	459,108,765	788,171,388
Balance	220,880,331	256,359,286	286,780,635	479,555,911	721,392,616

Suriname

Exports to	10,701,965	16,414,824	28,410,302	35,895,094	31,467,838
Imports from	2,621	0	737,000	12,500	23,258,247
Balance	10,699,344	16,414,824	27,673,302	35,882,594	8,209,591

Uruguay

Exports to	412,541,589	405,791,591	670,581,906	853,137,754	1,012,597,766
Imports from	484,847,356	537,868,366	522,855,590	493,653,258	618,224,941
Balance	-72,305,767	-132,076,775	147,726,316	359,484,496	394,372,825

Venezuela

Exports to	798,974,175	608,229,076	1,469,802,005	2,223,705,818	3,565,424,415
Imports from	633,060,045	275,154,451	199,083,320	255,605,407	591,553,378
Balance	165,914,130	333,074,625	1,270,718,685	1,968,100,411	2,973,871,037

Source: MDIC; SECEX.

The problem for the architects of Brazil's foreign policy was that the reality of the country's trading relations on the continent stood in marked contrast to its rhetoric, especially Lula's comment that "no country wants to buy. All want to have a trade surplus, no one wants a trade deficit" (da Silva 2004d). Lula continued to focus on the need for Brazil to consciously buy from its smaller South American neighbors, suggesting a willingness to forgo a trade surplus with these countries.

Lula's foreign policy team during his first term was not unmindful of these growing tensions and the need to restore balance to key trade relationships (da Silva 2003d; Amorim 2003c). As early as May 2003 discussions were taking place within BNDES about the possibility of the bank's financing Argentine exports to Brazil (*OESP* 7 May 2003). Demands for Brazilian assistance with the development of the other Mercosul countries continued to be considered in the context of using BNDES financing for activities ranging, chiefly, from the funding of major infrastructure projects and, by October 2005, assistance to Brazilian firms wishing to engage in new foreign direct investment ventures. This latter possibility, launched during the Cardoso presidency but brought to fruition during Lula's first term, particularly demonstrates the source of the growing frustration that the other South American countries felt with the economic aspects of Brazil's leadership project.

The bulk of BNDES' capital funds come from domestic payroll and corporate taxes and, as such, are legally mandated for exclusive use in activities that bring direct employment benefits to the country. Financing of FDI is thus problematic because it involves funding new opportunities in other countries with Brazilian money. To work around this potential legal stumbling block BNDES' FDI financing deploys two devices. First, the money it provides does not come from the bank's core capital, but is instead raised in international capital markets on five- to eight-year terms, with the size of the bank acting as a lever to extract interest rates close to the London Interbank Offered Rate (LIBOR). Second, Brazilian firms entering into a BNDES financing agreement for FDI in other countries must present and adhere to an approved strategy that will guarantee growth in their exports at least equal to the sum borrowed from BNDES. The result is a foreign economic policy package that appears to offer assistance for such ventures as a Brazilian firm–oriented business park outside Buenos Aires (*OESP* 12 March 2003), but in reality ensures that any such initiative provides at least equal benefits to the Brazilian economy.

Attention was also turned during Lula's first term to an extension of the diversionary trade practices used to strengthen relations with Argentina in the

1980s and early 1990s. Although Mercosul was soon to be hit with increased internal trade tensions stemming from the trade flows set out in Table 6.1, Amorim (2003d) is clear that Brazil had to recognize the validity of competing interests within the bloc and make space to absorb trade from and support growth and development within the other member states if the organization were to remain viable.

Significantly, during a 2004 trip to China Lula again explicitly acknowledged that, while all countries wished to export more than they imported, this was a mathematical impossibility. He then pointed to Brazil's responsibility to open its markets to those countries poorer than itself (da Silva 2004c). In this context the Cardoso-era South American project was given a framework for some of its missing substantive economic content through the creation in May 2003 of the Programa de Substituição Competitiva de Importações (PSCI—Competitive Import-Substitution Program). Yet the pattern of providing a strongly overt opportunity unmatched by actual possibilities was maintained.

Under the PSCI the government-run Brazil Trade Net seeks to help firms in other South American countries find new market opportunities by encouraging Brazilian firms to shift the suppliers of imports from extra- to intracontinental sources. In keeping with CEPAL's logic, which guided early attempts at Latin American integration (Prebisch 1986), the PSCI program sought to use the internal markets and economic space of the CSN to promote the development of a South American industrial capacity. PSCI's twist on the unsuccessful structuralist strategies of the past was that the state did not mandate a switch in suppliers. Instead, the role of the state, and the Brazilian state in particular, is to help identify what products might be substituted, bring potential trading partners together, and, through the IIRSA framework, seek to address whatever logistical and regulatory barriers might be artificially inflating the relative cost of the South American product. If a product offered by a firm in another CASA member country is uncompetitive in either cost or quality then that is the firm's problem and not a matter for public policy. While research institutes such as the Rio de Janeiro–based Fundação Centro de Estudos do Comércio Exterior (FUNCEX—Central Foundation for the Study of Foreign Trade) had completed studies identifying potential areas of expanded cooperation during the first three years of the Lula presidency, and MDIC had detailed data on what firms imported and where they imported it from, there was serious reluctance within the Brazilian state to make this information available to other South American countries (*Oxford Analytica* 26

Oct. 2005). A more pressing short- to medium-term problem was presented by the nature of products exported by South American countries, with the overwhelming majority of national exports being either in bulk agricultural or mineral commodities or energy sources such as electricity, gas, or oil (Burges 2005a, 440–442).

The continued asymmetrical pattern of Brazil's trade with the rest of South America—predominantly exporting manufactured goods and importing raw materials and energy—continued during Lula's first term. Dissatisfaction with this pattern was not only strong enough to prompt the charge of hegemonism from Argentina and keep Mercosul in a virtual state of institutional crisis (Malamud 2005), but also to incite violent public reaction against Brazilian imperialism, most notably in the form of the 2005 bombing of Petrobrás' offices in Santa Cruz, Bolivia (*OESP* 14 May 2005). Repeated dissatisfaction within Mercosul led to continued musings from Uruguay about the potential for a bilateral trade deal with the United States and precipitated a bit of a renaissance in Paraguay's foreign policy, first through the forceful advancement of national trading interests in the WTO as a leading member of the landlocked as well as small and vulnerable economy groups (Gauto Vielman 2005; *Oxford Analytica* 23 August 2005) and then via the granting of diplomatic immunity to U.S. military personnel working from a redeveloped base at Mariscal Estigarribia (*ABC Color* 6 July 2005).

Despite a rhetoric of expanded intra–South American linkages, including active progress on a bioceanic corridor through Peru (*Financial Times* 17 July 2005), much of the pattern seen during the Cardoso era was continued during the first Lula administration, with the emphasis being squarely placed on securing energy supplies for Brazil and protecting the internal, Mercosul, and South American market for Brazilian firms. While opportunities were certainly present and in theory were expanded by Lula, the economic pattern exhibited by Brazil's leadership failed to provide the carrots generally associated with the formation and management of a strong regional project.

Security

The area that demonstrated perhaps the greatest and, contradictorily, the least change was the security dimension of the Brazilian leadership project. Lula's foreign policy during his first term appeared to continue to focus tightly on the preservation of national autonomy and the prevention of new precedents that might serve to limit Brazil's freedom of action in the future. Thus, principles of nonintervention, multilateralism, and respect for sovereignty remained the central tenets expressed in the security dimension, although reality at times appeared to take a different course. Itamaraty continued its traditional game of attempting to balance the dominance of the United States in the hemispheric and global systems against Brazil's desire to be the chief actor on a continental level (Almeida 2004; Daudelin 2008).

Although not often framed in such explicit terms, particularly by the Brazilian diplomatic corps, the most apt comparison is with the foreign policy followed by Rio Branco (outlined briefly in Chapter 2). In order to retain the national and regional autonomy of action to pursue the consensual hegemony project, Brazil under Lula needed to continue providing what might best be described as classic middle-power behavior (Cooper et al. 1993; R. Cox, 1989). It also had to provide the United States assurances of basic levels of regional security in return for a continental environment relatively free of overt U.S. intervention.

Brazil's involvement in the Haitian situation is perhaps the clearest example of an attempt to demonstrate both to the United States and the wider international community that the country was capable of providing the security goods expected of a credible regional interlocutor and potential permanent member of the UNSC. It also can be read as an example of a new willingness by Brazilian foreign-policy actors to intervene explicitly in the affairs of other countries in order to advance Brazil's priorities. The significant point about Brazil's leadership of the UN military mission in Haiti launched in 2004 is that it occurred in almost total contradiction to attitudes adopted during the Cardoso era. Where Cardoso's Itamaraty was quick to denounce any attempt at imposing political outcomes on hemispheric democracies, the decision to accept leadership of the mission in Haiti in effect made Brazil complicit in what many have described as a Franco-U.S.-backed coup against the democratically elected Jean Bertrand Aristide (Daudelin 2008).

This rather blunt attribution of Itamaraty acquiescence and near-complicity in a coup, however, needs to be tempered with the example of Mahuad's ouster in Ecuador in 1999 and Fujimori's 2000 electoral manipulation in Peru, both of which saw Brazil adopt a rather tepid and passive reaction to events that were seriously questionable. The credibility of this proposition that events in Ecuador and Peru ran faster than Brazil could react is stretched somewhat by the particularly rapid reaction, via the Rio Group, to Chávez' temporary 2002 deposition, suggesting instead a rather pragmatic approach to prodemocracy foreign policy that would see Itamaraty seeking to extract the maximum national advantage from a given situation (Burges and Daudelin 2007). The pragmatism belied by the Haitian example combines with both Brazil's UNSC aspirations and the centrality of South America to the consensual hegemonic project to suggest that Brazil's direct intervention in Haiti had little bearing on Itamaraty's conceptions of how democracy might be pursued within the South American project.

On a procedural level, during his first term Lula's South American foreign policy remained remarkably consistent with the pattern of the Cardoso era. Preservation of autonomy and the prevention of potential sovereignty-infringing precedents remained his central formal goal; the protection of democracy was restricted to formulaic conceptions and a continued belief that forms of political representation were an internal question to be negotiated by a country's population. Here events at the 35th OAS General Assembly of 2005 in Fort Lauderdale, Florida, are particularly relevant.

The United States trumpeted the meeting as a democracy Summit and submitted a draft declaration that would in effect have given the OAS authority to pass judgment on the state of hemispheric democracies and order a collective intervention to prevent deviations from what was deemed the correct democratic path (OAS 2005). Deploying ALADI as a political tool, Brazil was quick to offer an alternate text that gutted the U.S. document of any suggestion that there was room for a regularized and institutionalized hemispheric intervention process to enforce democracy. The result, after much pointed debate, was a document that was little more than a bland restatement of the prodemocracy principles expressed at the 2001 Québec City Summit of the Americas (Burges 2005c).

Developments during the 35th OAS General Assembly ostensibly represent the exemplar moment of Lula's foreign policy's continuing the Cardoso pattern of protection of democracy and sovereignty, as was made clear by the reaction to Bolivian president Carlos Mesa's resignation from the presidency halfway through the meeting. Given that the constitutionally dictated pattern of succession was followed in Bolivia, Amorim's statement was unsurprisingly benign and bland, amounting to little more than a public expression of confidence in the Bolivian people's respect for their own institutions and procedures (*OESP* 8 June 2005).

Yet the reality was somewhat different. Brazil was playing a major and direct role behind the scenes, one that it was to continue throughout 2005, even if in an understated and quiet manner. Lula's key foreign-policy advisors kept a close eye on the ructions that led to Mesa's departure as well as the tumultuous political atmosphere before the 18 December 2005 general election; they also frequently met with key actors on both sides of the debate and eventually made not-so-veiled statements of confidence in central actors such as Evo Morales. While significant emphasis was consistently placed on encouraging all actors to at least respect pro-forma democratic principles, greater attention appeared to be given to ensuring the rise of figures ideologically sympathetic to Lula and protecting Brazilian access to Bolivia's natural gas deposits. In addition potential disquiet with MNCs' heightened energy taxation strategies was traded for guaranteed energy supply (*OESP* 17 May 2005; *Brazzil* 9 June 2005; *Mercopress* 2 Dec. 2005).

The pattern displayed in Bolivia was one of maintaining a reasonable degree of calm and preventing an uncontrolled and regionally destabilizing explosion of revolutionary fervor. This arguably key middle-power role exercised by Lula was particularly evident in Brazil-Venezuela relations. With ceaselessly heated rhetoric and strong indications of at least U.S. approbation of the 2002 coup against Chávez souring U.S.-Venezuelan relations to the point of diplomatic paralysis, Brazil engaged in a series of joint ventures with their northern neighbor. Bringing Venezuela into Mercosul was the culmination of a series of visits by high-level Lula advisors to Chávez and provided a slow, moderate, and controlled forum within which Chávez could make his proclamations and attempt to pursue his Bolivarian project for South America, all of which Brazil quietly worked to slow and undermine when it did not favor Brazilian interests (BBC 17 Oct. 2005).

A clear example of this is the November 2005 trilateral nuclear agreement between Argentina, Brazil, and Venezuela (*International Herald Tribune* 27 Nov. 2005). The agreement came after several years of rapid arms escalation in Venezuela, including the purchase of 100,000 AK-47 assault rifles as well as military aircraft and naval vessels. It drew on Argentina and Brazil's nuclear cooperation history to provide some substantial assurance to the United States that Chávez' latest ambitious venture would likely not lead to nuclear weapons proliferation in South America.

What was lost in the pattern of relations with Venezuela was Brazil's active attempts to look past operational democratic lacunae under Chávez' rule. Takes on the Venezuelan president's style of rule varied widely in Itamaraty, with Samuel Pinheiro Guimarães constantly asking ministry analysts for proof that Venezuela was a strong democracy. As one diplomat put it, "The United States says that Chávez was elected democratically, but governs undemocratically. We leave out the second clause."

Some diplomats pointed out that policymakers in Brasília were turning a blind eye to the weakness of the prodemocracy clauses in groupings such as Mercosul, the Rio Group, the OAS, and the Community of South American Nations. All of these groups had very strong measures in place to isolate authoritarian retrogressions, yet none were even vaguely equipped to deal with the sort of constitutional, ostensibly democratic, dismantling of democracy that some Brazilian diplomats saw occurring in Venezuela. Others in Itamaraty were further infuriated that Lula was actively departing from Brazil's long tradition of formal nonintervention in the politics of other countries by making clear statements of preference for presidential candidates throughout the region, particularly Néstor Kirchner in Argentina and Ollanta Humala in Peru.

The Cardoso era's problem of not being able to provide the muscle necessary to assist with concrete security tasks remained during Lula's first term. Even in instances where quick and detailed intelligence assistance could be provided, particularly through the use of Sivam to help Colombia and Peru with coca eradication and monitoring programs, information was provided on a fee basis, and an expansion of such resources into other, nontraditional, security areas such as the environment was greeted with some trepidation by Brazil (*OESP* 16 Oct. 2003; 18 June 2004). For a country with clearly stated regional leadership ambitions the silence in 2005 on the rekindling of Bolivia-Chile and Chile-Peru border tensions was particularly notable, especially when consideration is given to the potential knock-on effects the disputes might have had on the hallmark security achievement of the Cardoso era, the Ecuador-Peru peace agreement (Prensa Latina 7 Nov. 2005; Reuters 4 Nov. 2005). The pattern exhibited in Brazil's security policy during the initial years of the Lula presidency was one of continuing to seek the development of cooperative regional security institutions that would allow Brazilian preeminence and control, but minimizing the external influence of the United States and other extracontinental actors without incurring much in the way of fungible costs for Brazil.

Conclusion

The inauguration of the Lula presidency marked a critical point in Brazil's process of democratic consolidation, installing in the traditionally elitist office a representative of the left and the working class. It also brought a shift from an economics-grounded foreign policy to a politics-grounded agenda.

Indeed, the politicization of foreign policy (the consequence of handing it over to the traditional left as compensation for the continuation of Cardoso's liberal economic policies) had dramatic effects within Itamaraty. In an almost unprecedented move, a group of junior diplomats published an anonymous manifesto entitled "Guerra e paz no Itamaraty" (War and peace in Itamaraty). Their complaint was simple: promotions were being made on the basis of ideological conformity, not the merit criteria that had long set the Foreign Ministry apart as one of a handful of international-level elite public institutions in Brazil. Similar complaints were voiced by diplomats and business association observers who noted that many of the country's top diplomatic thinkers had been sent abroad because they failed to comply with the requisite political thinking.

Clearly, there is a very heavy element of political polemic in these criticisms of institutional evolution during Lula's first term. The point that some of these same critics acknowledged is that this might be a natural evolution of the rising importance of foreign policy in Brazilian politics and the wider population. A case in point is the Bolivian gas nationalization in 2006, a first because it intruded into and became an issue for the Brazilian presidential election that year. This represented something new in Brazilian politics and reflected the country's growing internationalization, both as consumer of continental energy supplies and as a global trader. The retrenchment and even near- explicit acceptance of the leadership strategy established during the Cardoso era was thus not wholly surprising. Where Cardoso was quiet about Brazilian ambitions to leadership, Lula was explicit, seeking overtly to deploy the currency of ideas as a device for leading a resurgent globally-oriented southern movement. The pattern of using regionalism, trade diversion, infrastructure integration, and consensus creation remained the dominant tactic for Itamaraty, with added emphasis being placed on the construction and dissemination of a common South American and southern identity. Brazil continued to provide the impetus and direction, pulling other states in a direction dictated by Itamaraty without actually having to expend notable quantities of resources.

The instructive point that emerges from a comparison of Cardoso's and Lula's use of the leadership strategies outlined in this book is the importance of being very modest about the ambition to lead. Throughout the Cardoso era extracting an admission from diplomats that Brazil was seeking and undertaking a leadership role in South America could prove a heroic task. Lula's Foreign Ministry, in contrast, was explicit in the early years about Brazil's willingness and desire to lead the continent and the global South. This did not, as traditional Brazilian doctrine suggests it might have, elicit loud protestations of imperialism and hegemonism from the rest of the continent. Indeed, there was a qualified and peaceful acceptance of Brazil's increasingly explicit leadership role that recognized the country's geographic, demographic, and economic preponderance. The problem for Lula's foreign-policy thinkers was that the other South American states, as Kirchner demonstrated at the Arab–South American Summit, were making new demands that Brazil provide the public goods and payoffs that make acquiescence to explicit leadership an attractive prospect.

The first Lula administration's response was a return to the same tactical style used during the Cardoso era, chiefly, the creation of new programs that offered other countries the prospect of satisfaction without incurring noticeable costs for Brazil. As proved the case with PSCI, success was far from overwhelming, but still substantive enough to at least retain the attention of other states when Itamaraty decided to present new ideas.

Conclusion

Nuance is important. Traditional conceptions of leadership as relying on forms of coercion and domination played little role in the approach adopted by Itamaraty during the Cardoso era. Instead, a new style of leadership was developed, one that found parallels in the Gramscian student-teacher dialectic's focus on consensus creation, discussion, and mutual internalization of new ideas and techniques. The intent was not to seek Brazilian leadership of a South American region through imposition, but to instigate a mutually beneficial ordering that would quietly embed Brazilian interests, aspirations, and strategies in the region. While this goal was sometimes hinted at in official statements (Cardoso 2000h; Lampreia 2000b) and academic analyses, it was not explicitly proclaimed or comprehensively examined until the transition to the Lula presidency (Almeida 2004; D. Costa 2003; H. Oliveira 2005; Vizentini 2003).

The theme that emerges from the political economy–based account of Brazilian foreign policy offered by this book is that Brazilian policymakers were seeking to use the principle of interdependence to fashion regional structures that would maximize national policymaking autonomy in the face of hemispheric and global pressures. The detailed discussions of economic and physical integration, leadership, ideas, and security issues demonstrate how initiatives in one area served to bolster and advance policy goals in another.

Of particular importance in this respect is the often-overlooked issue of infrastructure integration; it weaves through the discussion of both the economic and the security dimensions of Brazil's regionalist project, and is something that Cardoso himself has highlighted as central to his foreign policy (Cardoso and Lafer 2007). Brazil's foreign-policy makers sought to deploy ostensibly apolitical or technocratic agreements as a tool for reforming production structures and fostering the confidence and interdependence necessary to support Brazil-centered regional projects. This emerges most clearly in the security implications of IIRSA and the macroeconomic implications that regional energy matrices held for countries such as Bolivia, Paraguay, and, after the 2002 economic collapse, Argentina.

The inclusive nature of a Gramsci-inspired approach to leadership predicated on the notion of consensual hegemony, particularly in the fostering of substate-level interaction between countries, emerges clearly in the contrasting analysis of Mercosul, SAFTA, and IIRSA to strongly suggest that political intent is not enough to form a region. Rather, political initiatives must be married with leadership in concrete and seemingly apolitical policies such as infrastructure integration to bring about the mutual interpenetration necessary to incite pressure from civil society and business groups for a continuation and deepening of the regional project. The emphasis on cooperation and inclusion free of aggressive coercion is critical because, as has been argued here, the formation and operation of a successful region depends on decisions made by business independent of state influence.

In short, the ultimate decision by business and the wider population to embrace a regional project on a sustained basis will be based on a calculation of interests, not on political rhetoric. As the brief discussion of Lula's continuation of the consensual hegemony leadership strategy suggests, an important part of the approach adopted by Itamaraty during the Cardoso era was a clear and sustained willingness to actively disavow leadership ambitions when solid, fungible resources were not available consistently to offer payoffs in return for acquiescence to the regional project.

If we turn our attention to the successes and failures of Brazil's foreign policy during the Cardoso era it becomes possible to understand the formative dynamics of a regional project guided by consensual leadership. The evolution of a region is not a "big bang" appearance of a new order when a dominant state expends power resources to forcefully impose a particular structure on the international system. Instead, the process is more akin to the contrast between light and shadows. In areas of light what we might term the substance of a consensual hegemonic project—the regional project led by the predominant state—is accepted and in operation. The shadows offer metaphorical nuance to discussions about the uptake of the regionalist vision, with soft shadows indicating partial acceptance and the deepest shadow areas where the consensually hegemonic nature of the region has been rejected. A longer-term question that the researcher might then address is whether or not the "light" of a particular consensual vision will spread across the political landscape of a region, an event that would represent participating states' full acceptance of the "hegemon's" leadership and internalization of the "consensual hegemony" represented in the regionalist project.

The point here is that the region must be accepted by the participating states through a series of conscious decisions; the key is the reluctance to use direct or semidirect force to impose the project. Indeed, in the Brazilian case we might expand this proposition to suggest that the unwillingness to impose may well be accompanied by an inability to absorb the costs associated with imposition.

The suggestion that the leader is unwilling and potentially unable to impose its project is most evident in discussion of the ideas dimension. This discussion focuses on a reflexive relationship between internal and external notions of identity and leads to a self-conception that has a major impact on the formation of foreign-policy priorities and prerogatives. A significant element of this process, a state's position in the structure of the international political economy, is not something that can be imposed without inducing a reordering of the international system. The would-be creator of a regional project must therefore focus on framing a worldview and a set of core values and beliefs that might be used to formulate a common approach to international challenges. Moreover, the ideational basis of the project must be disseminated throughout the other states, which requires a dialogue reminiscent of Gramsci's student-teacher dialectic.

While force might compel other states to take up a particular ideational package, the goal of this process is to create an order that does not require continuous policing; this in turn requires the other states willingly to adopt and internalize the core values and beliefs underpinning the region. For this to take place there must exist not only a perceived consonance of interests, but also the prospect of positive returns in the economic and security dimensions.

In the Brazilian case the ideational basis was certainly not rejected by the other South American countries during the Cardoso era, but neither was it wholeheartedly embraced. The suggestion that national development might best be pursued through collective action via creation of a continent-wide region was viewed with some interest, but not to the extent that other states on the continent absorbed the substance of the project and unconsciously used it as the basis for the independent formulation of new policies. Nevertheless, partial dissemination of the ideas underpinning Brazilian foreign policy provided a common understanding that Itamaraty could use to frame regional economic and security strategies as well as to pursue the style of inclusive leadership necessary to advance the concept of South America as a viable geoeconomic and geopolitical actor.

It is in the economic dimension that the question of capabilities as a barrier to region formation becomes most apparent. In one sense the other South

American states were being asked to choose between closer approximation with the United States or greater continental integration, which implied tighter linkages to a very uncertain Brazilian economy during the Cardoso era and first years of the Lula era. Setting aside for the moment the question of the infrastructural networks necessary to deliver goods to market, the enduring reality is that the Brazilian economy was not capable of serving in the role of what Kindleberger (1989) in effect describes as the buyer of last resort. Indeed, the discussion of investment flows within Mercosul and the pattern of trade disputes among bloc members makes it clear that, while there was some capacity to absorb imports and provide capital, Brazil during the Cardoso era and the first Lula administration remained economically and politically unable to underwrite and sustain the development of neighboring countries. In this sense Brazil was unable to truly take on the costs of leadership and fulfill the role of economic engine for South America, a shortcoming demonstrated by the paucity of complex transnationalized production chains and the slow spread of Brazilian firms throughout the continent.

It would be wrong, however, to suggest that policy in the economic dimension was a failure. Just as the ideational basis of the regional leadership project offered positive returns, so did efforts aimed at tighter economic integration. The advent and preservation of Mercosul allowed a transformation in trade patterns and the consolidation of value-added industries in addition to providing an expanded market to entice sustained inward flows of foreign direct investment. Elaboration of a continental energy matrix allowed Brazil to convert its greatest economic weakness into a strategic strength as it transformed energy dependency into a device to deepen ties with neighboring countries, especially Argentina, Paraguay, Bolivia, and Venezuela. Indeed, the combination of an emergent industrialized market in Mercosul and the deepened economic ties on the continent precipitated by the energy matrix pointed toward the potential for expanded intra–South American trade. A major result was the regional infrastructure-integration agreement signed in 2000 in Brasília, intended to create the physical conditions necessary for expanded economic integration in the future. Thus, while Itamaraty did not succeed in forming an integrated economic space on the continent oriented toward Brazil, steps toward creating the preconditions for deeper integration were initiated, bringing with them expanded regional economic opportunities for Brazilian firms and investors.

The security dimension provides a more ambiguous account of Brazil's capacity to absorb the costs and fulfill the duties of a leader because armed conflict and interstate war were largely an anomaly in South America during the twentieth century. The Brazilian response to the one potentially serious armed clash—the border dispute between Ecuador and Peru—was managed by Brazil decisively and amicably, reinforcing the legalistic precedent that saw countries on the continent meet at the negotiating table, not on the battlefield. The need to expend scarce resources on military hardware in order to prevent conflict was therefore limited. Indeed, the security goods provided by Brazil were primarily political in nature and used to provide responses to democratic disruptions on the continent as part of a standing policy of attempting to preserve autonomy of action and national sovereignty as central principles in the inter-American system.

This concentration on sovereignty, however, also formed the basis for the largest shortcoming in Brazil's foreign policy in the security dimension, namely, the failure to create and coordinate an effective response to the new security threats of narco-trafficking, terrorism, and insurgency. At the core of the country's failure to deal adequately with these new security issues lies an unwillingness to employ the same logic in the security dimension that policy-makers applied in the economic dimension. The ideational proposition that economic questions must be thought of in transnational terms was not carried through to the realm of security policy, despite vague suggestions in the 1996 national defense policy statement that the nature of threats to the nation was changing. If we accept the notion that leadership requires provision of goods in the ideas, economics, and security dimensions of a possible hegemony, then analysis of the security dimension shows an inherent contradiction in the regional vision advanced by Cardoso's foreign-policy makers. The emphasis on transnationalization in the economic dimension clashed with the concentration on national sovereignty in the security dimension, creating an internal contradiction that retarded the emergence of a stable and sustainable regional order.

Elements of the internal contradiction in the Brazilian regionalist project—the clash between economic openness and the isolation seemingly required by security needs—filtered through to the leadership dimension. Brazilian leadership was accepted by the other South American countries when there were clear signs that a truly common project was being pursued, one that encapsulated the shared interests of the region. The two leading examples are the response to the 1994 Miami Summit of the Americas and the rapid agreement and take up the IIRSA project launched at the 2000 Summit of South American Presidents in Brasília. It was in the pursuit of the EU-Mercosul and CAN-Mercosul interregional agreements that the semipermeable openness seen in the security dimension once again became evident. As one Brazilian diplomat noted, an unwillingness to accept a larger share of the costs associated with a CAN-Mercosul deal presented a central barrier to progress in the negotiations. Indeed, the withdrawal at one point of the other Mercosul countries from the process suggested a perception that, despite a rhetoric of economic internationalization, Brazilian thinking was still guided by a direct concentration on immediate national interests.

Again, the suggestion is that Brazil was unwilling to absorb some of the costs alluded to in Kindleberger's discussion of the need for a leader to establish and maintain a system. In terms of the consensual hegemonic approach to leadership employed in this book the implication is perhaps more damaging because it sent a message to other states that might have participated that the proposed project was formulated in a manner that might embed Brazilian privilege and prerogative in the regional system.

Two theoretical elements, then, emerge from our discussion of Brazil's attempt to construct new regional arrangements during the Cardoso era. In the neorealist and neoliberal institutionalist conceptualizations of hegemony a great deal of emphasis is placed on the ability of a particular state to lead by imposing its preferred version of order on the international system. This suggests that pursuit of a hegemonic project requires a preponderance of power resources. Yet, as scholars such as Keohane point out, there may be problems with such a force-dependent approach because of the destructive potential of modern warfare (Keohane 1984, 9–10). The argument is pushed further by scholars such as Nye (2002), who suggest that ideational factors have assumed greater importance in the shaping of the operational reality of the international political economy. The argument that can then be made, and one that is taken up by Pedersen's (2002) model of cooperative hegemony, is that there is a new space for middle and emerging powers to fashion region-based order without having to threaten or exercise domineering power. Indeed, even if the political will were present, it is highly questionable that a Brazilian foreign policy predicated on the principles of dominance and coercion would have much chance of medium-term, let alone lasting, success in South America. Leadership along the lines suggested by consensual hegemony, thus, opens a middle ground, allowing policymakers to develop ideas that can be married with a modicum of resources to recruit regional cooperation for projects that the initiating state might otherwise be unable to sustain unilaterally.

The greatest strength of an analysis informed by a consensually hegemonic leadership style lies in the importance of cooperation and consensus generation it reveals in the construction of Brazil's foreign-policy project as outlined in these pages. Itamaraty's leadership project was not predicated on subsuming smaller actors under the will of the more powerful, but in seeking out ways of collectively addressing shared challenges and attempting to effect mutually desired outcomes, albeit with Brazilian interests at the fore. Here it can be suggested that the process of construction can be as, if not more, important than the realization of the completed project. The centrality of discussion and dialogue to the Brazilian leadership style was conducive to a rise of mutual understanding between the participating states and the formulation of joint positions on a range of issues. This has an immediate impact on regional-integration projects, drawing on the sort of approximation of interests and objectives crucial to the emergence of a stable regional bloc (Hettne 1999). Indeed, one consideration that might be entertained by future researchers is whether or not the ultimate expression of a consensual hegemony is the sort of deeply institutionalized regional arrangement typified by the European Union.

The suggestion that Brazilian foreign policy attempted to build on Mercosul and form some type of a SAFTA points to an often unexplored facet of regionalism that is critical to discussions of other groupings such as the South Asian Association for Regional Cooperation or the Southern African Development Community, namely, how a political decision to form a region can be translated into a pressing and desired socioeconomic reality for business and civil society groups. The suggestion here is that future research on emerging-market regional associations make fuller use of the political-economy approach and broaden the standard political-interest and economic-growth analyses to encompass the impact that supposedly technocratic issues such as infrastructure integration, regulatory approximation, and ideational diffusion have on the integration of production structures and the transformation of geoeconomic spaces. In a sense this is a loud call for scholars to put maps on their walls when they are analyzing the political and economic realities of a region to, it is hoped, prompt the logistical question that is first nature to the business activity essential for effective regionalization: How will goods get to market? As has been suggested here, the alteration of government's, business,' and civil society's attitudes is crucial to the consolidation of a regional space. The question for researchers is why a particular group of states might choose or decline to encourage the grass-roots linkages that will create pressure for greater integration.

Bibliography

Abdenur, Roberto. 1994a. "A política externa brasileira e o 'sentimento de exclusão." In Fonseca Júnior and Nabuco de Castro (1994).

———. 1994b. "Política externa e desenvolvimento." *Política Externa* 3 (3) (December): 51–71.

———. 1997. "Mercosul, Alca, União Européia—Reflexões para uma estratégia brasileira." *Política Externa* 6 (2) (September): 62–70.

Adler, Emanuel and Michael Barnett, eds. 1998. *Security Communities*. Cambridge: Cambridge University Press.

Alden, Chris, and Marco Antonio Vieira. 2005. "The New Diplomacy of the South: South Africa, Brazil, India, and Trilateralism." *Third World Quarterly* 26 (7): 1077–1095.

Aleixo, José Carlos Brandi. 1989. "Fundamentos e linhas gerais da política externa do Brasil." *Revista Brasileira de Ciência Política* 1 (1) (March): 7–44.

Almeida, Paulo Roberto de. 1993. "O Mercosul no contexto regional e internacional." *Política Externa* 2 (2) (September): 86–103.

———. 2001. "Relações internacionais e política externa do Brasil: Uma perspectiva historíca." *Meridiano* 47 (10–12): (April–June).

———. 2003. "A política internacional do Partido dos Trabalhadores: Da fundação à diplomacia do governo Lula." *Revista Sociológica Política* 20 (June): 87–102.

———. 2004. "Uma política externa engajada: A diplomacia do governo Lula." *Revista Brasileira de Política Internacional* 47 (1): 162–184.

———. 2005. "Políticas de integração regional do governo Lula." *Política Internacional*, no. 29 (November) 33–62.

Almeida-Medeiros, Marcelo de. 1995. "Relações externas do MERCOSUL: Uma abordagem brasileira." *Revista Brasileira de Política Internacional* 38 (2): 31–58.

Amann, Edmund. 1999. "Technological Self-reliance in Brazil: Achievements and Prospects: Some Evidence from the Non-serial Capital Goods Sector." *Oxford Development Studies* 27 (3): 329–357.

——— and Werner Baer. 2002. "Neoliberalism and Its Consequences in Brazil." *Journal of Latin American Studies* 34: 945–959.

Amann, Edmund, and F. I. Nixon. 1999. "Globalisation and the Brazilian Steel Industry: 1988–1997." *Journal of Development Studies* 35 (6) (August): 59–88.

Amatangelo, Gina. 2001. "Andean Regional Initiative: A Policy Fated to Fail." *Foreign Policy in Focus* 6 (29) (August): 1–4.

Amin, Samir. 1999. "Regionalization in Response to Polarizing Globalization." In Hettne, Inotai, and Sunkel (1999).

Amorim, Celso L. N. 1991a. "O Brasil e a ordem internacional pós-golfo." *Contexto Internacional* 13 (1) (January–June): 25–34.

———. 1991b. "Despacho ao Memorandum DAM-I/108" (27 February). Brasília: Secretaria de Estado das Relações Exteriores.

———. 1994. "Uma diplomacia voltada para o desenvolvimento e a democracia." In Fonseca Júnior and Nabuco de Castro (1994).

———. 2002. "Uma política firme, sem confrontos." Entrevista concedida pelo embaixador Celso Amorim à Gazeta Mercantil (18 December): www.mre.gov.br.

———. 2003a. *Celso Amorim (depoimento, 1997)*. Rio de Janeiro: CPDOC.

———. 2003b. Discurso proferido pelo embaixador Celso Amorim por ocasião da transmissão do cardo de Ministro de Estado das Relações Exteriores. Brasília (1 January): www.mre.gov.br.

———. 2003c. "Resultados, não prazos." Entrevista concedida a revista Istoé (2 June): www.mre.gov.br.

———. 2003d. "Indústria brasileira." Entrevista à revista CNI. Brasília (1 October): www.mre.gov.br.

———. 2004. Statement by Minister Celso Amorim at the G-90 Meeting. Georgetown, Guyana (3 June).

Anderson, Jon Lee. 2001. "The Revolutionary: The President of Venezuela Has a Vision, and Washington Has a Headache." *The New Yorker* (10 September).

Andrade, Virgílio Moretzsohn de. 1989. "Memorandum para Secretaria de Estado, Transporte Terrestre. Ligação Atlântico-Pacifico via Paraguai." Etra Loo Eo5, DTC/ DOC/DAM-I (26 October). Asunción, Paraguay: Brazilian Embassy.

Aquino, Ricardo Caballero. 1997. "A Most Unholy City in the East." *Hemisfile* 8 (6) (November–December): 6–7.

Arditi, Benjamín. 1995. "Cálculo y contingencia en las transiciones a la democracia: La experiencia paraguaya." *European Review of Latin American and Caribbean Studies*, no. 58 (June): 77–95.

Argentina, Ministerio de Relaciones Exteriores, Comercio Internacional y Culto. 2002. "Argentina, Brasil, Paraguay y EE. UU. ('3+1') analizaron cuestión 'triple frontera.'" Dirección de Prensa, Información para la Prensa, no. 197/2002 (18 December).

Arrighi, Giovanni. 1993. "The Three Hegemonies of Historical Capitalism." In Gill (1993).

Arroio, Ana Carolina Machado. 1995. "A política externa e o sistema brasileiro de telecomunicações por satélite." *Contexto Internacional* 17 (1) (January–June): 61–88.

Arvelaiz, Maximillien, and Temir Ponceleon. 2002. "Pushing for a Coup d'État." *Covert Action Quarterly*, no. 72 (Spring): 12–16.

Augelli, Enrico, and Craig N. Murphy. 1993. "Gramsci and International Relations: A General Perspective with Examples from Recent US Policy toward the Third World." In Gill (1993).

Bacha, Edmar L., and Pedro S. Malan. 1989. "Brazil's Debt: From the Miracle to the Fund." In Stepan (1989).

Banco Central do Brasil. 2002. "Capitais brasileiros no exterior": www.bancocentral. gov.br.

Banco Nacional de Desenvolvimento Econômico e Social (BNDES). 1998a. *Petrobrás: Cadernos de infra-estrutura: Fatos—estratégias*, no. 9. Rio de Janeiro: BNDES, October.

———. 1998b. *Petróleo: Cadernos de infra-estrutura: Fatos—estratégias*, no. 10. Rio de Janeiro: BNDES, December.

Barbosa, Rubens Antônio. 1993a. "SGIE memorandum para o Sr. secretário-geral, 'ALADI/GT ad hoc.' Revisão do TM-80. Futuro da ALADI." SGIE/035 (15 February). Brasília: Secretaria de Estado das Relações Exteriores.

———. 1993b. "Memorandum para o Sr. Ministro de Estado, interino: Presidente da Corporación Andina de Fomento. Encontro com o Ministro da Fazenda," SGIE/191 (17 August). Brasília: Secretaria de Estado das Relações Exteriores.

———. 1994. "O Brasil e suas opções internacionais: A articulação entre o universal e o regional." *Política Externa* 3 (3) (December): 101–116.

———. 1996. "O lugar do Brasil no mundo." *Política Externa* 5 (2) (September): 69–82.

———. 2001. "A View from Brazil." *Washington Quarterly* 24 (2: 149–158.

———. N.d. "The Evolution of the Integration Process in South America: From the Sixties to the Millennium." Washington, D.C.: Brazilian Embassy: http://www.brasilemb.org/embaixado_evolution_sa.shtml.

———. 2007. Author interview (São Paulo, 28 March): Former Brazilian ambassador to London and Washington and former lead figure in Mercosur relations.

Barbosa, Rubens Antônio, and Luís Panelli César. 1994a. "A integração sub-regional, regional e hemisférica: O esforço brasileiro." In Fonseca Júnior and Nabuco de Castro (1994).

———. 1994b. "O Brasil como 'global trader.'" In Fonseca Júnior and Nabuco de Castro (1994).

Barreto, Fernando de Mello. 2001. *Os sucessores do Barão, 1912–1964: Relações exteriores do Brasil*. São Paulo: Paz e Terra.

Barros, Sebastião do Rego. 1995. "Seminário Eixos de Integração sul-americana corredores de exportação, 13 de setembro de 1995." In Barros (1999).

———. 1997. "A política externa e a defesa nacional—XXXII Curso de Aperfeiçoamento de Diplomatas." 31 March. Reprinted in Barros (1999).

———. 1999. *Política externa em tempo real: A gestão do Embaixador Sebastião do Rego Barros no Itamaraty, 3 de janeiro de 1995 a 31 de dezembro de 1998: Discursos, palestras, artigos e relatório*. Brasília: FUNAG (Fundação Alexandre Gusmão).

Bato, Marcel. 1999. "O processo de paz Peru-Equador." *Parcerias Estratégicas*, no. 6 (March): 241–247.

Baumann, Renato, and Juan Carlos Lerda, eds. 1987a. *Brasil-Argentina-Uruguai: A integração em debate*. Brasília: Editora Universidade de Brasília.

———. 1987b. "A integração econômica entre Brasil, Argentina e Uruguai: Que tipo de integração se pretende?" In Baumann and Lerda.

Becker, Bertha K., and Claudio A. G. Egler. 1992. *Brazil: A New Regional Power in the World-Economy*. Cambridge: Cambridge University Press.

Beers, Rand. 2001. "Andean Regional Initiative: Testimony by Assistant Secretary of State for International Narcotics and Law Enforcement Affairs to the Senate Committee on Appropriations Subcommittee, Washington, D.C., 11 July 2001." *DISAM Journal* 23 (4) (Summer): 80–87.

Berger, Peter L., and Thomas Luckman. 1966. *The Social Construction of Reality: A Treatise in the Sociology of Knowledge*. New York: Doubleday.

Bernal-Meza, Raúl. 1999. "Políticas exteriores comparadas de Argentina e Brasil rumo ao Mercosul." *Revista Brasileira de Política Internacional* 42 (2): 40–51.

———. 2002. "A política exterior do Brasil: 1990–2002." *Revista Brasileira de Política Internacional* 45 (1): 36–71.

Bernier, Ivan, and Martin Roy. 1999. "NAFTA and Mercosur: Two Competing Models?" In Mace and Bélanger (1999).

Bieler, Andreas, and David Morton. 2001a. "Introduction: Neo-Gramscian Perspectives in International Political Economy and the Relevance to European Integration." In Bieler and Morton (2001b).

———, eds. 2001b. *Social Forces in the Making of the New Europe: The Restructuring of European Social Relations in the Global Political Economy*. Basingstoke, U.K.: Palgrave.

Bonelli, Regis. 1998. "Las estrategias de los grandes grupos económicos brasileños." In Peres (1998).

———. 1999. "A Note on Foreign Direct Investment and Industrial Competitiveness in Brazil." *Oxford Development Studies* 27 (3): 305–327.

Borja, Ivan. 1998. Author interview (Quito, 9 December): Colonel and public relations officer, Ministry of Defense, Ecuador.

Branford, Sue. 2003. "The Fernando Henrique Cardoso Legacy." In Branford and Kuchinski (2003).

———. 2003b. "The Making of a Leader." In Branford and Kuchinski (2003).

Branford, Sue, and Bernardo Kuchinski, eds. 2003. *Politics Transformed: Lula and the Workers' Party in Brazil*. London: Latin American Bureau.

Brazil. Itamaraty. Subsecretaria-Geral de Planejamento Político e Econômico. 1993. "Reflexões sobre a política externa brasileira." Working paper. Brasília: FUNAG/IPRI.

———. Secretaria de Assuntos Internacionais, Ministerio de Fazenda. "Convênio de Pagamentos e créditos recíprocos (CCR)": www.fazenda.gov.br/ sain/m_inf_ccr.htm.

Bresser-Pereira, Luiz Carlos. 2002. "The Second Washington Consensus and Brazil's Quasi-Stagnation": www.bresserpereira.org.br.

Brun, Diego Abente. 1998. "'People Power' in Paraguay," *Journal of Democracy* 10 (3): 93–100.

Bueno, Clodoaldo. 2002a. "Parte II: Da agroexportação ao desenvolvimento (1889–1964)." In Cervo and Bueno (2002).

———. 2002b. "O barão do Rio Branco e o Projeto da América do Sul." Brasília: FUNAG/IPRI/ IRBr (2002).

Bulmer-Thomas, Victor and James Dunkerley, eds. *The United States and Latin America: The New Agenda.* 1999. London/Cambridge: Institute for Latin American Studies, University of London, and David Rockefeller Center for Latin American Studies, Harvard University.

Burges, Sean W. 2005a. "Bounded by the Reality of Trade: Practical Limits to a South American Region." *Cambridge Review of International Affairs* 18 (3) (October): 437–454.

———. 2005b. "Auto-Estima in Brazil: The Logic of Lula's South-South Foreign Policy." *International Journal* 60 (4): 1133–1151.

———. 2005c. "The OAS as Democratic Policeman?" *FOCAL Point* 4 (6) (June): 1–2.

———. 2006. "Without Sticks or Carrots: Brazilian Leadership in South America during the Cardoso Era, 1992–2003." *Bulletin of Latin American Research* 25 (1) (January): 23–42.

———. 2007. "Building a Global Southern Coalition: The Competing Approaches of Brazil's Lula and Venezuela's Chávez." *Third World Quarterly* 28 (7): 1343–1358.

———. 2008. "Consensual Hegemony: Theorizing Brazilian Foreign Policy after the Cold War." *International Relations* 22 (1): 65–84.

Burges, Sean W., and Jean Daudelin. 2007. "Brazil: How Realists Defend Democracy." In Legler, Lean, and Boniface (2007).

Burns, E. Bradford. 1966. *The Unwritten Alliance: Rio Branco and Brazilian-American Relations.* New York: Columbia University Press.

Cabral, Otávio. 2007. "Nem na ditadura: Entrevista com Roberto Abdenur." *Veja* (5 February).

Cafruny, Alan W. 1990. "A Gramscian Concept of Declining Hegemony: Stages of U.S. Power and the Evolution of International Relations." In Rapkin (1990).

Calleya, Stephen C., ed. 2000. *Regionalism in the Post–Cold War Order.* Aldershot, U.K.: Ashgate.

Cammack, Paul. 1997. *Capitalism and Democracy in the Third World: The Doctrine for Political Development.* London: Leicester University Press.

Cannabrava, Ivan. 1997. "Memorandum para o Sra. DG do DCD. Processo de paz Equador-Peru. MOMEP. Equipamento e operador de comunicações." SGAP/96 (11 August). Brasília: Secretaria de Estado das Relações Exteriores.

Cardoso, Alberto Mendes. 2002. "Pronunciamento do Senhor Alberto Mendes Cardoso, chefe da delegação do Brasil ao II período ordinário de sessões do CICTE."

Organization of American States, Comitê Interamericano contra o Terrorismo, segundo período ordinário de sessões cicte/doc. 8/02 (30 January).

Cardoso, Fernando Henrique. 1973. "Associated-Dependent Development: Theoretical and Practical Implications." In Stepan (1973).

———. 1975. *Autoritarismo e democratização*. Rio de Janeiro: Paz e Terra.

———. 1979. "On the Characterization of Authoritarian Regimes in Latin America." In Collier (1979).

———. 1985. *A democracia necessária*. Campinas, Brazil: Papirus.

———. 1989. "Associated-Dependent Development and Democratic Theory." In Stepan (1989).

———. 1990. "New Approaches to Development in Latin America." In Cardoso with Font (2001).

———. 1993. "Toward a New Dialogue in North South Relations." In Cardoso with Font (2001).

———. 1995. "Democracy and Development." *CEPAL Review*, no. 56 (August): 7–12.

———. 1996a. "Impacto da globalização nos países em desenvolvimento: Riscos e oportunidades." Speech given at the Colegio de México, Mexico City (20 February).

———. 1996b. "The Impact of Globalization on Developing Countries." In Cardoso with Font (2001).

———. 1996c. "Globalization and International Relations." In Cardoso with Font (2001).

———. 1996d. "Globalization and Politics." In Cardoso with Font (2001).

———. 1997a. "Notas para a exposição do Senhor Presidente da República na Organização das Nações Unidas para a Alimentação e a Agricultura (FAO)." Rome (14 February).

———. 1997b. "Speech to the London School of Economics and Political Science." London (3 December).

———. 1997c. "As razões do presidente." *Veja* (1997): www.mre.gov.br.

———. 1997d. "Discurso do Senhor Presidente da República no banquete oferecido pelo Lord Mayor e a Corporação de Londres no Guildhall." London (3 December).

———. 1998a. "Discurso do Senhor Presidente na República na sessão comemorativa do cinqüentenário do Sistema Multilateral de Comércio." Geneva (19 May).

———. 1998b. "Speech to the Twentieth Special Session of the General Assembly Devoted to the Fight against Illicit Production, Sale, Demand, Traffic and Distribution of Narcotic Drugs and Psychotropic Substances and Related Activities." New York (8 June).

———. 1999a. Discurso na abertura da Primeira Reunião do Foro Empresarial Mercosul—Europa. Rio de Janeiro (21 February).

———. 1999b. Discurso na almoço com o Presidente do México na Fiesp. São Paulo (28 April).

———. 1999c. Discurso por ocasião da abertura da IX Conferência Ibero-Americana. Havana (15–16 November).

———. 1999d. "Progressive Governance for the 21st Century." Speech, Florence, Italy (20–21 November).

———. 1999e. Discurso por ocasião da Reunião do Conselho do Mercado Comum com Bolívia e Chile. Montevideo (8 December).

———. 2000a. "An Age of Citizenship." *Foreign Policy*, no. 119 (Summer): 40–43.

———. 2000b. Speech at the lunch hosted by António Guterres, prime minister of Portugal. Lisbon (8 March).

———. 2000c. Speech on the occasion of the official visit to the Republic of Costa Rica. San José (4 April).

———. 2000d. Speech at the opening ceremony of the Hannover World Exposition— EXPO-2000. Hannover (31 May).

———. 2000e. "Brazil and a New South America." *Valor Econômico* trans. Brazilian Ministry of Foreign Relations, Brazil (30 August).

———. 2000f. Speech to the German Society for Foreign Affairs. Berlin (5 October).

———. 2000g. Address by the President of the Republic, Fernando Henrique Cardoso, at the opening session of the Fourth Conference of Defense Ministers of the Americas." Manaus, Brazil (17 October).

———. 2000h. Speech by the President of the Republic, Fernando Henrique Cardoso, at the opening ceremony of the Sixth Economic Summit of Mercosur, Rio Palace Hotel, Rio de Janeiro.

———. 2000i. Final address to the Sixth Mercosul Summit. Rio de Janeiro.

———. 2001. "A política externa do Brasil no início de um novo século: Uma mensagem do Presidente da República." *Revista Brasileira de Política Internacional* 44 (1): 5–12.

———. 2002. "Towards a Democratic Global Governance: A Brazilian Perspective." The Cyrill Foster Lecture, Oxford University (13 November).

———. 2006. *A arte da política: A história que vivi*. Rio de Janeiro: Civilização Brasileira.

———. 2007. "New Paths: Reflections about Some Challenges of Globalization." Speech delivered at the University of North Carolina, Chapel Hill (26 March).

———, and William J. Clinton. 1997. "Remarks by President Clinton and President Cardoso at Reception, Brasília Room, Ministry of Foreign Affairs, Brasília, Brazil." Washington, D.C.: The White House, Office of the Press Secretary (13 October).

Cardoso, Fernando Henrique, and Enzo Faletto. 1979. *Dependency and Development in Latin America*. Trans. Marjory Mattingly Urquidi. Berkeley and Los Angeles: University of California Press.

Cardoso, Fernando Henrique, with Maurício Font. 2001. *Charting a New Course: The Politics of Globalization and Social Transformation*. New York: Rowman & Littlefield.

Cardoso, Fernando Henrique, and Celso Lafer. 2007. Author interview (São Paulo, 30 August).

Cardoso, Fernando Henrique, and Mário Soares. 1998. *O mundo em português: Um diálogo*. São Paulo: Paz e Terra.

Cardoso, Fernando Henrique, and Roberto Pompeu de Toledo. 1998. *O presidente segundo o sociólogo*. São Paulo: Companhia das Letras.

Cardoso, Fernando Henrique, with Brian Winter. 2006. *The Accidental President of Brazil: A Memoir*. New York: Public Affairs.

Carriço, Sérgio S. 1989. "Memorandum para o Sr. Chefe do DAA, 'Brasil-Bolívia. Gás.' Visita dos Ministros Bedregal e Illanes." DAM-II/18 (2 February). Brasília: Secretaria de Estado das Relações Exteriores.

Cason, Jeffrey. 2000. "Democracy Looks South: Mercosul and the Politics of Brazilian Trade Strategy." In Kingstone and Power (2000).

———. 2002. "On the Road to Southern Cone Economic Integration." *Journal of Interamerican Studies and World Affairs* 42 (1) (Spring): 23–42.

Cavagnari Filho, Geraldo Lesbat. 2002. "Introdução à defesa da Amazônia." *Carta Internacional* 10 (107–108) (January–February): 19–21.

Cervo, Amado Luiz. 1997. "Política de comércio exterior e desenvolvimento: A experiência brasileira." *Revista Brasileira de Política Internacional* 40 (2): 5–26.

———. 2001. *Relações internacionais da América Latina: Velhos e novos paradigmas*. Brasília: Instituto Brasileiro de Relações Internacionais.

———. 2002. "Relações internacionais do Brasil: Um balanço da era Cardoso." *Revista Brasileira de Política Internacional* 45 (1): 5–35.

———, and Clodoaldo Bueno. 2002. *História da política exterior do Brasil*. Brasília: Editora Universidade Nacional de Brasília.

Child, John. 1979. "Geopolitical Thinking in Latin America." *Latin American Research Review* 14 (2): 89–111.

Chohfi, Osmar V. 2002. Author interview (Brasília, 8 October): Secretary general of Itamaraty; ambassador to Ecuador for four years in the 1990s and during the settling of the Ecuador-Peru border conflict.

Chudnovsky, Daniel, and Andrés López. 1999. "Inversión extranjera directa y empresas multinacionales de países en desarrollo: Tendencias y marco conceptual." In Chudnovsky, Kosacoff, and López (1999).

———. 2000. "A Third Wave of FDI from Developing Countries: Latin American TNCs in the 1990s." *Transnational Corporations* 9 (2) (August): 31–74.

Chudnovsky, Daniel, Bernardo Kosacoff, and Andrés López, eds. 1999. *Las multinacionales latinoamericanas: Sus estrategias en un mundo globalizado*. Buenos Aires: Fondo de Cultura Económica de Argentina.

Cleaver, Vitória Alice. 1990. "DAM-I Memorandum para o Sr. Chefe do DAA, 'Hidrovia Paraguai-Paraná.' CIHPP. Objetivos, composição e natureza jurídica." DAM-I/108 (27 December). Brasília: Secretaria de Estado das Relações Exteriores.

———. 1991. "Memorandum para o Sr. Chefe do DA, 'Hidrovia Paraguai-Paraná.' IV Reunião do Comitê Intergovernmental (Colônia do Sacramento, 27 e 28/02 e 1/03 de 1991). Relatório. Questão da composição e natureza jurídica de comitê." DAM-I/13 (18 March). Brasília: Secretaria de Estado das Relações Exteriores.

Collier, David, ed. 1979. *The New Authoritarianism in Latin America*. Princeton, N.J.: Princeton University Press.

Collor, Fernando. 1991a. "Discurso por ocasião da assinatura do tratado para constituição do Mercado Comum do Sul (MERCOSUL), em Assunção, em 26 de março de 1991." *Resenha de Política Exterior do Brasil*, no. 68 (1st semester): 31–40.

———. 1991b. "Discurso pelo Presidente Fernando Collor no jantar oferecido em homenagem ao Senhor Andrés Rodríguez, presidente do Paraguai, no Palácio Itamaraty, em 26 de agosto de 1991." *Resenha de Política Exterior do Brasil*, no. 69: 93–95.

Comisión Económica para America Latina y el Caribe (CEPAL). *Economic Survey of Latin America, 1949*. 1951. Santiago: United Nations.

———. 2002. "El costo del transporte internacional, y la integración competitividad de América Latina y el Caribe." *Boletin FAL*, no. 191 (July): online edition.

Cooper, Andrew. 2001. "More Than a Star Turn: Canadian Hybrid Diplomacy and the OAS Mission to Peru." *International Journal* 56 (2) (Spring): 279–296.

———, Richard A. Higgott, and Kim Richard Nossal. 1993. *Relocating Middle Powers: Australia and Canada in a Changing World Order*. Vancouver: University of British Columbia Press.

Cooper, Andrew F., and Thomas Legler. 2001. "The OAS Democratic Solidarity Paradigm: Questions of Collective and National Leadership." *Latin American Politics and Society* 43 (1) (Spring): 103–126.

Corrêa, Luiz Felipe de Seixas. 1999a. "O Brasil e o mundo no limiar do novo século: Diplomacia e desenvolvimento." *Revista Brasileira de Política Internacional* 42 (1): 5–29.

———. 1999b. "Brazilian Foreign Policy." Lecture by Ambassador Luiz Felipe de Seixas Corrêa, External Relations secretary-general, at the Human Resources Training Center (CEFARH), Intellligence Department, Institutional Security Secretariat, Office of the President of the Republic (5 November).

Corsi, Francisco Luiz. 1999. *Estado novo: Política externa e projeto nacional*. São Paulo: Editora UNESP.

Costa, Darc. 2003. *Estratégia nacional: A cooperação sul-americana como caminho para a inserção internacional do Brasil*. Rio de Janeiro: Aristeu Souza.

Costa, Thomas Guedes da. 1996. "La sécurite collective: Pensée et politique du Brésil." *Relations Internationales*, no. 86 (Summer): 199–212.

———. 2000. *Brazil in the New Decade: Searching for a Future*. Washington, D.C.: Center for Strategic and International Studies.

———. 2001. "Strategies for Global Insertion: Brazil and its Regional Partners." In Tulchin and Espach (2001).

Cox, Michael. 2001. "Whatever Happened to American Decline? International Relations and the New United States Hegemony." *New Political Economy* 6 (3): 311–340.

———, G. John Ikenberry, and Takashi Inoguchi, eds. 2000. *American Democracy Promotion: Impulses, Strategies, and Impacts*. Oxford: Oxford University Press).

Cox, Robert W. 1987. *Production Power and World Order: Social Forces in the Making of Modern History*. New York: Columbia University Press.

———. 1989. "Middlepowermanship, Japan, and Future World Order." In Cox, with Sinclair (1996).

———. 1983. "Gramsci, Hegemony, and International Relations: An Essay in Method." In Cox, with Sinclair (1996)

——— with Timothy Sinclair. 1996. *Approaches to World Order*. Cambridge: Cambridge University Press.

Crone, Donald. 1993. "Does Hegemony Matter? The Reorganization of the Pacific Political Economy." *World Politics* 45 (4) (July): 501–525.

Cruz, Ademar Seabra de, Antonio Ricardo F. Cavalcante, and Luiz Pedone. 1993. "Brazil's Foreign Policy under Collo." *Journal of Interamerican Studies and World Affairs* 35 (1): 119–144.

Cunningham, Susan M. 1999. "Made in Brazil: Cardoso's Critical Path from Dependency via Neoliberal Options and the Third Way in the 1990s." *European Review of Latin American and Caribbean Studies*, no. 67 (December): 75–86.

Danese, Sérgio. 1999. *Diplomacia presidencial: História e crítica*. Rio de Janeiro: Topbooks.

da Silva, Luiz Inácio Lula. 2003a. Discurso no Conselho de Relações Internacionais, Nova York. New York (25 September): www.mre.gov.br.

———. 2003b. Discurso no encerramento do seminário sobre negócios e investimentos." Damascus (3 December): www.mre.gov.br.

———. 2003c. Palavras no encontro com estudantes brasileiros." Havana (27 September): www.mre.gov.br.

———. 2003d. Declaração à imprensa, durante visita do presidente do Equador, Lucio Gutiérrez. Brasília (27 May): www.mre.gov.br.

———. 2004a. Statement Opening the General Debate of the 59th Session of the General Assembly of the United Nations." (21 September): www.mre.gov.br.

———. 2004b. "Uma parceria de sucesso." Discurso no encontro com lideranças empresariais indianas. New Delhi (27 January): www.mre.gov.br.

———. 2004c. Discurso no encerramento do seminário Brasil-China: Xangai, China (26 May): www.mre.gov.br.

———. 2004d. "Palavras em encontro com representantes do Fórum da Sociedade Civil, na XI UNCTAD—part II." São Paulo (15 June).

Daudelin, Jean. 2008. "Joining the Club: Lula and the End of Periphery for Brazil." In Nitschack, Birle, and Costa (forthcoming).

Dávila-Villers, David R. 1992. "Competition and Co-operation in the River Plate: The Democratic Transition and Mercosur." *Bulletin of Latin American Research* 11 (3): 261–277.

Devlin, Robert, Antoni Estevadeordal, and Ekaterina Krivonos. 2003. "The Trade and Cooperation Nexus: How Does the Mercosur-EU Process Measure Up?" *INTAL-ITD-STA Occasional Paper* 22 (March).

dos Santos, Theotônio. 1989. "Integração latino-americana: Forças políticas em choque, experiências e perspectivas." *Revista Brasileira de Ciência Política* 1 (1) (March): 71–90.

———. 2000. *A teoria da dependência: Balanço e perspetivas*. Rio de Janeiro: Civilização Brasileira.

———and Laura Randall. 1998. "The Theoretical Foundations of the Cardoso Government: A New Stage of the Dependency Theory Debate." *Latin American Perspectives* 25 (1): 53–70.

Ecuador, Republic of. 2002. II Reunião de Presidentes da América do Sul, declaração sobre a Zona de Paz Sul-Americana. Guayaquil, 26–27 July 2002: www.mre.gov.br/daa/declaracao_ zonadepaz.htm.

Emmerij, Louis, ed. 1997. *Economic and Social Development in the XXI Century.* Washington, D.C.: Inter-American Development Bank.

Evans, Peter. 1979. *Dependent Development: The Alliance of Multinational, State, and Local Capital in Brazil.* Princeton, N.J.: Princeton University Press.

Fanon, Frantz. 1967. *Black Skin, White Masks.* Trans. C. L. Markmann. New York: Grove Press.

Farcau, Bruce W. 1996. *The Chaco War: Bolivia and Paraguay, 1932–1935.* Westport, Conn.: Praeger.

Faria, Vilmar, and Eduardo Graeff. 1999. *Progressive Governance for the 21st Century: The Brazilian Experience.* Brasília: Presidency of the Republic Special Advisory Body, November.

Fawcett, Louise, and Andrew Hurrell, eds. 1995. *Regionalism in World Politics: Regional Organization and International Order.* Oxford: Oxford University Press.

Feinberg, Richard E. 1997. *Summitry in the Americas: A Progress Report.* Washington, D.C.: Institute for International Economics.

Femia, Joseph V. 1987. *Gramsci's Political Thought: Hegemony, Consciousness, and the Revolutionary Process.* Oxford: Clarendon Press.

Ferraz, João Carlos, David Kupfer, and Franklin Serrano. 1999. "Macro/Micro Interactions: Economic and Institutional Uncertainties and Structural Change in Brazilian Industry." *Oxford Development Studies* 27 (3): 279–304.

Ferris, Elizabeth G. 1981. "The Andean Pact and the Amazon Treaty: Reflections of Changing Latin American Relations." *Journal of Interamerican Studies and World Affairs* 23 (2) (May): 147–175.

Ffrench-Davis, Ricardo. 1988. "An Outline of a Neo-Structuralist Approach." *CEPAL Review*, no. 34 (April): 37–44.

"Final Press Conference by President Clinton Following the Summit of the Americas." 1994. *Federal News Service* (11 December).

Flecha de Lima, Paulo Tarso. 1994. "O Brasil e o mundo após-guerra fria." Speech at Paul H. Nitze School of Advanced International Studies, 13 April 1994. In Flecha de Lima (1997).

———. 1997. *Caminhos diplomáticos: 10 anos de agenda internacional.* Rio de Janeiro: Livraria Francisco Alves.

Florêncio, Sérgio Abreu e Lima. 1992. "Memorandum para o Sr. Chefe do Departamento de Integração Latino-Americana. Tratamento do tema serviços no âmbito do Mercosul. Principais aspectos. Proposta de constituição de Grupo de Trabalho." Brasília: Secretaria de Estado das Relações Exteriores.

Flôres, Renato G. 1997. "Brazilian Trade Policy and the WTO 1996 Review." *World Economy* 20 (5): 615–631.

Foley, James B. 2000. "Ecuador: Change in Government." Press statement by James B. Foley, deputy spokesman, U.S. Department of State (22 January).

Fonseca, Gélson. 2004. *A legitimidade e outras questões internacionais: Poder e ética entre as nações*. 2nd ed. São Paulo: Paz e Terra.

Fonseca Júnior, Gélson, and Sérgio Henrique Nabuco de Castro, eds. 1994. *Temas de política externa brasileira II*. Vol. 1. São Paulo: Paz e Terra.

Fonseca, Luiz Henrique Pereira da. 1989. "Memorandum para o Sr. Chefe da DAA. Relações Brasil-Chile. Visita oficial do Senhor Secretário-Geral a Santiago." DAM-I/39 (14 June). Brasília: Secretaria de Estado das Relações Exteriores.

Font, Mauricio A. 2003. *Transforming Brazil: A Reform Era in Perspective*. New York: Rowman and Littlefield.

——— and Anthony Peter Spanakos, eds. 2004. *Reforming Brazil*. Lanham, Md.: Lexington Books.

Fontana, Benedetto. 1993. *Hegemony and Power: On the Relation between Gramsci and Machiavelli*. Minneapolis: University of Minnesota Press.

Forhmann, Alicia. 2000. "The New Regionalism and Collective Diplomacy in Latin America." In Hettne, Inotai, and Sunkel (2000).

Fournier, Dominique. 1999. "The Alfonsín Administration and the Promotion of Democratic Values in the Southern Cone and Andes." *Journal of Latin American Studies* 31: 39–74.

——— and Sean W. Burges. 2000. "Form before Function: Democratization in Paraguay." *Canadian Journal of Latin American and Caribbean Studies* 25 (49): 5–32.

Fowler, Will, ed. 1996. *Authoritarianism in Latin America Since Independence*. Westport, Conn.: Greenwood Press.

Franco, Itamar. 1993. Discurso na primeira sessão de trabalho, em assuntos políticos, durante a VII Cúpula Presidencial do Grupo do Rio (15 October).

Fundação Alexandre de Gusmão (FUNAG). 1997. *O Mercosul e a integração sul-americana: Mais do que a economia. Encontro de culturas*. Brasília: FUNAG.

Fundação Alexandre de Gusmão (FUNAG)/ Instituto de Pesquisa de Relações Internacionais (IPRI)/Instituto Rio Branco (IRBr). 2002. "Seminário: Modernização do Brasil." Mimeograph (28–29 August). Brasília: FUNAG/IPRI/IRBr.

G-20. 2005. "Bhurban G-20 Ministerial Declaration." Bhurban, Pakistan (9–10 September): www.wto-pakistan.org/statements/G20_Min_Declaration.doc.

Gallup, John Luke, Alejandro Gaviria, and Eduardo Lora. 2003. *Is Geography Destiny? Lessons from Latin America*. Palo Alto, Calif.: Stanford University Press.

Gamble, Andrew, and Anthony Payne, eds. 1996a. *Regionalism and World Order*. Basingstoke, U.K.: Macmillan.

———. 1996b. "Introduction: The Political Economy of Regionalism and World Order." In Gamble and Payne (1996a).

Garcia, Eugênio Vargas. 2000. *Cronologia das relações internacionais do Brasil*. Brasília: FUNAG.

Garcia, Marco Aurélio. 2003. "Brazilian Future." *openDemocracy.net* (17 July).

———. 2007. Author interview (Brasília, 22 March): Was the international secretary of the Partido dos Trabalhadores in Brazil and Special advisor on foreign affairs to president Luiz Inácio Lula da Silva.

Gates, Scott, Torbjøm L. Knutsen, and Jonathon W. Moses. 1996. "Democracy and Peace: A More Skeptical View." *Journal of Peace Research* 33 (1) (February): 1–10.

Gauto Vielman, R. 2005. "Facilitación del comercio." Presentation to the Trade Facilitation: A Tool for Development panel, 5th World Trade Organization Public Symposium, Geneva (21 April).

Giambiagi, Fábio, and Maurício Mesquita Moreira, eds. 1999. *A economia brasileira nos anos 90.* Rio de Janeiro: Banco Nacional de Desenvolvimento Econômico e Social.

Gill, Stephen. 1990. *American Hegemony and the Trilateral Commission.* Cambridge: Cambridge University Press.

———, ed. 1993. *Gramsci, Historical Materialism, and International Relations.* Cambridge: Cambridge University Press.

Gill, Stephen, and David Law. 1988. *The Global Political Economy: Perspectives, Problems and Policies.* Baltimore: Johns Hopkins University Press.

Gilpin, Robert. 1981. *War and Change in World Politics.* New York: Cambridge University Press.

———. 1987. *The Political Economy of International Relations.* Princeton, N.J.: Princeton University Press.

Goertzl, Ted G. 1999. *Fernando Henrique Cardoso: Reinventing Democracy in Brazil.* Boulder, Colo.: Lynne Rienner.

Golbery do Couto e Silva. 1967. *Geopolítica do Brasil.* Rio de Janeiro: José Olympia.

Goldberg, Jeffrey. 2002. "In the Party of God: Hezbollah Sets up Operations in South America and the United States." *The New Yorker* (28 October).

Goldstein, Judith, and Robert O. Keohane. "Ideas and Foreign Policy: An Analytical Framework." In Goldstein and Keohane (1993)

———, eds. 1993. *Ideas and Foreign Policy: Beliefs, Institutions, and Political Change.* Ithaca, N.Y.: Cornell University Press.

Gomes, Francisco de Paula Magalhães. 2001. Author interview (Brasília, 21 September): director, GEIPOT, Brazilian Transportation Planning Company, Ministry of Transport. GEIPOT has since been closed.

Gonçalves, Antonino Mena. 2002. Author interview (Brasília, 27 September): career Brazilian diplomat (ambassador rank), director-general of the Department of the Americas, Ministry of Foreign Affairs.

Gonçalves, José Botafogo. 1995. "Memorandum para o Sr. Chefe de Departamento de Integração. Brasil-Paraguai. Comércio." SGIE/166 (9 October). Brasília: Secretaria de Estado das Relações Exteriores.

Gordon, Lincoln. 2001. *Brazil's Second Chance: En Route toward The First World.* Washington, D.C.: Brookings Institution.

Gramsci, Antonio. 1957. *Antonio Gramsci: The Modern Prince & Other Writings.* Trans. Louis Marks. New York: International Publishers.

———. "The Modern Prince." 1957. In Gramsci (1957).

———. 1971. *Selections from the Prison Notebooks*. ed. and trans. Quiton Hoare and Geoffrey Nowell Smith. London: Lawrence and Wishart.

Grugel, Jean, and Marcelo de Almeida Medeiros. 1999. "Brazil and MERCOSUR." In Grugel and Hout (1999a).

Grugel, Jean, and Wil Hout, eds. 1999a. *Regionalism across the North-South Divide: State Strategies in the Semi-Periphery*. London: Routledge.

———. 1999b. "Regions, Regionalism and the South." In Grugel and Hout (1999a).

Grupo do Rio. 1995. *Grupo do Rio: Documentos do mecanismo permanente de consulta e concertação política*. Brasília: FUNAG.

———. 2002. "Declaración del Grupo de Río sobre la situación en Venezuela" (12 April): www.oas.org/OASpage/press2002/sp/Año2002/abril2002/Declaracion RioVE.htm.

Grupo Executivo de Integração da Política de Transportes (GEIPOT). 2001. "Facilitação fronteiriça no transporte rodoviário internacional Brasil-Mercosul." Ministério dos Transportes de Brasilia (*November*).

Guimarães, Samuel Pinheiro. 1999. *Quinhentos anos de periferia: Uma contribuição ao estudo de política internacional*. Porto Alegre, Brazil: Editora da UFRGS (Universidade Federal do Rio Grande do Sul).

Guimarães Reis, Fernando. 1990. "Memorandum para o Sr. Secretário-Geral de Política Externa: Grupo do Rio, IV Reunião de Presidentes, Caracas 11 a 13 de outubro. Projeto de documento final." DAA/60 (24 August). Brasília: Secretaria de Estado das Relações Exteriores.

Gutiérrez, Lino. 2002. Remarks by Lino Gutiérrez, principal deputy assistant secretary for Western Hemisphere affairs, to the North-South Center Roundtable, Carnegie Endowment for International Peace, Washington, D.C. (17 April): www.state.gov/p/wha/rls/rm/9573.htm.

Guyana. Ministry of Foreign Affairs. 2000a. Press Statement (29 July): www.sdnp.org.gy/minfor/pr/ foraff_venez.html.

———. 2000b. "Guyana/Suriname." Posted online June): www.sdnp.org.gy/.

Haggard, Stephen, and Robert R. Kaufman. 1995. *The Political Economy of Democratic Transitions*. Princeton, N.J.: Princeton University Press.

Hakim, Peter. 2002. "Democracy and U.S. Credibility." *New York Times* (21 April).

Hashmi, M. Anaam. 2000. "Role of Mercosur in Regional Trade Growth." *Managerial Finance* 26 (1): 41–52.

Hausmann, Ricardo, and Eduardo Fernández-Arias. 2000. "Foreign Direct Investment: Good Cholesterol?" Paper prepared for the seminar The New Wave of Capital Inflows: Sea Change or Just Another Tide? Annual Meeting of the Board of Governors, Inter-American Development Bank and Inter-American Investment Corporation, New Orleans (26 March).

Heritage Foundation. 1994. "Heritage Foundation Discussion." Federal News Service (14 November).

Herman, Edward S., and Noam Chomsky. 1994. *Manufacturing Consent: The Political Economy of the Mass Media*. London: Vintage.

Herz, Monica, and João Pontes Nogueira. 2002. *Ecuador vs. Peru: Peacemaking Amid Rivalry*. International Peace Academy Occasional Paper Series. Boulder, Colo.: Lynne Rienner.

Hettne, Björn. 1995. "Introduction: Towards an International Political Economy of Development." *European Journal of Development Research* 7 (2) (December): 223–232.

———. 1999. "Globalization and the New Regionalism: The Second Great Transformation." In Hettne, Inotai, and Sunkel (1999).

Hettne, Björn, András Inotai, and Osvaldo Sunkel, eds. 1999. *Globalism and the New Regionalism*. Basingstoke, U.K.: Macmillan.

———. 2000. *The New Regionalism and the Future of Security and Development*. Basingstoke, U.K.: Macmillan.

Hettne, Björn, and Fredrik Söderbaum. 2000. "Theorising the Rise of Regionness." *New Political Economy* 5 (3) (November): 457–473.

Hey, Jeanne A. K. 1997. "Three Building Blocks of a Theory of Latin American Foreign Policy." *Third World Quarterly* 18 (4): 631–658.

———. 1998. "Is There a Latin American Foreign Policy?" Review essay, *Mershon International Studies Review* 42: 106–116.

Hilton, Isabel, and Eliana Cardoso. 1996. "Economic Reform in Brazil: An Interview with Eliana Cardoso." *International Affairs* 72 (4): 727–736.

Hilton, Stanley. 1981. "The United States, Brazil, and the Cold War, 1945–1960: End of the Special Relationship." *Journal of American History* 68 (3) (December): 599–624.

———. 1985. "The Argentine Factor in Twentieth-century Brazilian Foreign Policy Strategy." *Political Science Quarterly* 100 (1) (Spring): 27–51.

Hirschman, Albert O. 1945. *National Power and the Structure of Foreign Trade*. Berkeley and Los Angeles: University of California Press.

———, ed. 1962. *Latin American Issues: Essays and Comments*. New York: Twentieth Century Fund.

Hirst, Monica. 1992. "MERCOSUR and the New Circumstances for Its Integration." *CEPAL Review*, no. 46 (April): 139–150.

———. 2004. *The United States and Brazil: A Long Road of Unmet Expectations*. London: Routledge.

———, and Maria Regina Soares de Lima. 2002. "Contexto internacional, democracia e política externa." *Política Externa* 11 (2) (September–November): 78–98.

———. 2006. "Brazil as an Intermediate State and Regional Power: Action, Choice and Responsibilities." *International Affairs* 82 (1): 21–40.

Hoffmann, Andrea Ribeiro. 2002. "The Foreign Policy of the European Union towards Mercosur in Historical Perspective." *Cena Internacional* 4 (2) (December): 10–13.

Holanda, Francisco Mauro Brasil de. 2001. *O gás no Mercosul: Uma perspectiva brasileira*. Brasília: IRBr/FUNAG/Centro de Estudos Estratégicos).

Holsti, Ole R., Randolph M. Siverson, and Alexander L. George, eds. 1980. *Change in the International System*. Boulder, Colo.: Westview Press.

Hurrell, Andrew. 1986. "The Quest for Autonomy: The Evolution of Brazil's Role in the International System, 1964–1985." Ph.D. dissertation, Oxford University.

———. 1995. "Regionalism in Theoretical Perspective." In Fawcett and Hurrell (1995).

———. 1998a. "An Emerging Security Community in South America?" In Adler and Barnett (1998).

———. 1998b. "Security in Latin America." *International Affairs* 74 (3): 529–546.

Iglesias, Enrique. 2000. "Regional Cooperation for the Development of Infrastructure in South America and the Inter-American Development Bank." Speech to the Brasília summit of South American presidents (31 August–1 September).

Ikenberry, G. John. 1996. "The Future of International Leadership." *Political Science Quarterly* 111 (3) (Autumn): 385–402.

India–Brazil–South Africa Dialogue Forum(IBSA). 2004. "Agenda for Cooperation." New Delhi (5 March): www.mre.gov.br.

Inter-American Development Bank (IADB). Integration and Regional Programs Department. 2000a. *A New Push for Regional Infrastructure Development in South America*. Washington, D.C.: Inter-American Development Bank, December.

———. 2000b. "Integration and Trade in the Americas." Periodic note (December).

———. 2000c. "La contribución del Banco Interamericano de Desarrollo a la integración física de América del Sur." (August).

IRELA (Institute for European-Latin American Relations). 1999. "Paraguay after the Crisis: Will Democracy Prosper?" *IRELA Briefing* BRF-99/6–PRY (23 April).

Jagdeo, Bharrat. 2000. "Statement by His Excellency President Bharrat Jagdeo on the Recent Pronouncements by Venezuela and Its Claim to Essequibo" (28 July).

Jaguaribe, Hélio. 1994. "O Brasil e o sistema internacional contemporâneo." In Marcovitch (1994).

Kay, Cristóbal. 1989. *Latin American Theories of Development and Underdevelopment*. London: Routledge.

Keohane, Robert O. 1980. "The Theory of Hegemonic Stability and Changes in the International Economic Regimes, 1967–1977." In Holsti, Siverson, and George (1980).

———. 1984. *After Hegemony: Cooperation and Discord in the World Political Economy*. Princeton, N.J.: Princeton University Press.

———, and Joseph S. Nye. 2001. *Power and Interdependence*. 3rd ed. New York: Longman.

Kindleberger, Charles P. 1973. *The World in Depression, 1929–1939*. Harmondsworth, U.K.: Penguin Books.

———. 1981. "Dominance and Leadership in the International Economy: Exploitation, Public Goods, and Free Rides." *International Studies Quarterly* 25 (2) (June): 242–254.

Kingstone, Peter R. 2000. "Muddling through Gridlock: Economic Policy Performance, Business Response, and Democratic Stability." In Kingstone and Power.

Kingstone, Peter R., and Timothy J. Power, eds. 2000. *Democratic Brazil: Actors, Institutions, and Processes*. Pittsburgh: University of Pittsburgh Press.

Knorr, Klaus. 1975. *The Power of Nations: The Political Economy of International Relations*. New York: Basic Books.

Krasner, Stephen D. 1976. "State Power and the Structure of International Trade." *World Politics* 28 (3) (April): 317–347.

Krause, Merrick E. 2002. "Partnering for Hemispheric Security: A Combined Regional Operations Center in Brazil." *Aerospace Power Journal* (Summer): 60–74.

Lafer, Celso. 1990. "Reflexões sobre a inserção do Brasil no contexto internacional." *Contexto Internacional*, no. 11 (January–June): 33–43.

———. 1992a. "Perspectivas e possibilidades da inserção internacional do Brasil." *Política Externa* 1 (3) (December): 100–121

———. 1992b. "Opening Address to the 47th Ordinary Session of the United Nations General Assembly (21 September)." In *La palabra del Brasil*.

———. 1992c. "Ministro Celso Lafer na Comissão de Relações Exteriores da Câmara dos Deputados: Pronunciamento do ministro das relações exteriores na Comissão de Relações Exteriores da Câmara dos Deputados, em 6 de agosto de 1992." *Resenha de Política Exterior do Brasil*, no. 71 (2nd semester): 37–45.

———. 1994. "Política externa brasileira: Reflexão e ação." In Marcovitch (1994).

———. 1996. "Comércio internacional, multilateralismo e regionalismo: Temas emergentes e novas direções." *Política Externa* 5 (3) (December): 50–64.

———. 1997. "Brasil: Forjando um novo papel nas relações internacionais." *Debates: O Brasil a União Européia e as Relações Internacionais*, no. 13: 11–22.

———. 2000. "Brazilian International Identity and Foreign Policy: Past, Present, and Future." *Daedalus* 129 (2) (Spring): 207–238.

———. 2001a. *A identidade internacional do Brasil e a política externa brasileira: Passado, presente e futuro*. São Paulo: Editora Perspectiva.

———. 2001b. "O Brasil e sua inserção no mundo." In Lafer (2002a).

———. 2001c. "Repúdio ao terrorismo: Intervenção perante o plenário do Senado Federal em 3 de outubro." In Lafer (2002a).

———. 2001d. "Notas taquigráficas do depoimento do Ministro Celso Lafer no Senado, 13 de março de 2001." *RelNet—Relatório* 015/2001 (15 March).

———. 2001e. "Discurso de abertura ao seminário da FLACSO 'Processo de integração em curso: A agenda latino-americana e do Caribe." Brasília (24 July). In Lafer (2002a).

———. 2001f. "A América do Sul deve ter uma infra-estrutura integrada." *La Nación* (7 August). In Lafer (2002a).

———. 2001g. "A política externa para a agricultura: Ala magna por ocasião do centenário da Esalq, 7 de maio." In Lafer (2002a).

———. 2002a. *Mudam-se os tempos: Diplomacia brasileira, 2001–2002*. Brasília: FUNAG/IPRI.

———. 2002b. "Discurso ao fórum nacional 'Nova Ordem Internacional, Globalização e o Mundo Pós-11 de Setembro, realizado em Brasília, 9 de maio." In Lafer (2002a).

———. 2002c. "O poder da palavra: Discurso de saudação ao Dia do Diplomata, Instituto Rio Branco, Brasília, 12 de junho." In Lafer (2002a).

———. 2007. Author interview (São Paulo, 26 March): twice foreign minister—immediately before Cardoso in 1991–1992, and later for Cardoso, 2001–2002. Also served as Brazil's ambassador in Geneva during the 1990s and was minister for development, industry, and international trade during the Cardoso era.

——— and Gélson Fonseca Júnior. 1994. "Questões para diplomacia no contexto internacional das polaridades indefinidas (Notas analíticas e algumas sugestões)." In Fonseca Júnior & Nabuco de Castro (1994).

Lafer, Celso, Paulo S. Wrobel, and Alexandre de Mello e Silva. 1993. "Entrevista com Celso Lafer." *Estudos Históricos* 6 (12): 271–284.

Lake, David A. 1993. "Leadership, Hegemony, and the International Economy: Naked Emperor or Tattered Monarch with Potential?" *International Studies Quarterly* 37: 459–489.

Lambert, Peter. 1996. "Mechanisms of Control: The Stroessner Regime in Paraguay." In Fowler (1996).

———. 2000. "A Decade of Electoral Democracy: Continuity, Change and Crisis in Paraguay." *Bulletin of Latin American Research* 19 (3) (July): 379–396.

———, and Andrew Nickson, eds. 1997. *The Transition to Democracy in Paraguay*. New York: St. Martin's Press.

Lampreia, Luiz Felipe. 1995a, "Discurso de posse." In Lampreia (1999a).

———. 1996a. "O Brasil e o mundo no século XXI: Uma visão do Itamaraty." *Política Externa* 5 (3) (December): 37–49.

———. 1996b. "Conferência proferida no III Encontro Nacional de Estudos Estratégicos, 'O Brasil e o Mundo no Século XXI'" (October). In Lampreia (1999a).

———. 1997. "Conferência sobre 'A Política Externa Brasileira Frea à Democracia e à Integração,' proferida no Consejo Argentino de Relaciones Internacionales" (6 March). In Lampreia (1999a).

———. 1998a. "A política externa do governo FHC: Continuidade e renovação." *Revista Brasileira de Política Internacional* 42 (2): 5–17.

———. 1998b. "Discurso por ocasião da assinatura do cronograma de implementação da declaração de Brasília, entre os governos do Equador e do Peru" (19 January). In Lampreia (1999a).

———. 1998c. "Discurso na abertura da 53 sessão da Assembléia Geral das Nações Unidas." New York (21 September): www.mre.gov.br.

———. 1998d. "Discurso pronunciado por ocasião do almoço em homenagem ao embaixador Dido Florentín Bogado, ministro das relações exteriores do Paraguai." In Lampreia (1999a).

———. 1999a. *Diplomacia brasileira: Palavras, contextos e razões*. Rio de Janeiro: Lacerda Editores.

———. 1999b. Speech at the Opening of the General Debate of the 54th Session of the United Nations General Assembly." New York (20 September): www.mre.gov.br.

———. 1999c. Statement at the III Session of the WTO Ministerial Conference. Seattle (30 November): www.mre.gov.br.

———. 2000a. Entrevista do Senhor Ministro de Estado das Relações Exteriores, Embaixador Luiz Felipe Lampreia, ao Jornal Zero Hora" (18 June).

———. 2000b. "Brazil Leads Continent without Imposing." Interview with the Minister of Foreign Affairs, Ambassador Luiz Felipe Lampreia, published by *Correio Braziliense* (24 August): www.mre.gov.br.

———. 2000c. Speech to the Opening of the General Debate of the 55th Session of the United Nations General Assembly." New York (12 September): www.mre.gov.br.

———. 2001. "The Diplomatic Agenda after Lampreia." Interview, Valor Econômico, trans. MRE (12 January).

———. 2002. Author interview (Rio de Janeiro, 23 September): minister of foreign affairs, 1995–2001; secretary-general of Itamaraty when Fernando Henrique Cardoso was foreign minister, 1992–1993.

———, and Ademar Seabra da Cruz Júnior. 2005. "Brazil: Coping with Structural Constraints." In Robertson and East (2005).

Latin American Weekly Report, various issues.

Legler, Thomas, Sharon F. Lean, and Dexter S. Boniface, eds. 2007. *Promoting Democracy in the Americas*. Baltimore: Johns Hopkins University Press.

Lessa, Antônio Carlos. 1996. "A diplomacia universalista do Brasil: A construção do sistema contemporâneo de relações bilaterais." *Revista Brasileira de Política Internacional* 40: 29–41.

Lewis, Paul H. 1993. *Political Parties and Generations in Paraguay's Liberal Era, 1869–1940*. Chapel Hill: University of North Carolina Press.

Lievesley, Geraldine. 1999. *Democracy Promotion in Latin America: Mobilization, Power and the Search for a New Politics*. Manchester, U.K.: Manchester University Press.

Little, W., and E. Posada-Carbó, eds. 1996. *Political Corruption in Europe and Latin America*. New York: St. Martin's Press.

López, Andrés. 1999. "El caso brasileño." In Chudnovsky, Kosacoff, and López (1999).

Lowenthal, Abraham F., ed. 1991. *Exporting Democracy: The United States and Latin America, Case Studies*. Baltimore: Johns Hopkins University Press.

Mace, Gordon. 1999. "The Origins, Nature, and Scope of the Hemispheric Project." In Mace and Bélanger (1999).

Mace, Gordon, Louis Bélanger, et al. 1999. *The Americas in Transition: The Contours of Regionalism*. Boulder, Colo.: Lynne Rienner.

Machado da Silva, Heloisa Conceição. 2000. "Crise, ação e pragmatismo: A política de comércio exterior brasileira de 1934–1945." *Revista Cena Internacional* 2 (2): 96–116.

Machado e Costa, José Luiz. 1999. "Balanço estratégico na América do Sul e o papel do Brasil na construção de uma visão sul-americana de defesa: Condicionantes, singularidades e parâmetros." *Política Externa* 7 (4) (March): 67–95.

Magalhães, Fernando Simas. 1999. *Cúpula das Américas de 1994: Papel negociador do Brasil, em busca de uma agenda hemisférica.* Brasília: IRBr/FUNAG/Centro de Estudos Estratégicos).

Magnoli, Demétrio. 2000. *Manual do candidato: Questões internacionais contemporâneas.* 2nd ed. Brasília: FUNAG.

Main, Alexander, Maximillien Arvelaiz, and Temir Porras-Ponceleon. 2002. "Virtual Reality: Real Coup." *Covert Action Quarterly*, no. 72 (Spring).

Malamud, Andrés. 2005. "Mercosur Turns 15: Between Rising Rhetoric and Declining Achievement." *Cambridge Review of International Affairs* 18 (3) (October): 421–436.

Mansfield, Edward D. 1998. "The Proliferation of Preferential Trading Arrangements." *Journal of Conflict Resolution* 42 (5) (October): 523–543.

——— and Helen V. Milner. 1999. "The New Wave of Regionalism." *International Organization* 53 (3) (Summer): 589–627.

Mansfield, Edward D., Jon C. Pevehouse, and David H. Bearce. 1999–2000. "Preferential Trading Arrangements and Military Disputes." *Security Studies* 9 (1–2) (Autumn–Winter): 92–118.

Manzetti, Luigi. 1990. "Argentine-Brazilian Economic Integration: An Early Appraisal." *Latin American Research Review* 25 (3): 109–140.

Manzur, Juan Carlos Morales. 1998. "Comunidad andina y Mercosur: La integración posible." *Cuestiones Políticas*, no. 20: 141–166.

Marcella, Gabriel, and Richard Downes, eds. 1999. *Security Co-operation in the Western Hemisphere: Resolving the Ecuador-Peru Conflict.* Miami: North-South Center Press.

Marcovitch, Jacques, ed. 1994. *Cooperação internacional: Estratégia e gestão.* São Paulo: Editora da Universidade de São Paulo.

Mares, David R. 1988. "Middle Powers under Regional Hegemony: To Challenge or Acquiesce in Hegemonic Enforcement." *International Studies Quarterly* 32 (4) (December): 453–471.

Marini, Ruy Mauro. 1972. "Brazilian Subimperialism." *Monthly Review* 23 (9) (February): 14–24.

Marques, Renato L. 1991. "Despacho ao memorandum DAM-I/108" (25 February). Brasília: Secretaria de Estado das Relações Exteriores.

Martínez, Javier, and Álvaro Díaz. 1996. *Chile: The Great Transformation.* Geneva: U.N. Research Institute for Social Development.

Martins Filho, João Roberto. 2007. "The Brazilian Armed Forces in the Post–Cold War Era: What Has Changed in Military Thinking?" Working Paper CBC-85–07. Oxford: Centre for Brazilian Studies, Oxford University.

Mattli, Walter. 1999. *The Logic of Regional Integration: Europe and Beyond.* Cambridge: Cambridge University Press.

McClintock, Cynthia. 2001. "The OAS in Peru: Room for Improvement." *Journal of Democracy* 12 (4) (October): 137–140.

McConnell, Shelley A. 2001. "Ecuador's Centrifugal Politics." *Current History* 100 (643) (February): 73–79.

McKeown, Timothy J. 1983. "Hegemonic Stability Theory and the 19th Century Tariff Levels in Europe." *International Organization* 37 (1) (Winter): 73–91.

Meller, Patricio, ed. 1991. *The Latin American Development Debate: Neostructuralism, Neomonetarism, and Adjustment Processes.* Boulder, Colo.: Westview Press.

Mendel, William W. 1998. "Security on Brazil's Amazon Frontier." *Low Intensity Conflict and Law Enforcement* 7 (3) (Winter): 60–74.

———. 1999. "The Brazilian Amazon: Controlling the Hydra." *Military Review* (July–August): 18–28.

Mercado Comum do Sul (Mercosul). 1991. "Tratado para a constituição de um mercado comum entre a República Argentina, a República Federativa do Brasil, a República do Paraguai e a República Oriental do Uruguai (Tratado do Assunção, 26/03/1991)." *Resenha de Política Exterior do Brasil,* no. 68: 33–45.

———. Comunidad Andina. 2002. "Acuerdo de complementación económica celebrado entre la Comunidad Andina y el Mercado Común del Sur (Mercosur)" (6 December): www.mercosur.org.uy.

Ministerio de Defesa. Brasil. N.d. "Programa Calha Norte.": https://www.defesa.gov.br/programa_calha_norte/index.php

Mittelman, James H. 1999. "Rethinking the 'New Regionalism' in the Context of Globalization." In Hettne, Inotai, and Sunkel (1999).

——— and Richard Falk. 2000. "Global Hegemony and Regionalism." In Calleya (2000).

Miyamoto, Shiguenou. 2000. "O Brasil e segurança regional." *Carta Internacional,* no. 89 (July): 7–10.

Mollo, Maria de Lourdes Rollemberg, and Alfredo Saad-Filho. 2006. "Neoliberal Economic Policies in Brazil (1994–2005): Cardoso, Lula and the Need for a Democratic Alternative." *New Political Economy* 11 (1) (March): 99–123.

Moore, Barrington. 1966. *Social Origins of Dictatorship and Democracy: Lord and Peasant in the Making of the Modern World.* Boston: Beacon Press.

Mora, Frank O. 1996. "Victims of the Balloon Effect: Drug Trafficking and U.S. Policy in Brazil and the Southern Cone of Latin America." *Journal of Social, Political, and Economic Studies* 21 (2) (Summer): 115–140.

Morgenthau, Hans J. 1967. *Politics among Nations: The Struggle for Power and Peace.* 4th ed. New York: Alfred A. Knopf.

Morton, O. 2000. "Letter from Brazil." *International Journal* 55 (4) (Autumn): 655–662.

Muñoz, Heraldo. 1996. "Collective Action for Democracy in the Americas." In Muñoz and Tulchin (1996).

——— and Joseph S. Tulchin, eds. 1996. *Latin American Nations in World Politics.* 2nd ed. Boulder, Colo.: Westview Press.

Murphy, Craig N., and Roger Tooze, eds. 1991. *The New International Political Economy.* Basingstoke, U.K.: Macmillan.

Nahú, Maria Aparecida Lopes. 1992. "Memorandum para o Sr. Chefe, substituto, do DAA: Bacia do Prata. Ligação ferroviária São Paulo–Tucumán. Solicitação do Governador Ramón Ortega." DAM-I/83 (23 September). Brasília: Secretaria de Estado das Relações Exteriores.

Narlikar, Amrita. 2003. *International Trade and Developing Countries: Bargaining Coalitions in the GATT & WTO*. London: Routledge.

———. 2004. "The Ministerial Process and Power Dynamics in the World Trade Organization: Understanding Failure from Seattle to Cancún." *New Political Economy* 9 (3) (September): 413–428.

——— and Diana Tussie. 2004. "The G20 at the Cancun Ministerial: Developing Countries and Their Evolving Coalitions in the WTO." *The World Economy* 27 (7): 947–966.

Narlikar, Amrita, and Rorden Wilkinson. 2004. "Collapse at the WTO: A Cancun Post-Mortem." *Third World Quarterly* 25 (3) (April): 447–460.

Nascimento, Elma Lia. 1997. "Just Say Yes." Brazzil: http://www.brazzil.com/ cvrjan97. htm.

Nickson, Andrew. 1988. "Tyranny and Longevity: Stroessner's Paraguay." *Third World Quarterly* 10 (1) (January): 237–259.

———. 1989. "The Overthrow of the Stroessner Regime: Re-establishing the Status Quo." *Bulletin of Latin American Research* 8 (2): 185–209.

———. 1996. "Democracy and Institutionalized Corruption in Paraguay." In Little and Posada-Carbó (1996).

———. 1997. "Corruption and the Transition." In Lambert and Nickson (1997).

Nitschack, Horst, Peter Birle, Sérgio Costa, eds. 2008. *Brazil and the Americas: Convergence and Perspectives*. Frankfurt: Vervuert.

Nye, Joseph S. 2002. *The Paradox of American Power*. Oxford: Oxford University Press.

Ocampo, José Antonio, and Juan Martin. 2003. *Globalization and Development: A Latin American and Caribbean Perspective*. Palo Alto, Calif.: Stanford University Press.

O'Donnell, Guillermo, and Phillipe C. Schmitter. 1986. *Transitions from Authoritarian Rule: Tentative Conclusions about Uncertain Democracies*. Baltimore: Johns Hopkins University Press.

Oliveira, Eliézer Rizzo de. 1999. "Brazilian Diplomacy and the 1995 Ecuador-Peru War." In Marcella and Downes (1999).

Oliveira, Henrique Altemani de. 2005. *Política externa brasileira*. São Paulo: Editora Saraiva.

Oppenheimer, Andrés. 2003. "Latin America's 'Ungoverned Spaces.'" *San Diego Union-Tribune* (12 March).

Organization of American States (OAS). 2002. "Support for Democracy in Venezuela." AG/RES. 1 (XXIX-E/02): www.oas.org/OASpage/press2002/sp/resolución AGreng_1.htm.

———. 2005. "Draft: Declaration of Florida: Delivering the Benefits of Democracy." AG/doc.4476/05 (1 June).

———. Unit for the Promotion of Democracy. 2000. *Electoral Observation in Peru, 2000*. Washington, D.C.: Organization of American States

Ouriques, Lêda Maria de Oliveira. 2000. "Opções para o financiamento o comunitário de uma rede básica de transporte no Mercosul." M.A. thesis, University of Brasília.

La palabra del Brasil en las Naciones Unidas, 1946–1995. Brasília: FUNAG, 1995.

Palmer, David Scott. 1997. "Peru-Ecuador Border Conflict: Missed Opportunities, Misplaced Nationalism, and Multilateral Peacekeeping." *Journal of Interamerican Studies and World Affairs* 39 (3) (Autumn): 109–148.

Park, J. 1995. "The New Regionalism and Third World Development." *Journal of Developing Societies* 11 (1): 21–35.

Payne, Anthony. 1994. "US Hegemony and the Reconfiguration of the Caribbean." *Review of International Studies* 20 (2): 149–168.

Pedersen, Thomas. 2002. "Cooperative Hegemony: Power, Ideas, and Institutions in Regional Integration." *Review of International Studies* 28: 677–696.

Penna Filho, Pio. 1999. "A pesquisa histórica no Itamaraty." *Revista Brasileira de Política Internacional* 42 (2): 117–144.

———. 2002. "Política externa e desenvolvimento: O Brasil de JK." *Revista Cena Internacional* 2 (1): 2–21.

Pereira, Lia Valls. 1999. "Toward the Common Market of the South: Mercosur's Origins, Evolution, and Challenges." In Roett (1999).

Peres, Wilson, ed. 1998. *Grandes empresas y grupos industriales latinoamericanos.* Mexico City: Siglo Veintiuno Editores.

Perruci, Gamaliel, Jr. 1995. "The North-South Security Dialogue in Brazil's Technology Policy." *Armed Forces and Society* 21 (3) (Spring): 371–394.

Perry, William. 2000. "Has the Future Arrived for Brazil." *Orbis* 44 (3) (Summer): 399–415.

Phillips, Nicola. 2001. "Regionalist Governance in the New Political Economy of Development: 'Relaunching' the Mercosur." *Third World Quarterly* 22 (4): 565–583.

———. 2003. "Hemispheric Integration and Subregionalism in the Americas." *International Affairs* 79 (2): 327–349.

———. 2004. *The Southern Cone Model: The Political Economy of Regional Capitalist Development.* London: Routledge.

Pinheiro, Leticia. 2004. *Política externa brasileira.* Rio de Janeiro: Jorger Zahar Editor.

Pion-Berlin, David. 2000. "Will Soldiers Follow? Economic Integration and Regional Security in the Southern Cone." *Journal of Inter-American Studies and World Affairs* 42 (1) (Spring): 43–69.

Polanyi, Karl. 1944. *The Great Transformation: The Political and Economic Origins of Our Time.* Boston: Beacon Press.

Porter, Roger B. 1990. "The Enterprise for the Americas Initiative: A New Approach to Economic Growth." *Journal of Interamerican Studies and World Affairs* 32 (4) (Winter): 1–12.

Powell, Colin. 2002. "Remarks of the Secretary of State Colin L. Powell to the Special Session of the General Assembly of the Organization of American States" (18 April): www.oas.org/speeches/Speechother02/2002/eng/041802–Colin_Powell_VE.htm.

Prado, Marica Clara R. M. do. 2005. *A real história do real: Uma radiografia da moeda que mudou o Brasil*. Rio de Janeiro: Editora Record.

Prebisch, Raúl. 1951. "Growth, Balance and Disparities: Interpretations of the Economic Development Process." In *CEPAL* (1951).

———. 1986. "Notes on Trade from the Standpoint of the Periphery." *CEPAL Review*, no. 28 (April): 203–214.

———. 1988. "Dependence, Interdependence, and Development." *CEPAL Review*, no. 34 (April): 197–205.

Procópio Filho, Argemiro, and Alcides Costa Vaz. 1997. "O Brasil no contexto do narcotráfico internacional." *Revista Brasileira de Política Internacional* 40 (1): 75–122.

Quadros, Jânio. 1961. "Brazil's New Foreign Policy." *Foreign Affairs* 40 (1) (October): 19–27.

Quintão, Geraldo Magela da Cruz. 2000. "Audiência pública do ministro da defesa na Comissão de Relações Exteriores e defesa nacional do Senado Federal." (22 November).

Rapkin, David P., ed. 1990. *World Leadership and Hegemony*. Boulder: Lynne Rienner.

Reis da Silva, André Luiz. 2000. "Interdependência, segurança e desenvolvimento na política externa do governo Castello Branco (1964–1967)." *Revista Cena Internacional* 2 (2): 137–164.

Rezende, Fernando. 1998. "The Brazilian Economy: Recent Developments and Future Prospects." *International Affairs* 74 (3): 563–575.

Ricupero, Rubens. 2000. *Rio Branco: O Brasil no mundo*. Rio de Janeiro: Contraponto Editora.

Roberston, Justin L., and Maurice A. East, eds. 2005. *Diplomacy and Developing Nations: Post–Cold War Foreign Policy-making Structures and Processes*. London: Routledge.

Robinson, William I. 1996a. *Promoting Polyarchy: Globalization, US Intervention, and Hegemony*. Cambridge: Cambridge University Press.

———. 1996b. "Globalization, the World System, and 'Democracy Promotion' in U.S. Foreign Policy." *Theory and Society* 25 (5): 615–655.

Rocha, Geisa Maria. 2002. "Neo-Dependency in Brazil." *New Left Review*, no. 16 (July–August): 5–33.

Roett, Riordan, ed. 1999. *Mercosur: Regional Integration, World Markets*. Boulder, Colo.: Lynne Rienner.

——— and Richard Scott Sacks. 1991. *Paraguay: The Personalist Legacy*. Boulder, Colo.: Westview Press.

Rose, Nikolas. 1999. *Powers of Freedom: Reframing Political Thought*. Cambridge: Cambridge University Press.

Rosenthal, Gert. 1997. "Development Thinking in Latin America and the Caribbean: Past and Future." In Emmerij (1997).

Rueschemeyer, Dietrich, Evelyne Huber Stephens, and John D. Stephens. 1992. *Capitalist Development and Democracy*. Cambridge: Blackwell Publishers.

Russet, Bruce. 1993. *Grasping the Democratic Peace: Principles for a Post–Cold War World*. Princeton, N.J.: Princeton University Press.

Santander, Sebastián. 2002. "EU-Mercosur Interregionalism: Facing up to the South American Crisis and the Emerging Free Trade Area of the Americas." *European Foreign Affairs Review* 7 (4) (Winter): 491–506.

Sardenberg, Ronaldo da Mota. 1998. "O Brasil e a nova ordem mundial." *Debates*, no. 16 (a projeção do Brasil face ao século XXI: Anais do IV Simpósio Brasil-Alemanha, Centro de Estudos Konrad Adenauer Stiftung): 9–17.

Sarney, José. 1989. "Discurso do Presidente José Sarney na cerimônia de condecoração, no Palácio do Governo, em Assunção, em 13 de novembro de 1989." *Resenha de Política Exterior do Brasil*, no. 63 (October–December): 24–26.

Schwartz, Gilson. 1998. "The Privatization Process and Foreign Direct Investment in Brazil: Results and Perspectives." *International Spectator* 33 (3) (July–September): 69–84.

II Reunião de Presidentes da América do Sul. 2002. "Declaração sobre a zona de paz sul-americana." Guayaquil (26–27 July): http://www2.mre.gov.br/daa/declaracao_zonadepaz.htm.

Selcher, Wayne A. 1985. "Brazilian-Argentine Relations in the 1980s: From Wary Rivalry to Friendly Competition." *Journal of Inter-American Studies and World Affairs* 27 (2) (Summer): 25–53.

———. 1986. "Current Dynamics and Future Prospects of Brazil's Relations with Latin America: Toward a Pattern of Bilateral Cooperation." *Journal of Interamerican Studies and World Affairs* 28 (2) (Summer): 67–99.

Siffert Filho, Nelson, and Carla Souza e Silva. 1999. "As grandes empresas nos anos 90: Respostas estratégicas a um cenário de mudanças." In Giambiagi and Mesquita Moreira (1999).

Silva, Paulo Azzi da, and Ángela de Rocha. 2001. "Perception of Export Barriers to Mercosur by Brazilian Firms." *International Marketing Review* 18 (6): 589–611.

Silveira, José Paulo. 2000. "Eixos de integração da América do Sul: A contribuição brasileira." Brasília: Secretaria de Planejamento e Investimentos Estratégicos, Ministério do Planejamento, Orçamento e Gestão (29 August).

———. 2001. Author interview (Brasília, 19 September): Secretary of planning and strategic investment, Ministry of Planning, Budget, and Management, Brazil.

Simões, Antônio José Ferreira. 2001. "O Brasil e a ALCA no limiar do novo milênio: Algumas reflexões." *Carta Internacional*, no. 106 (December): 4–5.

Sistema Económico Latinoamericano y del Caribe (SELA). 2002. "El consenso de Guayaquil sobre integración, seguridad y desarrollo: Elementos para el análisis de la viabilidad de sus propuestas." *Integración* SP/Di, no. 17–02 (August).

Smith, Joseph. 1991. *Unequal Giants: Diplomatic Relations between the United States and Brazil, 1889–1930*. Pittsburgh: University of Pittsburgh Press.

Smith, Peter H. 2000. *Talons of the Eagle: Dynamics of U.S.-Latin American Relations*. 2nd ed. Oxford: Oxford University Press.

Snidal, Duncan. 1985. "The Limits of Hegemonic Stability Theory." *International Organization* 39 (4) (Autumn): 579–614.

Soares Carbonar, Orlando. 1990. "Ofício para o Secretaria de Estado: Brasil, Paraguai. Visita do Senhor Ministro de Estado." *Ofício*, no. 383 (26 October). Brasília: Secretaria de Estado das Relações Exteriores.

Soares de Lima, Maria Regina. 1986. "The Political Economy of Brazilian Foreign Policy: Nuclear Policy, Trade and Itaipú." Ph.D. dissertation, Vanderbilt University.

———. 1990. "A economia política da política externa brasileira: Uma proposta de análise." *Contexto Internacional*, no. 12 (July–December): 7–29.

———. 1999. "Brazil's Alternative Vision." In Mace and Bélanger (1999).

———. 2005. "A política externa brasileira e os desafios da cooperação sul-sul." *Revista Brasileira de Política Internacional* 48 (1) (January–June): 24–59.

———, and Mônica Hirst. 2006. "Brazil as an Intermediate State and Regional Power: Action, Choice and Responsibilities." *International Affairs* 82 (1): 21–40.

Sodré, Roberto de Abreu. 1987. "Opening Statement to the XLII Ordinary Session of the United Nations General Assembly (21 September)." In *La palabra del Brasil*.

Sørensen, Georg. 1992. "Kant and Processes of Democratization: Consequences for Neorealist Thought." *Journal of Peace Research* 29 (4): 397–414.

Sorger, Carmen, and William A. Dymond. 1997. "Sisyphus Ascendant? Brazilian Foreign Policy for the Coming Century?" *Canadian Foreign Policy* 4 (3) (Winter): 37–49.

Souto, Cíntia Vieira. 2001. "A política externa do governo Médici (1969–1974): Uma nova proposta de inserção internacional para o Brasil." *Revista Cena Internacional* 3 (1): 43–61.

Spektor, Matias. 2002. "O Brasil e Argentina entre a cordialidade oficial e o projeto de integração: A política externa do governo de Ernesto Geisel (1974–1979)." *Revista Brasileira de Política Internacional* 45 (1): 117–145.

Spíndola, Lytha. 2002. Author interview (Brasília, 2 October): foreign trade secretary, Ministry of Development, Industry, and Foreign Trade, Brazil.

Stein, Arthur A. 1984. "The Hegemon's Dilemma: Great Britain, the United States, and the International Economic Order." *International Organization* 38 (2) (Spring): 355–386.

Stepan, Alfred, ed. 1973. *Authoritarian Brazil: Origins, Policies, and Future*. New Haven: Yale University Press.

———. 1989. *Democratizing Brazil: Problems of Transition and Consolidation*. Oxford: Oxford University Press.

Stopford, John, and Susan Strange, with John S. Henley. 1991. *Rival States, Rival Firms: Competition for World Market Share*. Cambridge: Cambridge University Press.

Strange, Susan. 1986. *Casino Capitalism*. Oxford: Basil Blackwell.

———. 1991. "An Eclectic Approach." In Murphy and Tooze (1991).

———. 1994. *States and Markets*. 2nd ed. London: Pinter.

———. 1998. *Mad Money*. Manchester, U.K.: Manchester University Press.

Sunkel, Osvaldo, ed. 1993. *Development from Within: Towards a Neostructuralist Approach for Latin America*. Boulder, Colo.: Lynne Rienner.

——— and Gustavo Zuleta. 1990. "Neo-structuralism versus Neo-liberalism in the 1990s." *CEPAL Review*, no. 42 (December): 35–51.

Svetlicic, Marjan. 1996. "Challenges of Globalisation and Regionalisation in the World Economy." *Global Society* 10 (2) (May): 107–123.

Tarzi, Shah M. 1999. "Dynamics of the Rise and Spread of Transnational Enterprises from the Emerging Market Economies." *Indian Journal of Economics*, no. 315 (April): 513–536.

Taylor, Lewis. 2001. "Alberto Fujimori's Peripeteia: From 'Re-Election' to Regime Collapse." *European Review of Latin American and Caribbean Studies*, no. 70 (April): 3–24.

Thorstensen, Vera. 1993. "Brasil: 'Global trader' ou 'regional trader': O dilema de política de internalização." *Síntesis*, no. 19 (January–June): 117–136.

Tulchin, Joseph S., and Ralph H. Espach, eds. 2001. *Latin America in the New International System*. Boulder, Colo.: Lynne Rienner.

United Nations Conference on Trade and Development (UNCTAD). 2000. *FDI Determinants and TNC Strategies: The Case of Brazil*. New York: United Nations.

———, 2001. *World Investment Report, 2001*. New York: United Nations.

United States. Central Intelligence Agency (CIA). 1953. "Probable Developments in Brazil." National Intelligence Estimate NIE-86 (4 December). Washington, D.C.: Central Intelligence Agency.

———. 1961. "Short-term Prospects for Brazil under Goulart." Special National Intelligence Estimate 93-2-61 (7 December). Washington, D.C.: Central Intelligence Agency.

United States. Department of Energy. 2002. "Country Analysis Brief—Paraguay" (September): http://www.eia.doe.gov/emeu/cabs/paraguay.html.

United States. Office of the White House Press Secretary. 1997. "Remarks by President Clinton and President Cardoso at Reception." Brasília Room, Ministry of Foreign Affairs, Brasília (13 October).

United States. State Department. 2002. "Visit to Brazil: Marc Grossman, Under Secretary of State for Political Affairs," Media Briefing, Brazilian Ministry of Foreign Affairs, Itamaraty Palace, Brasília, Brazil (7 March). Washington, D.C.: U.S. State Department.

United States Trade Representative (USTR). 2002. "U.S. and Chile Conclude Historic Free Trade Agreement." Press release, Executive Office of the President (11 December): http://www.ustr.gov/releases/2002/12/02-114.htm.

Valenzuela, Arturo. 1997. "Paraguay: The Coup That Didn't Happen." *Journal of Democracy* 8 (1): 43–55.

Vaz, Alcides Costa. 1999. "Parcerias estratégicas no contexto da política exterior brasileira: Implicações para o Mercosul." *Textos de Política e Relações Internacionales*, no. 14 (October). Brasília: Fundação Universidade de Brasília, Instituto de Ciência Política e Relações Internacionais.

———. 2002. *Cooperação, integração e processo negociador: A construcção do Mercosul*. Brasília: Instituto Brasileiro de Relações Internacionais.

Veliz, Claudio. 1966, ed. *Obstacles to Change in Latin America*. London: Oxford University Press.

Vieira, Marco Antônio Muxagata de Carvalho. 2001. "Idéias e instituições: Uma reflexão sobre a política externa brasileira do início da década 90." *Contexto Internacional* 23 (2) (July–December): 261–273.

Vigevani, Tullo, and Gabriel Cepaluni. 2007. "Lula's Foreign Policy and the Quest for Autonomy through Diversification." *Third World Quarterly* 28 (7): 1309–1326.

———and Marcelo Fernandes de Oliveira. 2007. "Brazilian Foreign Policy in the Cardoso Era: The Search for Autonomy through Integration." *Latin American Perspectives* 34 (5) (September): 58–80.

Vizentini, Paulo Fagundes. 2003. *Relações internacionais do Brasil: De Vargas a Lula*. São Paulo: Editora Fundação Perseu Abramo.

Warren, Harris Gaylord. 1985. *Rebirth of the Paraguayan Republic: The First Colorado Era, 1879–1904*. Pittsburgh, Pa.: University of Pittsburgh Press.

Webb, Michael C., and Stephen B. Krasner. 1989. "Hegemonic Stability Theory: An Empirical Assessment." *Review of International Studies* 15: 183–198.

Weidner, Glenn R. 1999. "Peacekeeping in the Upper Cenapa Valley: A Regional Response to Crisis." In Marcella and Downes (1999).

Weintraub, Sidney. 1991. "The New US Economic Initiative toward Latin America." *Journal of Interamerican Studies and World Affairs* 33 (1) (Spring): 1–18.

Wendt, Alexander. 1992. "Anarchy Is What States Make of It: The Social Construction of Power Politics." *International Organization* 46 (2) (Spring): 391–425.

———. 1999. *Social Theory of International Politics*. Cambridge: Cambridge University Press.

Whitehead, Laurence. 1991. "The Imposition of Democracy." In Lowenthal (1991).

———, ed. 1996. *The International Dimension of Democratization: Europe and Latin America*. Oxford: Oxford University Press.

———. 1999. "The European Union and the Americas." In Bulmer-Thomas and Dunkerley (1999).

Wilkinson, Rorden. 2000. *Multilateralism and the World Trade Organization: The Architecture and Extension of International Trade Regulation*. London: Routledge.

Wilson, Dominic, and Roopa Purushothaman. 2003. "Dreaming with BRICs: The Pat to 2050." *Goldman Sachs Global Economics Paper*, no. 99 (1 October).

Wrobel, Paulo S. 1996. "Brazil and the NPT: Resistance to Change?" *Security Dialogue* 27 (3) (September): 337–347.

Yopo, Boris H. 1991. "The Rio Group: Decline or Consolidation of the Latin American Concertación Policy?" *Journal of Interamerican Studies and World Affairs* 33 (4) (Winter): 27–44.

Zelner, Júlio. 1991."Despacho ao Memo DAM-I/108" (26 February). Brasília: Secretaria de Estado das Relações Exteriores.

Zirker, Daniel. 1994. "Brazilian Foreign Policy and Subimperialism during the Transition of the 1980s: A Review and Reapplication of Marini's Theory." *Latin American Perspectives* 21 (1): 115–131.

Index

Lula presidency, 158–83; cabinet appointments, 160–61; continuity of, 158–62; economic dimension, 172–78; ideas dimension, 169–72; leadership in global arena, 162–68; national self-confidence (*auto-estima* concept), 163, 169–70, 171; neoliberal economic policy, 158, 171; security dimension, 178–82; visit to China (2004), 177

Mahuad, Jamil, 134, 141, 179
Marginalization. *See* economic marginalization
MDIC (Ministério do Desenvolvimento, Indústria e Comércio Exterior), 101, 105, 111, 177
Médici presidency, 24–26
Menem, Carlos, 34, 47, 96, 104, 106–7, 123
Mercado Comum do Sul (Common Market of the South). *See* Mercosul
Mercosul: antiterror programs, 155; associate members, 38, 57, 113; Brazilian leadership in, 15, 54–59; creation of, 18, 31, 54; democratic preservation and, 132–33; EU relations, 44, 54–57; evolution and expansion of, 6–7, 33–38, 42, 50, 52, 70–71, 93, 95, 96, 113, 124, 166, 173; intergovernmental bodies of, 97; interregional agreements, 44, 54–59; intra-Mercosul investment flows, 108–13; membership in, 34, 35; membership for Venezuela, 181; political nature of, 73, 186; preservation and revitalization of, 165, 188; prodemocracy clauses, 182; security community, 125, 127, 130, 134, 153, 155; trade patterns, 97–103, 173–75
Mercosul-CAN negotiations, 61, 119, 123–24, 189–90
Mercosul-EU meetings (1999), 55–56
Mercosul Trade Commission, 97
Mesa, Carlos, 180
Mexico: economic leader in South America, 50; Gore vice presidential visit, 40; and NAFTA, 38, 39, 50
Miami Summit Meeting. *See* Summit of the Americas
Military Observer Mission Ecuador/Peru (MOMEP), 142–43, 156

MNCs. *See* multinational corporations (MNCs)
MOMEP. *See* Military Observer Mission Ecuador/Peru
Morales, Evo, 164, 165, 181
Müller, Lauro, 20
Mulroney, Brian, 29
Multilateralism and solidarity, 88–89, 179
Multinational corporations (MNCs), 38, 78, 79, 84, 109

NAFTA. *See* North American Free Trade Agreement
Narco-trafficking: in Amazônia, 149–50, 151; Brazilian Programa Calha Norte, 149, 154; Brazilian Sivam (Sistema de Vigiláncia), 150–52, 182; Colombia-Venezuela border area (Dog's Head), 150; and insurgency in Colombia, 153–54; Paraguay antidrug programs, 152–53; Plan Colombia, 149, 151, 152, 156; as security issue, 4, 15, 48, 126, 130, 148–53, 189; U.S. counternarcotics policy, 128
National autonomy preservation, 2, 4, 10, 15, 17, 25–26, 162, 178
National defense policy: and democracy, 126–30; Política de Defesa Nacional (PDN), 126–27, 128. *See also* security; security dimension of South American project
National development. *See* economic development
National identity, 69–74, 75; concept of self-identity and, 68–69, 88–89; South American rather than Latin American, 76
National Social and Economic Development Bank. *See* BNDES
National sovereignty, 74, 129–30, 133, 136, 156, 179, 180, 189
Neoliberalism, 81–85; in Cardoso presidency, 74, 81–85; conceptualization of hegemony, 190; in Latin America, 34; and leadership styles, 44; in Lula presidency, 158, 171; in Mercosul, 164
New world order: Brazil's position in, 3, 18; and changes in leadership, 45; Itamaraty's diplomatic views on, 5–6, 74
Noboa, Gustavo, 134